TEACHER EDUCATION

Making Education Effective

Editor

Sarita and Monika Tomar

ISHA BOOKS

DELHI-110 033

Teacher Education: Making Education Effective

(Education)

ISBN: 81-8205-094-4

Published in 2006 in India by
Isha Books, D-45, Prithviraj Road,
Adarsh Nagar, Delhi-110 033

Laser Typesetting at : Shree Vaishnavi Creations, Delhi
Printed at : **Sudha Offset Press, Delhi.**

Contents

Preface

Teaching is one of the most influential professions in society. In their day-to-day work, teachers can and do make huge differences to children's lives: directly, through the curriculum they teach, and indirectly, through their behaviour, attitudes, values, relationships with and interest in pupils.

Teaching is a creative, intellectually demanding and rewarding job, so the standards for joining the profession must be high too. Skilled practitioners can make teaching look easy but they have learned their skills and improved them through training, practice, evaluation and by learning from other colleagues.

Teacher development is a process, not an event. It means comprehensive growth and support. From the time teachers begin any initial preparation and/or teaching, provision needs to be made for ongoing development of knowledge of subject matter; concrete skills to teach, observe, assess, and reflect; incentives; and career growth. There also needs to be a linkage with other teachers and supervisors to help solve problems and to support each other through discussion, modelling, and coaching, and an involvement with other aspects of school and educational change.

Teacher educators at all levels, whether school or college-based, need to have induction and continuing professional development. This should ensure that they are aware of recent developments, can judge whether these should be incorporated into training, have perspectives that run beyond their direct experience, and have a rich range of material to draw on to support and stimulate trainee teachers. Teacher education programs must have a strong emphasis on academic rigor and provide challenging intellectual experiences for student teachers.

The present volume provides a comprehensive analysis of the principles and trends of teacher education. It will serve as a highly informative reference tool for teachers, educators, students and all concerned.

Editor

1

Teacher Training and Social Empowerment

Teacher development is a process, not an event. It means comprehensive growth and support. From the time teachers begin any initial preparation and/or teaching, provision needs to be made for ongoing development of knowledge of subject matter; concrete skills to teach, observe, assess, and reflect; incentives; and career growth. There also needs to be a linkage with other teachers and supervisors to help solve problems and to support each other through discussion, modeling, and coaching, and an involvement with other aspects of school and educational change.

The reality is that there are a variety of ways to prepare and support teachers in a variety of environments. Just as there is no single type of effective teacher, but there are common elements associated with successful teachers, there is no single type of effective initial preparation course, but there are common elements that should be discussed and incorporated where appropriate in design and implementation.

Initial preparation of teachers varies greatly across countries. Where programs do exist, they have worked well when they have ranged from fifteen days as in the BRAC schools in Bangladesh, twenty-five days in the rural community schools in Egypt, two years in Botswana, three years in Namibia, to the five-year programs found in some U.S. institutions. Success depends on how the courses are structured and what support accompanies them.

Programs that have shorter initial training tend to need more concentrated on-the-job followup; however, all programs need ongoing job support. Where there is an issue with getting females trained in restricted social regions, mobile teacher training has proved helpful. Well designed distance education programs can provide training to teachers, especially to large numbers of teachers. The rural community schools in Egypt, and the mobile teacher training program in Pakistan offer ideas for addressing particular needs for getting more teachers quickly into schools in particular social contexts.

All these projects demonstrated flexibility in selecting local people for training, taking them where they are at in experience, providing basic preparation, providing strong on-the-job support, and encouraging teachers to meet and work together to solve classroom problems all contribute to their success. A disservice is done to both teachers and the teaching profession if all teachers do not have the opportunity to gain equal professional qualifications, no matter what route is taken to attain them.

According to Hartwell, this Ministry of Education and UNICEF-supported program selects two women from the vicinity of the community school to serve as facilitators for each class. The women are usually secondary or technical school graduates, not university-trained teachers.

Selection is based on an initial personality test in which a woman's aptitude for teaching is assessed based on her ability to work with children, her disposition toward teaching, and her acceptability and openness to the community.

The initial training the women receive comprises twenty-five days over a three month period, including an initial eight to ten days of team building and enhancing the women's confidence in oral communication. This training is provided by the faculties of education staff in the elected governorates. Sessions cover developing multigrade teaching strategies and making of teaching resources, child-centered methods, and building self-confidence. Since two facilitators work together in the same classroom, the training also helps to establish the idea of continually discussing issues, developing shared materials, and consulting each other on ideas to improve the children's learning.

Practices for discussion are focused on child-centered, action-based activities, and the teacher as a learning facilitator. Self and peer evaluation of teaching are strongly encouraged. The facilitators are paid by the Ministry of Education for the nine months that schools are in session. During the summer months, the schools continue to function and inservice training continues. Costs for these three months are covered by NGO contributions from an inservice budget line. The NGO also provides field workers and supervisors who supplement the work of the Ministry by visiting teachers to provide support and guidance and to deliver school supplies.

Degree programs housed at general, multipurpose universities. These programs usually emphasize subject matter preparation more than pedagogical preparation.

These are generally three or four-year programs leading to a bachelor's degree, with the teaching preparation portion lasting one to two years. In Botswana, several key factors to be considered in an educational system that is still at a maturing stage of development. Because this program is part of an international donor-funded project, some of the "success" elements concerning donors are also noted.

Teacher education has suffered from a widespread perception that no special knowledge base is required for teaching, that anyone can teach as long as they understand the mechanics of chalkboard use. Lax admission standards have reinforced these misconceptions. Teacher education programs must have a strong emphasis on academic rigor and provide challenging intellectual experiences for student teachers.

The move towards a general education degree for primary teachers has opened up opportunities for teacher trainees throughout the world who start off with the intention of becoming teachers but then wish to enter other professions. The effects in the United States have not been severe, due to a surplus of qualified teachers, but there have been rather severe consequences in many developing nations where both graduates of secondary and superior level teacher training programs use the often "free" education in teacher training as a stepping stone to higher paying or more prestigious occupations.

In Hong Kong, training primary school teachers must specialize in two subject areas. One of the key issues faced by educational planners is how to do the following tasks with few resources: a) recruit sufficient numbers of qualified and committed teachers into the profession, b) retain these teachers in the educational system, and c) raise the quality of their instructional practice. Findings from the research suggest that while the incentives often provided by education systems help to improve teachers' overall career satisfaction and might help stimulate recruitment and encourage retention, they do not typically improve the quality of teaching practices.

Most national systems of education use more than one criterion for selection of candidates into teacher education programs. Common processes include:

— Successful completion of the minimum required period of schooling. Such a requirement is not always expected of primary teacher candidates in some developing countries where teacher education programs may still be part of the upper secondary education system;

— Sitting for an entrance examination that might consist of scholastic achievement and general knowledge;

— Personal interviews to look for such characteristics as communication skills, language proficiency, commitment to teaching, prior preparation, and personality; and

— Submission of letters of reference for character and academic checks.

In the United States and Canada, program size depends on the number of interested candidates meeting entry requirements and the admission policies of individual institutions. In many Canadian provinces, faculties of education have intake quotas for specific areas of concentration. While there is a national standard in many regions that candidates are usually expected to meet, the demand for teachers in many countries is so great that standards are not always maintained.

Even in higher income countries, the difficulties of recruiting sufficient teachers in particular subject areas and in certain geographical locations is often severe. The importance of having command of the subject matter knowledge, the skills to communicate effectively and create and sustain a learning environment, the language proficiency, and the commitment to teaching are identified frequently in the research literature as ideal criteria for the selection of candidates for teaching positions.

In desperate circumstances, a willingness to learn and a commitment to teaching are essential; the subject matter knowledge and appropriate skills can be developed through on-the-job support and inservice programs. The "licensed" and the "articled" teacher schemes in the United Kingdom are growing sources of new entrants.

Kemmerer defines the term "incentives" as all the direct and indirect benefits offered to teachers as intrinsic motivators. More specifically, he states that direct monetary benefits are the package of teacher salary, allowance, and fringe benefits; indirect monetary benefits are all other financial resources offered to teachers. These might include: i) professional support such as initial and ongoing training programs, teacher guides, textbooks, instructional supervision; and ii) personal support such as free or subsidized housing, food, or transportation.

Nonmonetary benefits include professional status in the community, location of teaching position, recognition and approval by significant people associated with the teacher, etc. Different incentives work for different people at different stages of their careers. It is important to look at each community of teachers and to find out what would make a difference for those individuals to improve their teaching as well as their career satisfaction.

Many countries provide incentives such as salary differentials, transportation funds, extra vacation time for traveling long distances, bicycles, or housing to encourage teachers to work in isolated rural areas. However, for improving the instructional skills of teachers, some suggestions that have monetary implications are to provide:

— release time to observe and work with peers in one's own school as well as in other schools or districts;

— release time for ongoing inservice programs;

— additional planning or preparation time for teachers; and

— institutional support for teachers, (induction programs, ongoing.support and guidance, rewards, providing instructional materials, providing orientation "programs" to the school/new region etc.) particularly in the first few years of teaching.

"Status" depends on how society and prospective teachers perceive the extrinsic compensation and conditions of the workplace, and the intrinsic rewards of professional accomplishments. Low status is often linked with low salaries, poor working conditions, and few opportunities for advancement and rewards. Therefore, the most able students are often attracted to other professions that will offer these attractive and needed incentives.

Teacher professionalism begins with instructional competence and commitment and extends into a number of related issues dealing with the degree of decision-making autonomy and accountability. Therefore, initial steps in developing teacher professionalization should focus on helping teachers develop basic instructional competencies. Ingersoll found that schools with more faculty influence over decision-making had distinctly lower rates of turnover than those with less staff influence over decision-making.

As a result, a host of reforms have been promoted that are designed to upgrade the working conditions of teachers, such as teacher empowerment initiatives, evaluation of performance, merit pay plans, career ladders, mentoring programs, and other professional development plans. One of the few studies dealing with the issue of teacher education faculty in the developing world was conducted by Schiefelbein and Tedesco. The study found that among education professors, a higher proportion were female, older, had a lower percentage of doctorates but a higher percentage of master's degrees, possessed degrees acquired nationally rather than internationally, and preferred teaching to research more than did professors in other disciplines.

Induction programs that guide and support beginning teachers in their first year or two of teaching are essential to develop sound teaching practices as well as to retain teachers in the system. Some countries prefer school-based induction programs, while others such as Israel, have induction programs run by teacher colleges and the academic schools of education. Some key guidelines for running induction programs, as summarized by Odell are presented here:

— Provide continuing assistance for beginning teachers to reduce the identified common problems that typically occur in the early stages of teaching.

— Support development of the knowledge and the skills needed by beginner teachers to be successful in their initial teaching position, and provide resources for instructional materials.

— Integrate beginning teachers into the social system of the school, the school district, and the community.

— Provide an opportunity for beginning teachers to analyze and reflect on their teaching.

— Accompany reflection time with coaching from veteran support teachers.

— Increase the positive attitudes of beginning teachers toward teaching.

— Provide incentives and compensation to those participating in the program, including the mentor teachers.

— Provide release time for observations of other teachers-coaching and planning is necessary for both mentors and beginning teachers.

— Waive formal appraisals and evaluations during the first year of teaching.

APEC countries such as Hong Kong, the Peoples' Republic of China, the Republic of Korea, the United States, Canada, New Zealand, and Japan have or are developing induction programs, transition periods, and on-the-job support for beginning teachers. In Chinese Taipei, teacher candidates, prior to licensure, undertake a year-long internship following their course work. In mainland China, responsibility for training new teachers Induction Programs.occurs through a minimum three-year apprenticeship, which some schools extend to five years.

In the Republic of Korea, the rate of teacher participation in school-based induction has risen from less than 10 percent in 1992 to about a quarter of all teachers in 1994-95. Incorporating induction programs within the more general framework of school-based inservice education is common in the United States and other western industrial countries, particularly where initial teacher preparation has been upgraded and lengthened.

New Zealand and Japan offer examples of highly developed induction and internship programs. In New Zealand, it is generally accepted that the first years in the classroom are a continuation of the initial training students received in college, and the first stage of their ongoing professional development. Though registration is not a compulsory requirement, new teachers are not eligible to become fully registered until they have completed at least two years of classroom experience.

In Japan, beginning teachers are given a lighter work load; attend in-school training two times per week with assistance from designated guidance teachers; and receive out-of-school training once per week. Out-of-school training covers a wide range of activities including volunteer work, lectures, seminars, and visits to other schools, child welfare facilities, private cooperation, and social education facilities.

To support induction activities, schools employing one beginning teacher are assigned a part-time lecturer; those employing two beginning teachers are assigned a full-time teacher. The appointing authorities cover funding for induction programs, and the national government covers one half of all personnel and out-of-school training costs. In Canada, the provinces of Quebec and New Brunswick are currently piloting induction programs.

In the United States, approximately twenty-five states have started some kind of induction program, although only a few have provided funding for mentors, release time, or graduated responsibility for new teachers. In these programs, teachers are generally employed full time on provisional licenses and are observed and evaluated on their teaching performance as a condition for receiving a professional license after one to three years. Several schools in Australia have their own induction and support programs for beginning teachers. The Australian Education Union has recently created policy guidelines for launching induction programs.

Many international projects have attempted to change the supervisory and teacher evaluation systems in order to improve instruction and to weed out weaker teachers. However, supervisors face a conflict caused by performing both roles of evaluator and facilitator. Supervisors often ask how they can both help teachers grow as classroom instructors when they must also make a written evaluation of their effectiveness.

This conflict is so great, that some countries have attempted to separate the roles, with some supervisors evaluating teachers in a traditional "inspector" role and others promoting teacher development. Teachers often feel the conflict too, not knowing whether to rely on the supervisor for support or to avoid the supervisor for fear of receiving a poor evaluation. The conflicting roles are almost inevitable: just as a classroom teacher must be both a facilitator and an evaluator of student progress, so most supervisors are thrust into both roles.

In 1990, international agencies, governments, NGOs, professional bodies and the private sector convened at two major world events to give the highest priority to Universal Primary Education (UPE). The World Conference on Education for All, held in Jomtien, Thailand and the World Summit for Children, in New York crystallized a world movement that had been growing over the past several decades. They provided a new impetus to the universally acknowledged central role of education in development and a better understanding of its frustratingly slow pace in many countries.

For UNICEF, which played a central role in both meetings, 1990 became the start of a decade in which education would become not only a high programming priority but also a call signal for evolving direction and policies. This included increased intersectoral work and a broadened definition of education that expanded its scope from traditional academic study to life skills, peace and conflict resolution, rights and empowerment. In addition, UNICEF incorporated into its new programming efforts a broadening of the focus on children of primary school age to include both very young children and adolescents.

In the years following Jomtien, the implications of the shift in vision widened with a growing acceptance of the legal and ethical right of all children to have access to school and to the opportunity for quality education. At the same time, the arguments about the economic and social benefits of education began to receive greater attention and entered into common political parlance. The traditional methods were just not working. The rise in enrolment was not matched by a rise in learning, retention or completion of school, especially among girls. What was needed to reach UPE was a major reform of educational goals, methods, and power relations. Such reform would reflect an expanded vision and new model of education that included improved and more relevant curricula and textbooks, teaching methods, and better trained teachers and administrators. Reform would require whole systems that were sensitive and relevant to gender and to powerless excluded populations of children, including the poor, ethnic and racial minorities and working children. Still, no commitment to new methods, schedules and curricula would succeed if education systems only resulted in perpetuating the status quo and replicating the western model of education installed and instilled in the psyches of most developing countries.

An educational system that goes hand in hand with social transformation was and is still needed. Such a system moves students and teachers from passive recipients and donors of knowledge to active participants in their own learning. It results in a full understanding and acceptance that a major shift in power structures at all levels is required to bring real change and the possibility of achieving EFA. The international community met again in Dakar in 2000 when new commitments to learners were made. These commitments, as laid out in the Dakar Framework for Action, not only reflect the expanded vision of education as first articulated in Jomtien, but also address some of the new challenges that have exploded since 1990, such as the HIV/AIDS pandemic. The broadened vision of education has called for new and revitalized partnerships, and that is as true post Dakar as it was a decade ago. There is now a plethora of stakeholders involved in basic education efforts at the global level. They include multilateral and bilateral international development organizations central and local governments, NGOs, teachers, parents and communities.

The best partnerships recognize independence, entitlements, and indigenous knowledge; express mutual respect and trust; and work within the framework of national development and educational priorities. In theory, at least, serious attempts have been made to move away from the practices of earlier decades when grants for education projects usually restricted the receiving country's equipment, experts, and other needs to choices preselected by the donor country or agency.

To be involved in the dialogue about education systems around the world today is to understand and articulate the key role played by teachers. Through teachers can flow the ideology, values, and culture of a nation, state, and its people. Misinformation and constricted learning behaviours that students internalize can also be filtered through teachers' lack of knowledge, misjudgements, or biases. Calls for educational reform must therefore emphasize the education and empowerment of teachers that includes the real opportunity for them to share perspectives, power and decision-making. One critical area in which all teachers must be educated is gender equity.

Among international agencies and donors, Education For All (EFA) reform efforts have heavily targeted girls and women calling for the elimination of gender gaps in access, learning and retention. Numerous programmes have also been initiated that either focus entirely on females or make a special effort to ensure their inclusion. Education for girls, however, in strongly patriarchal countries will not result in empowered women who will participate in critical decision making-unless their teachers are empowered supporters of gender equity. This is especially true of women teachers who must serve as positive role models. Although they are the front-line participants and critical to successful quality schooling, teachers often form a silent majority; they are excluded not only from policy-making, governance and management, but also from day-to-day instructional strategies and decision making.

Teachers as a whole, especially in less developed countries, have held minimal power in educational systems that are organized in hierarchical ways. Women teachers in particular are even less able to participate in decision-making and have even less voice in creating the institutional structures and policies that affect their lives—in and out of school —and the success of their students. Education researchers point out that the structural and institutional aspects of schools, rather than teachers, perpetuate the barriers to empowerment and equity. Structural obstacles encourage the reproduction of current power relations rather than stimulate changes. Even in many educational reform efforts, for example, teachers are often the forgotten or taken-for-granted vehicles used to implement but not to create or initiate reforms.

Pre-service and in-service training are often not planned or integrated into reform efforts; in many developing countries, teachers have no formal pre-service education at all. Yet, in spite of these arguments, it is also true that in many countries teachers are becoming increasingly accepted as essential partners in a dynamic education system. But if efforts to increase student access, learning and retention in primary education are to succeed, relevant and empowering teacher education is crucial. Teachers must become active, fulfilled and empowered professionals themselves. If an educational system is to engender normative change, the entire system must be restructured to allow all actors to participate more democratically.

The education system in India remains at a critical juncture. The world's second most populous country, with current estimates of over one billion people, India has a literacy rate of approximately 51 per cent. The history of India's educational system is complex, marked by deep debate and many contradictions between policy and practices and between laws and their enforcement. Elements of continuity and tradition have battled those of change and innovation. The power of cultural and historic barriers to change, including nearly two centuries of colonialism and many more centuries of a rigid caste system, have maintained a stubborn barrier to meaningful social transformation. However, well before the past decade and even the past century, a populist movement continued to challenge very powerful traditional educational values and practices. A brief look at the diverse historical trends and currents can help to illuminate both the deep cultural roots of tradition and the strong reform elements that are critical to the current situation. This history reveals that progress is slow and uneven, and that the future is embedded in the past. Necessary changes must be perceived within the larger historical perspective.

Historical links between women's teacher training and girls' education viewed through a gender lens, India's history of educational reform reveals more than a century of policies that seemed to anticipate and support the needed links between women's teacher education and education for girls. As early as 1882, the Indian Education Commission supported teacher-training institutes for women. In 1913, the government of India (GOI) passed a resolution that both established teaching universities and emphasized the education of girls. Primary school teachers were required to pass a vernacular middle examination, receive one year of training and take refresher courses. They would receive a salary of not less than 12 rupees, and teach classes with no more than 30 to 40 students. During the struggle for independence in 1947, and in the years following, a growing number of women activists struggled with the ideas of gender and social change, internally, with each other and with society. These women demanded a revision of the norms perpetuating inequities that would include the right to vote and equal rights to education. In 1944, the women's literacy rate had grown only to 3.4 per cent from 0.9 per cent in 1901. Their demands went far beyond the goals of national leaders and male reformers who promoted a limited view of female education that left the basic patriarchal social structure unchanged. Male leaders aimed to use education to make women more capable of fulfilling their traditional roles as wives and mothers and not to make them more efficient and active units in the process of socio-economic or political development.

After independence, official GOI policies reflected the development of democratic ideology and institutions. The 1950 Constitution of independent India promised "universal, free, and compulsory education to all children up to the age of fourteen". Within this educational commitment, women were specifically named among "weaker others" to be given special protection and the opportunity to advance. To further these goals, the GOI established committees to reform the system including the Women's Education Committee, which addressed the training and employment of women teachers. Almost twenty years later, in 1968, India's first National Policy on Education (NPE) recommended that "the education of girls should require emphasis, not only on grounds of social justice, but also because it accelerates social transformation."

The 1985 "Challenge of Education," a Ministry of Education policy perspective review, cited many shortcomings of the education system and criticized the government's failure to carry out reform. It drew attention to the continuing authoritarian, centralized and monolithic management approach that impeded decentralization and local participation. The system, it said, also created an environment of anonymity and widespread apathy of teachers and the community in regard to primary school. The role of teachers reflected the many, often opposing, currents of tradition, caste, colonialism and reform. On the one hand, teachers held the status of guru deriving from the Brahman ideal of moral authority and sacred knowledge, subduing the curiosity and questioning of students. Yet teachers received poor quality teacher training, low pay and had little decision-making power in regard to substantive or administrative issues.

The education system would play an interventionist role in promoting women's studies and empowering women to become actively involved as decision makers and administrators. The elimination of women's illiteracy and the removal of obstacles inhibiting their access to, and retention in, elementary education will receive overriding priority, through provision of special support services, setting of time targets, and effective monitoring.

In 1992, further policy change continued to promote the end of gender discrimination and the empowerment of women to full participation. The NPE and Programme of Action (POA) viewed education as an instrument of social transformation that would eliminate curriculum biases and enable professionals such as teachers, decision makers, administrators and planners to "play a positive interventionist role for gender equality".

To achieve this would require a large-scale overhaul of policies and practices. Such measures included: training all teachers and instructors as agents of women's empowerment; developing gender and poverty sensitization programmes for teacher educators and administrators; developing gender-sensitive curriculum; removal of sex bias from textbooks. They also included giving preference to female teacher recruitment to motivate parents to send girls to school. The NPE set explicit goals for women teachers' recruitment at a minimum of 50 per cent and urged that training facilities ensure an adequate, though unspecified, number of qualified women teachers in subjects that included mathematics and science.

Yet a stark contradiction has remained between policy commitments to women's equality and actual reform. Little real change has occurred despite the clear articulation by Indian educational policy and planning of what is necessary to create democratically structured programmes that will facilitate gender sensitivity and equity. Changing the ideology of a country steeped in cultural, social and economic inequities requires constant struggle. Over the years, the absence of political initiative and funding accompanied by changes in political control has hindered steady progress toward these goals.

Women's national literacy rates remain at 42 per cent compared to the rate of 69 per cent for men. The limited scope of women's roles must be replaced with a 21st century ideology that makes them full participants in socio-economic and political development. Programmes that attempt to incorporate gender equitable policies, including those for teachers, have been increasing. Because they play a pivotal role in transmitting equality to their students, women teachers must be high on the list of women who participate in more gender equitable programmes.

Teacher Empowerment Programme (TEP)

The teacher empowerment programme emerged as one important programme that focused increasingly on gender equity for teachers. This in-service programme began in the Dhar district of Madhya Pradesh in 1992 as a grassroots effort designed to meet the immediate needs of teachers for new content and skills that would increase their influence on the process of education. Focused on interactive participation and decision-making of teachers, the TEP aimed to place power in their hands and facilitate its responsible use. Innovative and imaginative, the TEP did not reject official education policy; its general objectives and processes are consistent with the guidelines of the National Policy on Education (NPE) and its Programme of Action (POA).

The TEP began as a UNICEF initiative yet was enabled through a long standing relationship with the Government of India, familiarity with government policies and practices, and a deep understanding of the needs and conditions of teachers. Through combined goals and efforts, the partnership of UNICEF, the GOI, and the teachers' union capitalised on an increasingly conducive environment and was able to put stated policy goals into practice. For teachers, this meant improved status, teaching skills and materials, greater participation and decision-making in governance and programme development and more joyful training in pedagogy. The empowerment of teachers would also have a direct and positive bearing on achieving the goals for students that included increased attendance, retention through class five—especially for girls—and higher levels of achievement.

The TEP ties educational developmental theory to practice as teachers learn a child-responsive approach that is joyful and experiential. They learn that teachers must be nurturing and caring and offer concrete contexts so children can learn through play and various hands-on activities. They learn to provide opportunities for children to express themselves verbally and artistically through singing, dancing, and drama and to allow ample time to tell and listen to stories that make sense of their environment and their lives.

Unlike most previous in-service trainings, the TEP addresses the lack of joy in teaching, the overburdened curriculum and the unmotivated teachers—all criticisms in various GOI and other education reports. The unshakeable foundation of the Joyful Learning approach is that teachers participate and collaborate through an interactive, hands-on approach. The choice of districts in which to implement the TEP was linked to indicators showing the poorest literacy rates. UP is India's most populous state and one of the five lowest literacy states where the rate stands at about only 41 per cent—55 percent for males and only 25 percent for females. When the TEP expanded to the State of UP, teachers themselves chose the name Ruchipurna Shikshan or Joyful Learning (JL) for their training, reflecting both their ownership of the programme and a new attitude it motivated. Just one month before the training began in UP, on the day annually celebrated as Teachers' Day, over 12,000 teachers pledged and committed themselves to work toward UPE, to avoid absenteeism and drunkenness, and to become better teachers. Since that day, many teachers have pledged or re-pledged their commitment as part of the Joyful Learning Programme.

Teachers made their own teaching aids such as the cloth pocket board sewn to create rows and pockets. They used colour-coded cards for activities such as matching, categorizing, and sequencing, or word cards that enabled language arts skills such as vocabulary, syntax, or story telling. These activities have remained a part of the training throughout the history of the programme, and flourish today. Low-cost, low-tech and inclusive processes represent activities that teachers can initiate with the children themselves. The portable, pocket board teaching aid has proven particularly effective in environments where there is no classroom.

Yet just as important as providing teachers with new skills and content, the training in UP went beyond teachers and administrators. It included space for dialogue among teachers, trainers and government officials for reflection, sharing and discussion of concerns. In one training session, for example, teachers expressed concern about outdated syllabi and curricula in the pre-service Basic Teacher Training (BTT) programme. They expressed the need for better communication among department officials, monitors, and the DIET (District Institute of Education and Training) instructors to increase their understanding and ownership of the TEP. The intangible aspects and principles upon which the programme was based are evident during these dialogues— respect, trust, commitment, and equity. The in-service manual for Class One expresses these empowering foundations:

> Teachers are all creative, talented people and respond remarkably when they are respected and included in the decision-making integral to their work in the classroom. They gain a sense of ownership over their work and their classrooms, when they are involved in development of the curriculum, designing of the syllabus, making and selecting of teaching materials and in designing training programmes leading to their own intellectual and professional development.

Placing teachers in a central role, encouraging hands-on interactive activities and the making of teaching aids have garnered strong and wide teacher support in the districts in which the programme has operated. Although implementation is challenging, partners have learned to work together and make the best use of each others' diverse expertise, resources and knowledge. Furthermore, the TEP has begun to converge with other government-sponsored teacher training programmes to spread more widely the joyful learning that ultimately will benefit both the teachers and the students.

The training itself may empower to some extent all the teachers who participate. Listening closely to their life stories, related experiences and private views, brings into sharp focus the link between private and public, between life and education, between the personal and political. It also reveals the complexities, nuances and entrenched attitudes and behaviours behind the theory and the statistics. The voices of these teachers help to reveal how their daily lives, thoughts and feelings fit into the larger public culture and system that helps or hinders women teachers' empowerment.

Underlying the implementation of the TEP is the philosophy that teachers must be trusted, respected, listened to, and encouraged to nurture their creative abilities. The emphasis was on the immediate participation of all teachers through activities that encourage open and equal male and female interaction and break down inhibitions that would obviate the need for specific attention to gender issues. This mainstreaming, or gender blind, strategy prevalent at the start of the movement for gender equality, acknowledged the need for equal female participation but emphasized that programmes should respond to the needs and concerns of women within the framework of broader human and social development objectives.

However, such an approach has also exposed the difficulties of translating mainstreaming goals into visible results and actions and has proven extremely limited in producing significant and speedy improvement in the status of women. This is true in the most socially progressive societies, but especially in country programmes where the national environment is not conducive to promoting social equity and empowerment of women.

Looking at the TEP through a gender lens, what arises as central to the discussion are the relative benefits and drawbacks to mainstreaming gender concerns through gender—neutral practices of equality or to promoting gender-specific analysis and activities. As the programme expanded from MP to UP, the need for specific discussion of gender issues was acknowledged and incorporated into the structure, design and implementation of the programme process.

Explicit targeting of gender equity became part of the TEP curricula in UP, opening space for depth of coverage and for additional content. Planners were aware that more time was needed to break down the barriers of women's silence and dispel misconceptions about their acceptance of the status quo. Longer training sessions evolved and the overall training increased in length from one to five days. To achieve equality and empowerment, it would also be necessary to address men's underlying attitudes towards gender.

Throughout the observations of the TEP, the interdependency of numbers of woman teachers and empowerment surfaced repeatedly. Reasons for restricted women's participation in teaching varied from practical to psychosocial—for example, from competing family obligations to feelings of unworthiness. Both are rooted in gender roles resulting from lifelong discrimination and socialization.

Yet attention to lived realities and explicit discussion of gender issues will support woman teachers and gender equity and help to increase the numbers of woman teachers. Many of the TEP's training procedures and materials were designed by a group of two trainers and ten teachers, a group, however, that included only one woman trainer and one woman teacher. Although two females were better than none, given the special focus on girls' education in the UP programme, more women teachers among this group should have been recruited for the training.

As gender-sensitive women teachers can be role models for girls, empowered women trainers can help teachers they train to understand and reduce stereotypes and prejudices by drawing on women's experience, or "lived realities." They can turn demeaned and devalued traditional female behaviours into respected assets that benefit themselves, their professions and their societies. All cultures have long recognized that "different" is too often a synonym for "deficient" and seen as a consequence of immutable female "nature." This can confine women to stereotyped and restricted gender roles. Feminism in the 1970's understandably accepted the "gender blind" argument that women's differences were a result of nurture (or lack of) rather than nature and if women were given the same opportunities as men, these differences would disappear. Since the 1980's a voluminous body of literature has acknowledged and heralded women's ways of doing things in which differences—such as skills in and attention to consultation, cooperation and facilitation; and process and consensus building—are celebrated and esteemed and their capacity to transform society is promoted.

Gender neutral participatory activities in the TEP brought to the surface many of the differences between men and women and the need to address them directly. Over the past two decades, the link between women's private and public lives has been at the heart of the international women's movement and the subject of worldwide media attention.

In private, women behave a certain way with a certain kind of freedom. When they are in public or around men, the behaviour change is significant. There is a consistent implication that the presence of men (in a setting outside the home) creates a public domain, even in an informal setting. When there are just women, there isn't this tension. In the early MP trainings, participants did not discuss these issues. Rather, there was a matter-off act environment of expectation that supported and trusted women's strengths without looking at the problem or its causes.

For men as well, performing helped to break down gender barriers. A key part of the curricula focuses on males and females teaching and singing songs that they will also teach to the children. The songs encourage girls' attendance and success in school. Men and women working together can provide role models for women and allow men to see and experience women in leadership roles as well as to experience their own histories and gender biases.

Continued exposure to gender equality can help to break down the hierarchical societal roles and facilitate men's respect for the women's skills, even as something they might emulate. This practice coincides with the essence of GID policies—a reinforcement of the necessity of programmes that target both women and men at the deeper structural level-rather than WID policies that had targeted primarily the integration of women.

Teacher Preparation Programmes

A crucial component of any training is the practicum, variously termed 'teaching practice' or 'school experience'. Traditionally, initial teacher preparation programmes which are college-based have sent students into schools for various lengths of time, under varying degrees of supervision from visiting tutors and 'co-operating teachers' or 'mentors'. Students commonly report this to be the 'most useful' part of their training; tutors find it exhausting and time-consuming; for the college it is expensive and difficult to organise; schools are often unsure of their role and seldom organise the time to the mutual benefit of trainee and school.

At one extreme, staff may take time off, leaving the trainee to sink or swim; at the other the teacher may re-teach each lesson so her class doesn't suffer. More recently, in high income countries, forms of training have developed which reverse the school-college relationship. The trainees are based in school and go out to a campus for academic and professional training sessions. In the UK, one can now gain 'qualified teacher status' via such a school-based training route, which is seen by some as preferable because of its practical bias and criticised by others as lacking academic rigour.

In low income countries, such training 'on the job' is mainly used to upgrade and certify unqualified serving teachers, rather than seen as a respectable pre-service route. There are often problems with providing good distance learning materials and adequate professional support in remote areas, especially where schools are poorly resourced and offer few good models of practice. Theorists of professional learning point to the situated, contextual nature of much professional knowledge, and how it can be developed and built up through experience, but stress also the role of public propositional knowledge and the need for support and guidance from more experienced others through several stages.

This suggests, ideally, that professional learning takes places through alternating periods of input and practice over a considerable period of time. In Ghana, Lesotho and Trinidad and Tobago the research looked at the 'traditional' type of teaching practice (TP), where students go out to schools for one or more 'blocks' of time and are visited by college tutors. In all of these places, the college organises and controls the practice, leaving the schools merely acting as - sometimes reluctant - hosts. Though different messages come from different studies, all provide some form of critique of this pattern, and show how difficult it is to bring theory and practice together in this way.

The Trinidadian colleges have a highly organised system of teaching practice (TP). Although structured slightly differently at the two colleges, TP takes up 12 weeks, arranged roughly in three block periods over the two years. Trainees have a 120-hour programme of preparation for TP; they visit the schools and prepare all lesson plans and units of work prior to each block. Trainees are supposed to teach only four lessons a day, but some do more.

Conditions in the schools are not always conducive to interactive and participatory teaching. The integration of theory and practice does not seem to take place as it is supposed to do. Only a few supervisors used a more holistic approach, encouraging the trainees to respond in a dynamic and creative way to the specific needs of the learners in that class. Even in these cases, the conversations would involve personal theories and experiences, rather than the theory taught in college.

There are contradictory assumptions operating here. The college curriculum is premised on the idea that after acquiring a corpus of knowledge, trainees will be able to apply this to their teaching. Yet supervising tutors talk about practice and experience, and implicitly suggest the need for personal theories developed over time which can use and apply situated knowledge. This suggests an altogether different model of learning to teach, one that focuses on the trainee's own developing understanding of what she is doing in the light of knowledge and of reflection on experience.

The Malawi study shows this is no easy option, particularly in resourceconstrained conditions. Much infrastructure has to be in place and all the support personnel trained before the schools can deliver effective training. The Trinidadian scheme originated from a concern to guide unemployed youth into teaching. It illustrates ways of providing school experience as an orientation to teaching, and perhaps as a selection mechanism, rather than as part of a formal training programme.

The school-based component of the MIITEP scheme is worth studying in detail because it shows the many constraints and problems of trying to upgrade large numbers of teachers 'on the job', as well as offering some pointers to good practice and potential starting points. The intention was that during this time they would receive support from the school, especially from the headteacher, and from the locally-based Primary Education Advisors (PEAs), who would run periodic zonal seminars. College tutors would make supervisory visits, and mark the 16 assignments to be completed during this period.

MIITEP was a huge, elaborate scheme devised to meet a crisis, without sufficient time to put into place the necessary administrative infrastructures; for example, some trainees' records were incomplete and it was not always known where they were. The disbursement of the external funds on which it depended did not always match the needs and timing of the programme.

A key training element - the complementary Malawi Schools Support System Programme (MSSSP) - which was to train headteachers and PEAs in management and supervision, began some time after MIITEP itself. Thus, while detailed criticisms have been made this account will focus on some of the emergent issues, looking at the constraints but also at the potentials, emphasising the prerequisites for such a scheme to work. The conditions in schools are one major constraint on such training.

In Malawi primary schools it is rare for pupils to have desks and chairs; many schools lack classrooms and children have to be taught in the open except when it rains. Since the advent of UPE, classes can range up to 200-300, especially when combined for lack of space or lack of teachers. The blackboard is the main teaching aid, though enterprising teachers collect bottle-tops, stones, etc. for counting.

Textbooks, if available, usually have to be shared between several children; some teachers do not have teachers' guides, and there are virtually no other published resources. In the lower grades, many pupils do not even have pencils or exercise books and infant grades sometimes practise writing in the sand. The head teacher has to coordinate the training, for example pairing the trainees with more experienced teachers - though in over half Malawi primary schools less than 50% of the staff are qualified - organising training sessions, supervising them regularly, and sending in reports.

The headteachers and schools need to organise support, through appropriate pairing, training activities, and supervision that includes formative feedback. In schools there are experienced teachers who have devised contextually useful strategies, which facilitate pupil learning, that could become starting points for working out improved methods that draw on international theories of learning but which are also culturally and economically appropriate.

In Trinidad and Tobago, where there is no pre-service training, some potential teachers undergo a year's apprenticeship in schools while being paid a small stipend. It was devised by the Ministry of Education (MOE) in 1993, as part of a wider national initiative for unemployed youth, to attract potential teachers and to act as a filter for unsuitable ones.

The OJT graduates who went later to college valued particularly the practical aspects, such as lesson planning, which they found very useful for their first teaching practice. Some found the limited amount of teaching frustrating, and all agreed a good relationship with the mentor was a crucial element for success. The main weakness was the lack of coherence within the course; there was no standard curriculum and no links between the theory classes and the practical training in school. Neither were there any links to the college curriculum. Mentors were not trained or supervised. Plans were in train, however, to develop a more coherent and better monitored system.

However, such an orientation course provides an interesting model that might be adapted elsewhere, perhaps in condensed form. The key elements are:

— the participation of the school principal and mentor in the training

— learning practical elements in the classroom, supported by more theoretical elements at induction, in vacations, evenings and weekends

— a phased introduction to teaching, through observation and team teaching before taking over the class

— an introduction which offers basic skills, strategies and confidence-building, which can be complemented later by more substantial academic and professional training.

In South Africa all training courses are therefore likely to involve a substantial practicum. The BAGET design gives an example of how an urban-based programme might develop. There are four short periods of practice teaching - one of which being in a teaching workplace other than a formal school, such as early childhood education, adult training, or community development - and the fourth year is a internship. Peripatetic lecturers would work in partnership with teachers in the schools to supervise the interns. Such a pattern would be difficult in rural areas.

As a result of the policy changes in South Africa, currently there is little development of preservice courses, and much emphasis on in-service and upgrading of underqualified teachers on the job. This will hopefully enhance the ability of the schools in future to play a more significant role in initial training.

School-based training can be cost-effective in that trainees are also teaching, but it needs to be complemented by sufficient external input, such as residential periods, local workshops and distance learning. This also requires considerable infrastructure and organisation to ensure the components are integrated. Schools undertaking training need substantial support in terms of professional development and basic resources.

In many low income countries, good practice does exist in local schools, where experienced teachers have developed their own ways of dealing with large classes and few resources. Such practice should be recognised, used in training, and developed so that innovations and reforms are built around what is possible. Some kind of orientation is essential before untrained recruits start teaching. A period of supervised on-the-job training can be used both as a filter and as a preparation for subsequent college-based courses, but there needs to be coherence between the two.

After training, the actual process of getting a job in a school differs widely between countries: in some the teachers apply, while in others they are 'posted' to vacancies. The system of deployment has wide implications for how the newly trained teachers are, or can be, utilised most effectively and encouraged to stay in the profession.

In a complex process, final year students state their preferences in terms of region and religion, and then they are assigned to schools by the Ghanaian Education Service (GES) in consultation with regional and district offices, and in some cases with religious educational units. As most students prefer the urban or developed regions where they grew up, when they are posted to the rural areas they try, sometimes by underhand means, to get a transfer.

Many practical concerns, such as poor accommodation, the lack of amenities such as transport, piped water and electricity, but they also highlighted cultural aspects, such as the different social values and norms of village life, and the ambivalent attitude of some rural parents towards education. One said he feared to become 'a village man' if he remained in the rural areas; this suggests that many young teachers perceive such postings as a threat to their very identity, and therefore will leave, by one means or another.

Women face additional problems, such as intrusive scrutiny and gossip, and for this reason among others are seldom posted to villages, although their presence would provide good role models for girls. Salaries can be up to nine months late, the posting system is seen as unfair, and little professional support is available locally. Thus new teachers find it difficult to settle down and feel comfortable in their posts and even those who do report for duty often manage to transfer within a couple of years, being replaced once more by untrained teachers.

Those who stay on mention a number of altruistic and intrinsic reasons, but many also indicate they intend taking study leave once their stipulated three years' service is over, and moving out of primary teaching. In Malawi teachers are also 'posted' to schools, and report similar practical difficulties; almost all had experienced late payment of salaries, and the majority also mentioned accommodation, food and transport, but they seem to have fewer problems with community relations, perhaps because they already knew the area.

All teachers in MIITEP had already been posted to schools when they were first recruited, and most returned to the school where they had previously taught, though some were posted to secondary schools and one became a head teacher! By contrast, in Lesotho graduating teachers apply directly to a school, or through the Church Secretariats who own most of the schools. This 'market system' probably means that rural schools get the least effective teachers, but the evidence suggests most teachers felt more satisfied and in control of their lives.

The Ghanaian teachers had a number of criticisms. The main one was that the colleges were out of touch with the reality of the schools, and they had not been taught strategies for coping with such things as the pupils' very low levels of achievement, their poor English, and the frequent absenteeism. Some felt the college curriculum was overly academic, especially in preparing Primary teachers.

Any effective system of teacher education has to recognise and build on the characteristics and motivations that trainees bring to the profession when they enter training programmes. Understanding what these characteristics are provides a basis for the development of curricula that address trainees' needs and capabilities. It is also a reminder to teacher trainers that the backgrounds and aspirations of those entering training now may not be the same as in the past. Where this is so it invites consideration of how training content and methods should change to reflect new realities.

The average age of entrants to teacher education in the samples vary. Ghana (21 years) and Lesotho (22.2 years) have the youngest entrants; Malawi (25.9) and Trinidad and Tobago (26.1) have the oldest. The most obvious explanation for this is that in the former cases most entrants are admitted directly from the school secondary system. Overall between 70% and 75% of teachers are between 19 and 22 years old in Ghana and Lesotho, and the same proportions are between 23 and 27 years in Malawi and Trinidad and Tobago.

Age may be significant for training in a number of ways. First, older trainees are more likely to likely to have some formal or informal experience of teaching, whether or not this is required for entry. Second, they are more likely to be married, or marry during training and have direct or indirect experience of child-raising. Third, older trainees are more obviously adult learners rather than young students arriving directly from school. Fourth, older trainees may be more fixed in their views about teaching and teachers, and clearer about their commitment to teaching as a career.

Over two-thirds of the student teachers were female in both Lesotho and Trinidad and Tobago. The reverse was the case in Ghana, where only onethird of the student teachers were female. Worldwide, the trend has been for primary teaching to become largely feminised; it is interesting that in Ghana and Malawi this has not yet happened.

All the teacher education systems have been influenced by institutions originally established by Christian denominations. Religious affiliation plays an important role in defining identity in each country. In Ghana some colleges, particularly the most prestigious ones like Presbyterian Training College and Wesley, retain strong religious affiliations, though the system of 38 colleges is formally under the control of the Ministry of Education.

Religiouslybased training colleges were amalgamated into a single secular institution in Lesotho in 1975. Two of the six colleges in Malawi remain affiliated to the Catholic church, though formal control over the Colleges was taken by the government in 1973. In Trinidad and Tobago most of the denominational institutions closed from the 1960s onward, while the government established Corinth and Valsayn Colleges on a secular basis. The religious affiliation of Ghanaian student teachers in the sample was predominately Christian with 36% Catholic, 16% Methodist, 15% other named denominations and 24% who just classified themselves as 'Christian'.

Muslims accounted for 4% of the student teachers, significantly less than their percentage of the population, perhaps reflecting the fact that colleges in the sample were selected from the predominantly Christian South. In Lesotho, the majority of Basotho student teachers were either Catholic or Lesotho Evangelical Church. About 16% were Anglican and a further 14% 'other'. In Malawi 41% were members of the Church of Central Africa and 29% were Catholic. About 15% were Seventh Day Adventists, and 3% Muslim.

Again this is significantly less than the national proportion of Muslims, which may reflect different attitudes to education. In Trinidad and Tobago 22% were Catholic, 19% Hindu, 16% Presbyterian, and 30% were distributed across various other Christian denominations; 6% were Muslim. The religious affiliation of student teachers, and the denominational history of many of the training institutions, carries implications for the training process. These are not simple to unravel, but are likely to have some influence on student teachers' attitudes towards learning, and their role as teachers.

Qualifications of Student Teachers

It is difficult to present the diversity of the educational experience and qualifications of the student teachers in the four different countries. The examinations in the different countries are often not equivalent and the levels of attainment differ across the sites. However it is possible to make some general statements about the educational qualifications of the student teachers on entry.

Overall, the student teachers in Trinidad had substantially higher educational qualifications than the student teachers in the other three countries. There was very little difference between the achievement of the male and female student teachers in Trinidad. In Ghana, the women had achieved similar results in English, whilst the men achieved better results in mathematics and science.

The overall picture is that most trainee teachers achieved relatively low results at the end of their secondary school career, leaving them underqualified for higher education. Teacher training colleges, it seems, take the next tranche down from the universities. The training programmes are for serving teachers in Trinidad and Tobago and Malawi so all the respondents had taught before. In contrast, in Lesotho and Ghana few had any teaching experience and were direct entrants from schools.

The student teachers' responses to statements about teaching and the teaching profession add another dimension to the biographical information that the students have supplied. The responses give some insight into the attitudes that these trainee teachers bring with them when they enter training.

In Ghana, trainee teachers may have more sympathy with didactic approaches to teaching than in the other countries. Ghanaian trainee teachers were much more likely than others to agree that 'Teachers cannot do much to improve the academic performance of low achieving students' with over 80% strongly agreeing or agreeing. These trainees appear not to have high expectations of their ability to improve children's capabilities. Language issues are well established as a problem in all the African countries in the sample. Surprisingly, teacher education curricula seem to give little emphasis to it in the training process.

Teaching is a very difficult job to do well also gives some indication of how entering trainees perceive their intended profession. There was little agreement from the Malawian trainees, implying that most thought teaching was easy, whilst a majority of the Trinidadian trainees felt teaching was difficult. Malawian trainees are anxious not to be seen as having difficulties since all have been teaching as untrained teachers for several years before entering MIITEP. In Trinidad trainees have also been teaching prior to enrolling on the training programme and they are better qualified. It may be that they regard teaching as more difficult because expectations of them are high, but this possible explanation remains at the level of a speculation. An aspect of trainees' career preferences are partly indicated by responses to statement.

A majority of Ghanaian trainees agreed with this statement, possibly reflecting the fact that primary teachers become qualified for upgrading training and study leave after a few years teaching in primary schools. This is not such an established pattern in the other countries. Three-quarters of Basotho trainees disagreed with this statement, with a strong difference between males and females, suggesting females were more enthusiastic about remaining as primary school teachers.

Overall the great majority of Ghanaian trainees agreed with this, as did a small preponderance of those in Trinidad. About a quarter of those in Lesotho agreed and the Malawi sample was evenly split. This may partly reflect the chances of trainees actually getting into university—opportunities appear very limited in Lesotho. These results are not easy to interpret, but they suggest that many trainees enter college with ambivalent attitudes to the profession and that they may be confused about some of the key pedagogic concepts. Teacher educators need to be aware of such views and inconsistencies so that they can deal constructively with them.

A good teacher, was very punctual to the class every morning all the lessons he taught were very challenging, [and] he taught clearly. He was very intelligent in .... explanations. He was having a parental love to each and every student in his class. He knew how to treat both fast learners, medium-learners as well as slow learners. He knew how to influence his students to perform very well ... he succeeded in making every pupil to obtain better pass-marks.

Views from Malawi and Ghana are broadly similar, though interestingly there is rather less emphasis on the nurturing role. This may be related to the fact that primary teaching in these two countries is much less heavily feminised than in Lesotho. But there is the same emphasis on personality—the ability to encourage and inspire - and on commitment-patient, hardworking, ready to help individuals—rather than on professional skills.

In Ghana the emphasis on the teacher as social role model extends beyond the individual to the community. In Lesotho, the student views of the ideal teacher - the kind of teacher they would like to be - provide support for the thesis that students model themselves on their own teachers. In Trinidad and Tobago the images of the good teacher that emerged from the open-ended survey questions were not dissimilar to those found elsewhere: caring, helpful, encouraging, maternal and dedicated.

Again there was little mention of cognitive or pedagogic skills, though a strong theme emerged, different from the African sites, about 'making learning fun'. First and foremost a good teacher must be able to establish caring relationships, understand the children's needs, act as an exemplar, be patient but firm - in other words, taking on a parental role. Many of these qualities are felt to be innate. However, professional and pedagogic skills are also necessary, and the good teacher has to be trained, so they can work effectively in the classroom. After a year, most of the respondents felt they had gained useful knowledge about handling children and delivering lessons, though they still held ambivalent views on corporal punishment.

Teacher as responsible for everything; A primary teacher has to be an 'all-rounder', capable of doing everything on their own. This seems to emphasise the burden on the individual, rather than a collective responsibility. Teachers have to make sacrifices, taking a job with relatively low professional status and poor salaries, while being expected to perform a multi-faceted role in the classroom. George et al conclude that underlying these images and metaphors are powerful cultural myths about being a teacher in Trinidad and Tobago, which have their roots far back in the society's historical experiences. Such myths describe teachers as engaged in self-sacrificing work which they do because of a love of children and a sense of altruism.

On the one hand teachers are seen as powerful individuals capable of effecting change through love and selfless dedication, and earning respect; on the other hand they have to forego high salaries and status. Both college curriculum and the myth project a certain desired scenario, while trainees experience something much less rewarding. While the substantive self embraces the cultural myth, the situated self has difficulties with the low status and rewards. Teacher as a:

— role model in the community

— self-reliant and independent individual

— a stepping stone to better jobs

— duty to family

— a moral or religious ideal of service

— isolation and fear of becoming 'a village man'

— an opportunity for strong friendships

— 'government work'

— an opportunity to pursue other interests like farming and business

Unsurprisingly, students gave a mixture of motives for wanting to train as a teacher. In Africa, general altruistic reasons such as 'to impart knowledge', to 'bring light' and 'raise the standard of education in the country'. Some of these ideas seemed linked to the Christian traditions of both students and colleges, others to development discourses.

A few students expressed an intrinsic interest in working with children, or wanted to win respect from the community as a role model. The qualitative studies confirm these broad patterns, but show more clearly how their idealistic and altruistic motives conflict with their realistic assessment of difficult conditions in the schools and the low status of primary teachers. Students' ideals need to be nurtured and rewarded if they are to act as lifelong motivators.

2

Learning: Towards Teacher Development

When teachers are involved in appropriate decision-making processes, are able to reflect on and change their circumstances, enjoy being around children, have the skills needed to impart appropriate knowledge and manage their classrooms, and understand their role in the broader community, they are usually highly motivated and student achievement tends to rise. These elements are usually developed over time and with practice.

The principals cited student-centered learning, a democratic learning environment, outstanding leadership, high standards and expectations and a range of other factors. The principal of perhaps the most student-centered, democratic school in the country shocked everyone when he said that he built his school around his teachers. When teachers were motivated, committed, and happy to be there, the rest of the work would fall into place.

In considering raising the quality of teaching, one must begin at the teacher level. Teacher development must be seen as a continuum of learning, with teachers located at various places along the continuum. Teaching experience is gained over time. Long-term goals for excellence in teaching should be ambitious, but short and mid-term goals must reflect the reality of the everyday working situation for teachers.

Even if only very modest changes are produced, such as getting a teacher to come to class each day and undertake basic skills training with rote methods, this represents progress if before the teacher did not even make it to class. While there are certainly better methods than rote to help children learn, the point is that planners and administrators may need to have modest goals in the initial stages of enacting a teacher development program.

However, they should never lose sight of moving forward to the goal of creating a teacher who will use a variety of interesting and effective learning methods. Almost twenty years ago, Husen, Saha, and Noonan published Teacher Training and Student Achievement in Less Developed Countries for the World Bank. However, how teachers were prepared and supported within the school system were critical elements of higher student achievement and retention.

For example, outside formal evaluations of the Basic Education Strengthening (BEST) project in Guatemala showed that teachers had been effective in advancing children through the primary schools, schools retained significantly more students than traditional rural schools, and students achieved at a higher level in mathematics and reading. It was also found that active pedagogy practiced by the teachers contributed to pupils' emotional growth and participatory behavior. Parental satisfaction was also higher-parents cited their children's ability to read and behave better at home.

Teachers had developed skills to diagnose the difficulties facing students, reflect on possible solutions, and make appropriate changes to student learning environments. In the BRAC Non-Formal Primary Education program, teaching staff are provided with a high level of practical on-the-job support. A formal evaluation of the program showed that more than 90 percent of the children who start the school program finish.

Specific factors such as the years of teacher training, the teacher's verbal fluency, subject matter knowledge, having books and materials and knowing how to use them, teacher expectations of pupil performance, time spent on classroom preparation, and frequent monitoring of student progress are known to affect student achievement. Most of these skills can be learned through teacher education programs and on-the-job supervision.

Darling-Hammond and Cobb summarized several trends revealed in the large teacher development study on some of the Asia-Pacific Economic Cooperation (APEC) countries. While these trends were reported from the APEC countries, they reflect issues that are being discussed in many other countries around the world. These trends include:

— Across APEC countries, women make up the bulk of the teaching force at the pre-primary and primary school levels. While women also predominate at the secondary level in many member countries, in Japan and the Republic of Korea men make up the bulk of the teaching force in secondary schools. In most APEC countries men continue to outnumber women in senior administrative positions such as head teachers.

— Teacher wages often compare unfavorably with salaries in other professions.

— Several countries find it difficult to meet demand for teachers in remote areas. On the other hand, in the United States, the highest demand for teachers is in inner cities and in growing areas of the country where immigration is high and teacher salaries tend to be lower.

— Countries facing teacher shortages use a variety of ad hoc solutions, including hiring teachers without full preparation by establishing emergency and alternative routes to licensing.

— Some countries report that teaching is still a field with little opportunity for advancement and promotion, i.e., to advance, one must leave teaching.

— Efforts are underway to strengthen preparation programs and induction support for teachers.

— There are few external incentives to participate in professional development activities.

— Some APEC countries are trying to establish national frameworks for professional development to expand beyond its use for licensure or registration, and credentialing for promotion, and to encourage professional development as an integral and ongoing component of the profession. What the countries are aiming for is a continuum of professional development and growth for teachers that spans their careers from preparation to retirement.

— Teaching in most APEC countries is a highly regarded profession.

There are efforts in the United States, Australia, and some provinces in Canada foster greater collaboration among institutions of higher education, school districts, and teacher organizations in efforts to improve teacher preparation and support. Professional development school relationships and mentoring programs are examples of increased collaboration between schools and colleges of education.

Most developing nations are forced to employ some underqualified- and often unqualified-teachers in order to achieve universal primary education. This has generally been a major factor in the decline of the overall quality of education and the increase in recurrent budget expenditure. In countries where teacher salaries are perceived as being a "step up" from other nonagricultural salaries, parents will often encourage their children to attend a teacher training program.

In addition, when salaries are competitive, graduates of teacher training programs are more likely to enter the teaching profession rather than the private sector. Numerous factors help determine what salary will attract and retain quality teachers. Salaries need to support at least basic living conditions, to attract and maintain teachers with the desired levels of qualifications, and to minimize "moonlighting" and lack of professional commitment. Coombe notes the high departure rates, absenteeism, neglect of duty, and lack of discipline among teachers in Africa, all of which contribute to lack of discipline, absenteeism, and repetition among pupils.

Núnez reports that primary school teachers in Chile in the early 1980s received the lowest salary on the national scale, a problem that worsened in subsequent years as decentralized responsibilities for hiring and firing teachers meant increased work instability. High rates of inflation in countries such as Venezuela can erode the purchasing power of comparatively high salaries for public servants such as teachers.

Countries that have had rapid economic growth in the past decade, such as Chile and Thailand, have found it necessary to raise teachers' salaries more rapidly to keep them from defecting to the private sector. Many African economies have remained stagnant and even declined over the past twenty years, which has made it almost impossible to raise teachers' salaries. Moreover, with the contintent's massive unemployment and underemployment, there has not been the economic pressure to raise salaries.

During massive deflations such as that experienced by Mexico in the mid-1990s, teachers and other civil servants bear a large portion of the burden and, when the economy recovers, make strong demands on the political system for greater salary equity. Up to 90 percent of all recurrent educational expenditures are allocated to teachers' salaries in many formal government systems. However, some successful nonformal basic education school programs have managed to greatly reduce the proportion of the budget spent on teachers' salaries.

BRAC's Nonformal Primary Education program in Bangladesh, for example, supports about 35,000 schools, with 27 percent of its program budget going to management and supervision and only 29 percent to teachers' salaries. The remainder of the budget supports students' books and supplies, rental of classroom space, training, teaching aids and equipment, and staff offices and housing. While teachers-particularly those at the primary level-in most developing nations are notoriously underpaid, no clear relationship between teacher salary and student achievement has been discovered.

However, salaries do correlate highly with qualifications and experience in almost all school systems. Thias and Carnoy and Carnoy and de Moura Castro found significant relationships between the average teacher salary and examination outcomes at both the primary and secondary levels in Kenya, but salaries accounted for only a small fraction of the total variance in performance.

Recent research shows that on average only about half of teachers' time is devoted to direct teaching and lesson preparation. Administrative and other duties take up the largest part of teachers' time, and many of those activities might potentially be delegated to support staff.

On intra-institutional studies, teacher training ranked consistently at or near the bottom in reference to other academic disciplines, often with expenditures far below those in the sciences,.engineering, or business. The studies all conclude that teacher education is underfunded in comparison to not only other disciplines, but even within departments of education. Peseau, Backman, and Fry point out that traditional funding formulas do not accurately reflect the complexity of teacher education programs.

Clinical programs in teacher education encompass several functions not generally characteristic of traditional didactic courses. Among these functions are such things as student placement, travel, communications, clinical supervision, support services and materials, simulation and microteaching expenditures, and payments to cooperating teachers. Monk and Brent also found that in the United States, it is likely that classes in teacher education programs are instructed by the least senior faculty members and contain twice as many students as other department courses.

There has been very little research conducted on either the direct or indirect costs of teacher education or the cost-benefit ratios of particular forms of preservice and inservice education as they affect various indicators of school improvement or student achievement. The studies from Guatemala and Bangladesh however, indicate that comparatively inexpensive teacher training models can lead to significant change in teacher classroom pedagogy and in higher retention rates, both important indicators of school improvement.

Distance education, when carefully designed for large numbers of students, appears to be significantly less expensive than traditional residential programs in producing "qualified" or "certificated" personnel. Some APEC countries report a trend of increasing expenditures for professional development activities. New Zealand, for example, reported a 30 percent increase in funding for professional development between 1991 and 1993. In New Zealand in 1992, primary and secondary schools spent approximately $14 million on professional development. The bulk was spent on teacher release time.

In 1993, Australia announced the federally funded National Professional Development Program, which provided $60 million for staff development activities over a three-year period. In general, U.S. school districts spend less than 0.5 percent of their budgets on professional development.

The Basic Education Strengthening Project (BEST) in Guatemala has developed two low cost, innovative educational reforms, the Nueva Escuela Unitaria (NEU) and National Bilingual Intercultural Education (DIGEBI).

The costs of these two programs for rural, predominantly Mayan-speaking students were compared by Chesterfield and Rubio to regular Ministry of Education schools serving similar populations in the same regions. The indicators of cost-effectiveness were the percentage of children in the base year who progressed normally through primary education and the average cost per student to produce a sixth-grade graduate in 1996.

The cumulative costs per student for all years were divided by the number of students in sixth grade in 1996. Both NEU and DIGEBI schools had higher percentages of children making normal progress through the primary grades than comparison groups. In both cases, the innovative programs had higher percentages of first graders who were enrolled in second grade than the comparison schools and in each case this translated into higher percentages of children in sixth grade.

Independent cost studies confirmed BRAC costs for schooling are much lower, even without considering the extra private costs of formal schools that make them more expensive and lead to high dropout and low enrollment rates. In addition, unlike the formal school system, which allocates the vast majority of its resources to teacher salaries and school facilities, BRAC allocates almost 27 percent of the NFPE budget to management and supervision of teachers. Only 29 percent is allocated to teacher salaries.

Rugh and Bossert add that the BRAC teacher earns about US$12 per month, which is twice that of an agricultural laborer. In their study they concluded that BRAC demonstrated that paraprofessional teachers trained in the short fifteen-day initial period and given strong on-the-job support were capable of becoming effective primary-level teachers. As far as other aspects of the program are concerned, because poverty is identified by Bangladeshi parents as a major reason for their children dropping out or not enrolling in the formal schools, the NFPE program is designed so that parents incur practically no direct costs for sending their children to BRAC schools.

Books and supplies are provided free, uniforms are not required, school hours are varied to home and agricultural cycle needs, and schools are located in proximity to the students' homes. BRAC school attendance results in less income loss to the families than does formal school attendance. BRAC students achieve as much as or more than formal school students. During a three-year period, BRAC students completed the NFPE program and entered the formal school Class IV at a higher rate than did the students who began in the formal system.

BRAC students are scoring the same or higher than formal school students on basic education assessment and basic literacy tests..Even with annual costs per enrolled student in BRAC and the formal schools system approximately equal, the relatively higher attendance rates, lower repetition rates, higher Class III completion rates, and higher Class IV continuation rates for BRAC students mean that BRAC schools are substantially more cost efficient per graduate than the government schools.

Effective teachers have different styles and personalities, and are considered effective for varying reasons. In many communities, teachers are considered effective if many of their students attain some of the following: sound academic achievement; an enjoyment of learning; and skills to continue to learn, solve problems, and functionally operate in and contribute to their societies. Effective teachers give students appropriate attention when needs arise.

Whatever other worthwhile results are achieved because of teachers' work, teacher effectiveness is usually expressed in terms of pupils' academic achievement, something that is more easily measured than some other valued outcomes of good education. The measurable gains in student progress are some of the strongest indicators of improvement in educational quality. Improving the learning environment will help raise student achievement. Teachers who are able to develop sound academic achievement with their pupils tend to share many of the following characteristics. Effective teachers at a mature stage of development tend to:

— know their subject matter;

— use pedagogy appropriate for the content;

— use an appropriate language of instruction, and have mastery of that language;

— create and sustain an effective learning environment;

— find out about and respond to the needs and interests of their students and communities;

— reflect on their teaching and children's responses and make changes to the learning environment as necessary;

— have a strong sense of ethics;

— are committed to teaching; and

— care about their students.

Effective teachers tend to have confidence in their ability to teach, care about teaching and their students, and cooperate with each other. These characteristics are reflected in the teachers' comfort in using learning materials and in trying new ideas, low teacher absenteeism and tardiness, and a high level of group involvement in planning teaching and in resolving whole-school issues. However, classrooms where teachers lack general subject mastery and confidence in their ability to teach, the development of positive teacher attitudes is often hindered.

Children who spend more time studying in school tend to learn more. A distinction needs to be made between the established number of days and hours per day, the actual time the school is in operation, and how the available hours are used. In some settings, the policy on the school calendar and daily hours may need to be revised to have schools in session more.

Effective teachers waste less class time in starting and ending instructional activities; they select materials that are appropriate to student abilities; they emphasize academic instruction and active learning strategies; and they provide immediate constructive feedback to students. The patterns that have emerged from studying schools reveal that high achieving schools have safe, orderly environments that are conducive to learning. Since order and discipline are an indication of the seriousness and purpose with which a school approaches improving student learning, effective teachers pay attention to developing well ordered classrooms, and constructively disciplined students.

Classrooms and classes are well organized and facilities are clean and in good repair. School and classroom rules are clearly articulated, are agreed upon by both teachers and students, and are fairly and equitably maintained. Also, positive behavior is reinforced, and students and teachers attend classes regularly and according to an established timetable. There is a great deal of evidence to indicate that low expectations are the norm in too many classrooms around the world.

Educational researchers and anthropologists have pointed to the academic success of many newly industrialized Asian nations as examples of the importance of setting high standards for learning and expecting all students to achieve them. There is particular evidence in the research literature that high staff expectations for all students to do well contribute to making a school effective.

The concept of the school as a place of commitment to learning is communicated clearly by the principal and teachers, and student performance is monitored regularly in effective schools. Also, student assignments are sufficiently frequent and difficult to convey this high expectation and teachers' confidence in students' abilities, and confidence in students is reinforced by giving them many opportunities to take responsibility for school activities. These expectations translate into more positive self-concepts and greater self-reliance among students.

The few studies that have investigated whether head teachers and teachers in developing countries who expect high achievement receive stronger commitment and performance from students whose self-concepts are positive suggest confirmation of the findings from industrialized countries. However, in all too many developing country classrooms, particularly in the early primary grades, there is an almost palpable expectation that up to half the students will desert or fail.

This has led many policymakers to push for automatic social promotion policies, but in the absence of appropriate remedial instructional programs, this has only helped to continue the lowering of educational quality. Neither automatic promotion in the absence of remediation, nor failure and retention policies have proven successful in most nations. Effective teachers throughout the world genuinely care for their students, but the frustrations of large classes, students who need special care and attention, and the requirements of day-to-day existence often turn even the most caring teacher into a frustrated and, at times, punitive individual.

Research has indicated the need for teachers to pay special attention to student interests, problems, and accomplishments. Self-responsibility and self-reliance on the part of students are also emphasized in the research literature, but once again the lock step curriculum, whole-class instruction, and teacher-controlled classroom management that so dominate developing world classrooms prevent students from developing these skills. There are, of course, exceptions to this bleak picture, the most outstanding being the NEU schools in Guatemala and the Escuela Nueva in Colombia, where students are given exceptional levels of responsibility, and in fact, democratically administer much of what goes on in the school.

Some studies shows that effective teachers and schools develop a well organized curriculum that emphasizes the acquisition of basic skills and is designed to ensure academic success by defining learning objectives that are matched to identified teaching strategies, available materials, and an integrated sequence of topics across grade levels. Dalin et al. particularly emphasize the production of teaching and learning materials by the school. Lockheed and Verspoor support the importance of an organized curriculum, but they caution that textbooks do not constitute the curriculum.

In developing countries, textbooks and other instructional materials are sometimes poorly designed, often have factual inaccuracies and problems with readability, and tend not to promote higher-order thinking skills. However, the evidence is strong that children in developing countries who have access to textbooks and other reading material learn more than those who do not.

Textbooks are the single most important instructional material, and are particularly effective where teachers use teaching guides with them. The provision and use of paper, pencils, chalkboards, chalk, posters, filmstrips, and audiotapes also facilitate student learning. While most curriculum guides in both the developing and industrialized countries contain a range of instructional resources and teaching activities, too often in the poorer nations teachers either have no access to the necessary materials, or they have not received sufficient training to make use of more active, creative pedagogies.

Teachers often are frightened of straying from traditional teaching behavior or utilizing nontraditional activities for fear of school-director or supervisor criticism. Another major concern in rural, multigrade schools in developing countries is the utter impossibility of a teacher preparing separate lessons for each and every grade and subject area. Rural teachers complain that they spend several hours daily writing detailed lesson plans for each class and subject. The carefully designed student workbooks in Colombia and Guatemala (NEU) appear to be a way of maintaining high curricular integrity, while not forcing unrealistic planning on the teacher.

Children need to be appraised of what is to come, both verbally and in writing, as appropriate. Given children's varying attention spans and ability to understand, it is critical to repeat instructions and key points. This repetition, however, should not necessarily be in the same words or with the same specific instructional activity. Classrooms in developing countries, ethnographers have observed that the teacher has only mastered one approach to a lesson, topic, concept, or skill, and keeps repeating it over and over again without using different language, new approaches, or another attack on the topic to help all children understand.

This becomes a key teacher education role, to provide the classroom teacher with sufficient underlying academic information to assist all children to understand the concept. "Trained" teachers are capable of delivering a particular lesson, but it is only as teachers gain sufficient academic knowledge and background experience that they are generally capable of approaching the same concept in new and creative ways to help each child master it. This is where "teacher education" rather than just teacher training comes into the picture.

A systematic approach to teaching that both increases student achievement and student engagement in the classroom is described in Rosenshine and Stevens, who note the following characteristics of effective directed teaching lessons:

— Begin a lesson with a short review of previous prerequisite learning.

— Begin a lesson with a short statement of goals

— Present new material in small steps with student practice after each step.

— Give clear and detailed instructions and explanations.

— Provide a high level of active practice for all students.

— Ask a large number of questions, check for student understanding, and obtain responses from all students.

— Guide students during initial practice.

— Provide systematic feedback and corrections.

— Provide explicit instruction, practice, and supervision for seatwork exercises.

The teaching practices might include individual assignments with worksheets, class discussion, group work explaining, drill-and-practice, asking questions, and cross-age tutoring. When available, teachers may also make use of interactive radio or programmed materials. An emphasis on higher order thinking is important. In developing countries, Fuller found confirming when a teacher spent more hours preparing for class, the preparation raised the quality of instruction and improved student achievement. Lockheed and Verspoor suggested that, while the use of worksheets and homework is also effective in developing countries. Instead, they suggest an emphasis on small, cooperative-group learning, cross-age peer tutoring, and the use of interactive radio, where possible, as cost-effective alternatives.

They also note that instruction such as drill and practice, asking questions that stimulate student thinking, presenting information in small hierarchical steps, having students repeat information, and giving constructive feedback can raise academic performance. Teachers have been encouraged to go beyond the usual drill and practice and checking for understanding and into the realm of creative problem solving. Stallings and Kaskowitz's research on classrooms reported that student scores on group-administered tests of nonverbal problem-solving skills were higher where the structure allowed students to take more initiative.

In these classrooms students asked more questions, worked more independently with manipulative materials, and worked more often on group tasks in cooperative activities. When given the instructional training materials, teachers in even the most difficult of circumstances can provide students with a problem-solving, inquiry-based learning environment. Effective teachers have also learned when to give rewards immediately and when to delay them in order to teach persistence.

Effective teachers and schools also keep parents regularly informed about student progress, and seek parent's help in keeping students working towards excellence. Effective teachers attempt to define excellence by objective standards, not by peer comparison. While research in psychology has presented overwhelming evidence of the importance of rewards, rather than punishment, classroom teachers throughout the world still apply an inordinate number of negative consequences for poor academic work or inappropriate student behavior.

Sarcasm, labeling, corporal punishment, shaming, grouping by "intelligence," and a wide array of other teacher behaviors still characterize thousands of classrooms, despite preservice course work in educational psychology, and countless inservice programs on how to motivate students and maintain control in the classroom. Rewards at the whole school level are also most important. When schools publicly honor and reward academic achievement and positive social behavior, this encourages all students to follow a similar pattern. Effective schools have clearly defined academic standards, and academic success is recognized through regular public rewards and incentives for achievement.

Teacher development is a process and, therefore, different training and support is needed at different stages of this continuum. The education that teachers receive has the potential to make a difference to children's learning and therefore warrants careful attention. The features listed above that are associated with effective teaching are critical when planning and implementing support for teachers. While only a few of these features might be addressed in the early stages of some teacher development programs, small first steps are important beginnings in the process of improving teacher quality.

Teacher Training Curriculum

The teacher training curriculum was linked quite closely to the primary school syllabus and there was little specialisation either by subject or school phase. There were considerable inconsistencies within the curriculum with regard to aims, objectives, pedagogy, teaching-learning materials and assessment. Most teaching followed a transmission style, with lecturing and question-and-answer sessions being most common. Students were generally assessed by tests, essays and end-of-year exams.

Teacher education programmes can only be understood and evaluated within the historical, socio-economic, political and cultural contexts in which they have developed, including the perceived role of the teacher in society, current views of knowledge, and the level of economic development.

Teacher education programmes, like other curricula, are built up around various theories of learning, though these are not always made explicit. Theories of learning rest on assumptions about the nature of knowledge. For example, the behaviourist psychology had its roots in the positivist epistemology which sees knowledge as objective, existing apart from the individual and social context, and capable of transmission and application in more or less fixed forms. This view underlies what Schon criticises as the 'technical rationality' model of professional education, where the student acquires discipline-based knowledge and is then expected to apply it routinely to what are often unique and confused situations, that require artistry and individual judgement as well as scientific understanding.

Constructivist learning theories, while not denying the scientific basis of much modern knowledge, stress also its situated and contextual nature, and the way individuals reconstruct what they hear and experience before they can use it effectively. Social constructivists emphasise how the social, cultural and political structures permeate the contexts and affect the way knowledge is acquired and used. Such views suggest putting more emphasis on an extended and supported 'practicum' in professional learning.

In many traditional societies knowledge was seen as something fixed, finite and to be handed down, rather than something to be explored, questioned and developed along new lines. The elders were respected because they had this knowledge, and could teach it to the young, whose role was to listen rather than ask questions. Tabulawa argues that these deeply-rooted cultural assumptions have contributed to the resistance to educational change in African classrooms, particularly where this involves the idea of teacher and learner entering into dialogue and pursuing enquiries together. It may well be that under the influence of international discourse such cultural assumptions are breaking down, particularly in urban areas.

Another international trend is towards bringing theory and practice closer together through campus-school partnerships, using mentor teachers and school internship to complement or even replace the academic studies in university or college. In the UK this has gone so far that graduate teachers may now train entirely on the job, working under supervision and attending seminars in local Teachers' Centres. It seems questionable whether this is a satisfactory way of preparing professionals who have sufficient intellectual grasp of educational issues to ensure their teaching remains dynamic and responsive to social change; it seems more likely to be a recipe for maintaining the status quo.

Such training methods also presuppose a high level of both infrastructure and professional development at school level. They are more difficult to introduce into education systems which are poorly resourced and where the teachers in the host schools may themselves not be fully qualified. Teacher education is a politically contested area. Most governments seek to control the teacher education curriculum, either directly by having the colleges under ministerial control, or indirectly through setting centralised standards and guidelines for university departments of education to follow.

The state has many, sometimes conflicting, expectations of the teachers. They may be viewed as conservers of traditional values or moral exemplars, and at the same time be expected to act as agents of development. Governments driven by the global imperative to compete successfully in world markets may see teachers as just another set of technicians who are supposed to prepare a skilled and obedient workforce. Where transformation is on the political agenda, teachers are expected to lead the creation of new citizens, having themselves undergone political change.

The term 'curriculum' is here defined as the entire experience throughout the training programme, as taught by college tutors, as organised both on and off campus, and as learnt by trainee teachers. The curriculum existed in different forms, viz:

— On paper, as designed and set out in the documents

— In the minds of the tutors

— As experienced by trainees

— As perceived by external observers

Eraut's model of curriculum design, which identifies the interrelations between aims, objectives, content, teaching/ learning resources, pedagogy, and assessment; this is useful for evaluating how far the programme embodies a consistent and coherent curricular strategy. The actual content of a professional curriculum, however, is more complex than this model allows for, involving a strategic balancing of different academic and practical components, and ways of fitting them into a structure of time and place.

The last major comparative studies of teacher education curricula in low income countries took place in the 1980's and these gave an impression of stasis and neglect. In South Africa, the entire system of teacher development is being transformed and moved into the Higher Education sector. The curriculum of the new 4-year Bachelor of General Education and Training (BAGET) degree introduced in January 1999 at the University of Durban-Westville (UDW), this has been designed from scratch, with new ways of linking content and methods, and with a large element of schoolbased training.

It is not typical of current South African practice, but will be used as an example of reconceptualisation. It is consistent with the new South African 'Norms and

Standards for Educators' which set out the threefold competences -academic, practical and reflexive - needed to enable teachers to take on multiple roles as 'critical professional educators'and contrasts with other longer standing forms of provision.

However, the curriculum is evolving slowly, mainly through incremental changes brought about by the lecturers themselves, in the direction of more reflective practice. It is hoped to link it more closely to the year-long the 'on-the-job' apprenticeship training given to unqualified entrants to teaching. Internationally, it is common for teachers to follow (at least partly) different courses to prepare them for, respectively, Infant/Lower Primary, Upper Primary, and Secondary, on the grounds that different subject content and different methods are appropriate for each phase.

In Ghana recent practice has been to have just one programme to prepare teachers for the whole Basic School cycle, comprising both Primary and Junior Secondary Schools (JSS), even though primary schools need class teachers and JSS require specialists. In Malawi and Trinidad and Tobago the programmes train class teachers for the whole of the primary years; in Lesotho there was for a short time an elective course for 'Early Years' which has been dropped in the new Diploma in Education (Primary).

In South Africa primary teachers have traditionally been trained as part-specialists, which is reflected in their curricular patterns. In Ghana colleges might specialise in either Primary or Junior Secondary. The curricula in Ghana and Trinidad and Tobago state no overall aims. This leaves the tutors free to develop the curriculum on the one hand, but on the other gives no impetus for change. But the teachers' role is also related to political, epistemological and ideological perceptions which permeate the education system more generally. It is generally agreed that the key components of any initial teacher training programme must include:

— *Subject content*: adequate knowledge and understanding of the subject(s) to be taught in school

— *'pedagogic content knowledge' or 'methods'*: ways of teaching and assessing the subject(s) appropriate to the learners' level

— *education & professional studies*: a basic understanding of how children develop and learn, plus some 'craft knowledge' on how to manage the teaching process

— *a 'practicum'*: opportunities to bring all these together and practise performing the role of teacher.

— *general education*: courses designed for personal growth and enrichment.

In the African countries language content has to include both English and the local language. In such multi-lingual contexts, it is disturbing to find so little attention paid to developing trainees' own language skills, both in English as the main medium of instruction, and in other local or national languages needed for teaching in the lower grades. Lesotho's curriculum attempts some remediation in the bridging course and within the English syllabus, but observation revealed an old-fashioned grammar approach which did little to enhance communication.

A major dilemma is whether to give the trainees just the content needed to teach the syllabus, or to teach them the discipline to as high a level as possible. Close scrutiny of curriculum documents suggest that even when syllabi are supposedly designed to a common pattern, subject teams interpret and teach them differently; often the sciences put more emphasis on content, and teach methods separately, while the humanities more often combine them.

In broad terms, Ghana, Lesotho and Trinidad and Tobago try to teach content and methods separately, while Malawi and UDW try to integrate them. This is related to the question of academic level, but in interesting ways. The MIITEP course mainly teaches subject content and methods together, apart from science, using an approximate balance of 1:2. Thus methods, generally in the form of routine skills and prescriptive advice, predominate. At the other end of the academic scale the UDW team conceptualised 'Science Education', 'Maths Education' and 'Language Education' as disciplines in their own right, and designed the programme around such courses with the explicit intention of developing the students' academic and pedagogical knowledge together.

The Trinidad and Tobago curriculum is in general heavily oriented towards giving trainees a 'knowledge base', with well over half the modules devoted to content, but the subject approaches vary; in science and maths the modules are set out as separate, while in arts and humanities knowledge and pedagogic aspects are more likely to be treated within the same unit. Classroom observation, however, suggest that experienced tutors interpret the curriculum in their own way, and the most effective integration was observed in a science lesson.

From an international perspective, the four college syllabi appear both outdated and conservative, caught in an intellectual time-warp. The old 'foundations of education' or 'ologies' are still apparent. In psychology, behaviourist and Piagetian concepts are taught, but much recent work on cognitive development and on constructivism is missing, and Vygotsky's name appears unknown to the tutors, some of whom are clearly recycling their university notes of years ago.

The sociology modules, where they appear, seem to take a functionalist perspective, though Trinidadian tutors have developed new modules. In spite of the rhetoric, little real integration of theory and practice. In general, the educational theories seem to be taught, and learnt, for their own sake, rather than as a means of understanding and enhancing practice. Child development and learning theories are not related to specific subjects, such as language acquisition or misconceptions in science.

The general professional and pedagogic skills are taught separately from the theory, and the only opportunity to bring these together, in teaching practice, is seldom exploited for this end. The educational theories are drawn from Western sources, and not subjected to critique in the light of local culture and norms.

The curriculum documents often list a range of student-centred, interactive and participatory methods - demonstrations, group work, role play, fieldtrips, project work - but observations in three of the African sites revealed a predominantly teacher-centred transmission mode. Teaching 'subject content' resembled traditional high school methods: the tutor would present information orally, using the board or textbook, interspersed with (tutor) questions and (student) answers; only occasionally were attempts made to develop a class discussion. The levels of cognitive demand seemed low; in places students' poor language skills inhibited debates. In English and maths students might do individual exercises; in science experiments were usually demonstrated by the tutor, probably because of shortage of both time and equipment.

In most places, at least some tutors used group work of some kind, with varied levels of effectiveness, as few tutors were clear about what they wanted to achieve through groups. What was striking was that quite similar styles of teaching predominated in 'methods' lessons, although there tended to be more student activity, and more group work. But in the main, trainees were told about how to handle primary classes, and occasionally shown, as when the tutor did a demonstration lesson, or showed a video, but very seldom did they actually experience the kind of student-centred methods that were preached.

It is ironic that the pedagogy of teacher education courses themselves should be so neglected, and that teacher educators so seldom apply their espoused theories to their own practice. Several reasons may be adduced for this situation. Firstly, in some places large numbers made interactive work more difficult, but not impossible, as there were isolated examples in both Lesotho and Trinidad and Tobago of tutors handling large groups in participatory ways.

Lack of resources was certainly a factor, particularly in Malawi. The exam pressure and the consequent need to cover the syllabus, were clearly important in both Malawi and Ghana. The Ghanaian tutors said that because of the overcrowded syllabus, extra curricular activities and the looming exams, there was simply no time to engage in activities requiring extensive exploratory work by students. In addition, Ghanaian tutors did not set students collaborative work for fear it would lead to 'copying' in the exam.

In short, primary teachers need to be confident of their subject knowledge, but the academic ambitions of some of the curricula are often mismatched to the students' levels of achievement. In particular, the difficulties of learning in a second language are underestimated. The pedagogy is ill-matched in several ways: it does not use adult learning methods where appropriate; it seldom practises the kinds of learnercentred methods it preaches; it copies secondary schools, and does not teach trainees to become independent learners.

Challenges and Opportunities

Teacher educators at all levels, whether school or college-based, need to have induction and continuing professional development. This should ensure that they are aware of recent developments, can judge whether these should be incorporated into training, have perspectives that run beyond their direct experience, and have a rich range of material to draw on to support and stimulate trainee teachers.

In Ghana, Lesotho, and Malawi the challenge posed for teacher education by national targets for enrolment and pupil-teacher ratios for primary schooling is immense. None of these systems can produce enough new teachers to meet projected demand. Each needs to increase the output of trained teachers several-fold. In Ghana output would have to increase three or four times if all children were to be enrolled at primary level and taught by trained teachers. In Lesotho, more than five times current output is needed.

Projections of demand in South Africa suggest substantially rising demand for teachers which is very sensitive to the demographic impact of HIV/AIDS. Demand is rising as the numbers entering primary teacher training have fallen to minimal levels. Malawi has already adopted a mixed-mode approach to training that is relatively low cost and high volume which could meet demand with imaginable levels of expansion.

However, quality is widely questioned, the programme cannot be delivered as originally intended, and places are unlikely to be filled without recruiting from those completing just two years of secondary schooling. The Millennium Development Goals (MDG) relating to education cannot be met unless the supply of teachers is adequate to keep pupil-teacher ratios within reasonable limits, and the quality of their training is sufficient to result in minimum acceptable levels of pupil achievement. The costs of existing methods of training are such that simple expansion of existing capacity is often not financially viable.

Improvements in efficiency and effectiveness are needed that can lower costs and expand output within sustainable budgets. It may also be necessary to consider alternatives to two or three years full-time, pre-career training. Traditional teacher education programmes are heavily 'front-loaded' with most investment at the beginning of a teaching career. Their unit costs can exceed those of university education and may be 50 or more times the annual cost of a primary school place. If the average length of teachers' careers is declining, as it is in some cases as a result of HIV/AIDS, and if the numbers which have to be trained are much larger than current capacity, teacher education programmes with lower costs are needed.

The alternative is to revise MDG targets for universalising access and achieving gender equity in primary schooling. Despite the obvious importance of policy on teacher education to the achievement of nationally and internationally agreed goals to universalise primary schooling, improve quality, and enhance equity in access and retention, the development of coherent, medium term, financially sustainable teacher education policy, tailored to meet the demand for new teachers, has been widely neglected. In Ghana, College reform has not been a priority since FCUBE (Free Compulsory Universal Basic Education) was announced.

The recent introduction of the 'In-In-Out' programme to replace three-year fully residential training has not evolved from a considered strategy to supply the number of teachers needed to meet the objectives of FCUBE. Lesotho continues to train far fewer teachers than it needs to implement Free Primary Education (FPE). It has also established a Task Force on Teacher Education to build on the MUSTER research and has ambitions to develop a strategic plan. Malawi has grappled with the implications of its FPE programme and has attempted to meet the need for trained teachers through the innovative Malawi Integrated Inservice Teacher Education Programme (MIITEP) programme of mixed college- and school-based training. The suspension of this programme, with the consequence that no new teachers were enrolled in training for more nearly three years, reflects the absence of national teacher education policy and of any real sense of urgency to address the problems of initial training.

The recent creation of a Teacher Education Division within the Ministry, the inclusion of teacher education more prominently in the Policy and Investment Framework, and the agreement on the funding of three extra MIITEP cohorts are positive signs. Trinidad and Tobago policy on teacher education has no clear locus of control or chain of accountability. Unlike other Eastern

Caribbean States, where partnerships exist between Ministries, Colleges and the University of the West Indies, responsibilities are ill-defined, as is policy.

Educational reform focused on schools often proceeds in advance of reforms in teacher education curricula. In principle teacher education should lead rather than lag behind wider reforms, so that new entrants can be prepared to adopt new curricula and teaching methods. It is, however, unrealistic to expect new teachers to be focal points for change as new members of the profession in junior positions. International borrowing is inevitable and often useful for the development of teacher education. However, models and theories developed in one context should not be imported uncritically to others. Some aspects will resonate more easily across cultures than others.

Teacher education curricula are needed that, while sometimes using cross-national insights as points of departure, also build on local teacher knowledge, experience, and examples of good practice, in order to develop culturally relevant and effective teaching strategies. If innovations are to work, they need to be grounded and contextualised, and to make sense to those expected to carry them out. Moreover, strategies for innovation should recognise the importance of establishing a favourable climate of opinion to adopt new practices.

Innovations that are pushed from the centre, rather than pulled by effective demand from communities of practice, will always be more difficult to sustain. Professional links with school system were often fragile or non-existent and practising primary teachers were conspicuous by their general absence from activities organised in the colleges. Many colleges can be characterised by physical and intellectual isolation and many appeared held down by the weight of tradition, by lack of vision, and poor management.

Any reconceptualisation of teacher education has to consider whether colleges have a role, and if so, what that role should be. Most colleges exist uneasily in an ill-defined area between Ministries, higher education, and schools. Forms of governance need to be identified that support an academic and professional atmosphere, and which might encourage the development of cultures of research on practice linking staff and programmes into problems of school development and students' achievement.

It is essential to develop a cadre of professional teacher educators, who are capable of working both within and outside the institution in creative and innovative ways. This implies a pay and career structure that recognises the kinds of work they do and the responsibilities they carry. It should be policy to recruit primary trainers from experienced and committed primary teachers and provide the necessary academic upgrading, or if taking secondarytrained teachers, to provide appropriate orientation including a period observing/teaching in primary schools.

Gender issues must be borne in mind to ensure women candidates are not disadvantaged by selection criteria or mode of training. The development of a cadre implies induction programmes for new recruits, and regular opportunities for continuing professional development, including where appropriate post-graduate degrees. Teacher educators should be expected to work with and in schools and carry out research, to keep up to date with international developments and to help adapt these to local conditions.

Teacher education systems develop within national contexts which condition their form. New ideas for methods and structures have to recognise the realities of differing needs, circumstances and resources. Suggested improvements have to be formulated within the assumptions, processes and expectations of the wider national education system. The basic structural issues for teacher education systems revolve around where training should take place, how long it should take, and what, if anything, should happen before and after periods of initial training leading to certification.

There are three common options as to institutional location. These are colleges of education, university education departments, or in schools. In reality the choices between these locations are not free. College-based systems for primary training are common in many low income countries and reflect how training systems have developed. Colleges are often the only post-secondary institutions in their geographic area and may be associated with post-secondary opportunities for particular groups who have a political stake in the continuity of the institutions.

College systems seem likely to persist unless or until essentially political decisions are taken to adopt another arrangement. South Africa has taken the step of making all initial training university-based or affiliated with universities. However, the circumstances under which this has come about are unique. College-based systems may have advantages in terms of local location linked to communities or clusters of schools, a focus on a single profession and a responsiveness to educational needs, a role in pre-service and in-service education, and lower costs than tertiary level institutions.

University-based training offers the prospect of inputs from staff with high levels of disciplinary expertise, connection to insights from research relevant to learning and teaching, multi-disciplinary perspectives, and superior teaching resources associated with large-scale institutions. On the other hand critics suggest that university-based training may be a long way removed from the issues of practice in primary schools, high levels of academic knowledge in disciplines are largely irrelevant, and tutors' career advancement is likely to depend more on research recognition than training competence.

School-based training has become increasingly common in rich country systems. There are many good pedagogic and professional development reasons why training located in the work environment is potentially attractive because of its direct links with practical problems, advice from successful teachers, and socialisation into professional norms and standards. However, the basic assumptions of school-based training - namely that there are sufficient schools to offer appropriate training environments and enough qualified teachers to act as professional mentors to trainees - are often difficult to meet in low income countries.

Most schools may not be appropriately resourced as training sites, lacking both qualified teachers and enough teaching and learning materials. Nor do staff necessarily see their role as including training new teachers and they are unlikely themselves to have any training as trainers. Under these circumstances, school-based training may simply become a form of 'sitting by Thabo', with new teachers simply copying what is done around them whether or not this is good practice.

School-based training is generally associated with various forms of distance education, as it is in MIITEP. Distance education methods are attractive because they allow teachers to be trained while on the job, which saves the costs of replacement. It should also reduce the direct costs if a proportion of the training is self-instructional and based on print or other low cost media. However, the problems of distance learning are well known. For primary teachers in rural Africa there are particular problems.

In so-called predominantly 'oral' cultures students may find book-based learning particularly difficult; aural media such as radio programmes or audio-cassettes may be more effective, if the technology is available and motivation can be maintained. Video is much more expensive, and unlikely to be as cost-effective as alternatives. Though new information technologies based on computers and the internet appear to offer many potential benefits, these are yet to be demonstrated in practice in mass systems of teacher education in Africa. They have high initial costs and carry risks of rapid obsolescence of hardware and software.

Teacher education appears to be one of the most conservative parts of many education systems. It seldom is the source of curriculum innovation, theorised pedagogy, or radical reconceptualisations of professional learning. It often lags behind schools in the adoption of new practice and patterns of learning and teaching. This is a signifier that political will and bureaucratic courage may be needed for the implementation of real changes designed to improve efficiency and effectiveness. The case of South Africa, where changes in teacher education were part of more general system-wide transformation, is instructive but unique. There the will and the vision has existed to challenge old orthodoxies, wasteful resource allocation, and ineffective training methods.

Pre-training teaching experience as an untrained teacher is common. Only in Trinidad and Tobago is this institutionalised as an On-the-Job Training Scheme. The development of OJT-like schemes has several attractions - trainees can be selected partly on the basis of their performance over time, rather than initial academic qualification; trainees contribute to reducing teacher shortages through the work they do; managed OJT schemes could greatly enrich the skills and competencies of those entering training. At the same time, pay and conditions of service need to be improved to the point where they can attract and retain people with appropriate qualities.

Teacher education curricula suffer in varying degrees from fragmentation. In most systems curricula are not developed dynamically or incrementally, neither are they suffused with contributions from teacher educators at college level. Revitalised teacher education systems could transform this situation through systematic and cumulative approaches to developing and enriching the curriculum and its learning materials base at college level, and through coherent national level programmes to generate more relevant core materials within an agreed framework.

Working practices in teacher education differ widely. Training institutions need to be much more demand-led, in terms of being responsive to the needs of trainees, rather than to the preferences, priorities and familiar practices of those who work in them. Few colleges make much use of experienced teachers drawn in to inform discussions about pedagogy, class management, and curriculum realities. Even fewer college staff spend periods in schools in a professional development role which could help inform their collegebased teaching.

Teacher educators may need to develop or rediscover culturally appropriate 'visions' of what an effective teacher is. They should provide opportunities for growth and development of personal attributes that can help trainees become confident and competent in their diverse professional roles. Student teachers need to be treated as adult learners and helped to study in more independent and proactive ways, so they experience themselves new ways of learning and teaching; they need to learn to reflect in ways that enable them to improve the quality and effectiveness of their teaching.

Radical reform requires vision, courage and persistence to reshape teacher education in fundamental ways. It will usually require substantial investment up-front before benefits are apparent, and the conversion to new approaches of those embedded in the comfort zones of the old. It is the most exciting but the most risky option as entrenched interests rarely embrace new practices without strong incentives; such changes are usually linked to wider political reforms.

Conventional teacher education systems are heavily front-loaded in terms of the investment of resources i.e. most if not all the resources are committed to pre-career full-time residential training. Where demand is high long periods of pre-career training will be expensive and slow to produce large numbers of new teachers. Alternatives which provide shorter periods of introductory training, followed by periods of work as assistant teachers, and interspersed with subsequent training inputs building on the base acquired from school experience, could be both more efficient, and more effective.

Teacher educators all over the world are an underdeveloped group. In few countries are there specific career paths or professional courses for them. From an academic point of view, little research has been carried out in this field and the available literature, even in the West, is very sparse. One exception comes from a group of (mainly) North American university teacher educators, working in the 'reflective practitioner' mode, who used self-study and action research approaches to theorise about their own professional learning and how to improve their practice.

Reports from high income countries suggest that most cadres of teacher educators tend towards a conservative ideology rather than a radical or transformative one. This is perhaps to be expected when they have themselves usually come up through the same system. Yet it seems obvious that if educational change is to take place, those who prepare the next generation of teachers must play a key role in innovation.

Beeby pointed out the self-perpetuating nature of educational systems and the problem of where to break the cycle: Teacher trainers in low income countries who do try to break with the old pattern usually get their ideas from travel in rich countries, or from books written there, and often hand them on, in the form of indigestible theory, to teachers who need practical guidance to take even simpler steps forward.

In many low income countries today this question is still very pertinent, and there are only a few reports of relevant research or action. One describes the concerted efforts made for colleges in Papua New Guinea. In Namibia, where teacher education was planned as the spearhead of reform, and all college tutors were invited to take a postgraduate higher diploma in teacher education. The theory and practice of this course were based on the same principles as those underlying the reforms in the rest of the system, so that tutors were better prepared to train future teachers in the new methods.

Almost all primary college tutors have come up through the teaching ranks, but in different ways and from different starting points, so that not all have relevant experience. Most of the older Malawian tutors began as primary teachers, but as nowadays college staff must have degrees, the younger ones are secondary-trained. For similar reasons, in Lesotho less than half the staff have any primary experience and most of those surveyed agreed that 'most tutors do not know much about teaching primary pupils'.

In Ghana most have had upper primary or junior secondary experience; fewer have worked in the infant grades. In Trinidad and Tobago most tutors have a secondary school background, again because they are degree-holders while primary teachers are not. Unsurprisingly, tutors' qualifications vary with the country's wealth and with the opportunities offered for academic and professional development in the education system as a whole.

Thus in Trinidad and Tobago half the tutors hold Masters degrees, in Lesotho almost all tutors are graduates, and about a third have Masters degrees, while Ghana about three-quarters hold a B.Ed and very few have Masters. In Malawi the majority of tutors have only diplomas; the rest have Bachelors degrees, with a sprinkling of Masters. While Malawian tutors are expected to be generalists, and may teach two or three subjects, including Education, elsewhere the tutors specialise either in one subject or in Education, though occasionally they may hold degrees in both.

In Ghana, most college tutors had attended either the University of Cape Coast (UCC) or the University College of Winneba but they were not specifically trained as teacher educators since it was assumed that anyone graduating in education would be capable of teaching at a college, even though most of the methods taught were for secondary level. However, in Trinidad and Tobago the UWI offers a teacher education option within the M.Ed., which includes training in supervision, and several tutors had received scholarships to undertake this degree.

The gender balance broadly reflects the more general participation of women in the local teaching force. In Lesotho most of the college staff are women - though the Director has always been a man - and in Trinidad and Tobago just over half the tutors are women, while in Ghana and Malawi they are mostly male. However, Malawi's policy of promoting suitable women is raising the proportion in the colleges, two of which had female principals at the time of the study.

Thus, while tutors come from the local teaching force and mirror many of its characteristics, this poses a particular problem for countries where primary teachers have low status and minimal training, making it difficult to find people to staff the colleges who have both academic standing and first-hand knowledge of primary schools. The lack of attention paid to specific training for the job is also a widespread phenomenon.

As in many other countries, the careers of teacher educators appear haphazard and unsupported. In Malawi, for example, tutors reported being 'picked' from their schools to fill gaps in the colleges and promotions depend on the MOE. In Trinidad and Tobago, where there were few material incentives to transfer, tutors seem to have applied out of personal interest, or via encouragement by others, some having already proved themselves as advisory teachers.

Elsewhere the moves seem to have been more deliberately planned; for example in Lesotho, tutors said they moved to get better conditions of service, less stress, and the opportunities for further study - not all of which actually materialised, since criteria for study leave and promotion were unclear. In Ghana, many teachers begin in the primary schools, further their studies by training as a secondary teacher, and then aspire to become a college tutor. This is seen almost as a 'natural progression' towards better conditions of service and more prestige; it also shows how training colleges in Ghana are regarded 'postsecondary' rather than tertiary or higher educational institutions.

In sum, very few people became trainers from an intrinsic interest in improving the preparation of teachers. One of the most troubling findings was the lack of any formal induction for college tutors. There seemed a general assumption that since you were a trained teacher, you would know how to train teachers yourself. The Malawian colleges offered some informal support; newcomers were given books and syllabuses and encouraged to seek advice, to observe others, or to be observed themselves.

In Trinidad and Tobago there was a system of informal mentoring where new tutors could 'sit in' on colleagues' lectures, and were paired with experienced tutors on Teaching Practice rounds. But at the NTTC peer observation was unknown and informal support apparently very sparse. It seemed that most staff had learnt on the job, drawing on memories of their own training. In the English department, tutors with only secondary training were allowed just to teach content at first, picking up the 'methods' courses later on.

In the case of Professional Studies, some tutors appeared to have relied largely on what they had been taught at the National University of Lesotho (NUL) in Educational Foundations courses; this would imply that what is being offered to NTTC students may be 15-20 years out of date. It was clear that when they had first come to the college many tutors had not known what to do, and relied on serendipitous help.

In the African countries studied in-service commonly takes the form either of local short courses, or long award-bearing courses that often require foreign travel. In Lesotho tutors exercised more personal initiative, but opportunities were sporadic, and the courses usually short. A notable exception was that six staff were trained to run a special programme in Early Learning, through a combination of short courses and regional study tours, which was perceived as very successful. Many tutors would like to upgrade their academic qualifications for both intrinsic and instrumental reasons, but opportunities are limited by funds and often by the lack of suitable local programmes.

While in Trinidad and Tobago tutors could study for an M.Ed. at the local UWI campus, the African colleges were still largely dependent on overseas scholarships. In these countries there were individual tutors who had done post-graduate study in the UK or the USA, and while such courses were stimulating they often found considerable problems in applying the ideas at home. For example, one who studied in the UK said, only half jokingly, that although the course had been an 'eye-opener', he had had to 'reverse what he had learnt' in adapting the ideas to Lesotho because of the lack of resources in schools.

In Ghana over a hundred college tutors were trained in British Universities under the Junior Secondary School Teacher Education Project (JUSSTEP), but they were able to make little impact on their return due to the deep-rooted conservatism of the colleges. Improvements in the college environment, its leadership and vision, are pre-requisites for change. Even the best in-service is only valuable if the lessons learnt can be applied in one's own classroom, and this depends on a number of other factors, such as basic resources, follow-up support, a critical mass of sympathetic colleagues, supportive management, and a culture conducive to change.

But the external environment is also crucial, since colleges are usually part of wider systems, and fall under the Ministries of Education. In both Ghana and Malawi traditional assessment practices, outside as well as inside the colleges, acted as a brake on efforts to change. In Trinidad and Tobago colleges there were both innovative tutors and supportive Principals, but the Board of Teacher Training maintained a conservative grip on the curriculum that the colleges were only just beginning to challenge.

While this ferment and international borrowing has many positive aspects, it also leads to disjunctions between rhetoric and actual practice. Colleges seem to be grappling with the paradigm shift towards constructivist teaching and learning so they could adapt it to local contexts and to development needs, but the shift comes into conflict with values, attitudes and beliefs about knowledge and schooling held by different stakeholders. There is a need for clearer models of training which incorporate recent developments in understanding of professional learning, but which also acknowledge local starting points, striking a balance between the old and new.

Malawian and Ghanaian tutors see their work as similar to high school teaching, and themselves as deliverers of a set curriculum. They regard their students in deficit terms, as empty vessels to be filled with the correct ideas and skills, even though in Malawi most students were in their late twenties and all had taught before. Many of their Basotho and Trinidadian counterparts by contrast feel themselves to be tertiary lecturers, have more control over what and how they teach, and expect more independent learning from their students, though this is not easily developed where the students' curriculum is overloaded, there is little time for personal study, and where students are used to 'transmission' teaching in high school.

One universal complaint from the tutors was the perceived low level of student academic standards. Yet the tutors had not developed pedagogic strategies for dealing with this, such as remedial classes, study skills, or training in independent learning. Lesotho's introductory upgrading semester partly addressed these issues, but the strategies were not continued into the main programme. A truly 'learner-centred' approach would suggest adapting the curriculum to student needs, both in terms of content and of process.

The studies explored, in different ways, how tutors perceived good primary teachers, in the hope this would reveal something of their personal views of teacher education. Several themes around the 'ideal' teacher emerged; in many ways these were similar to the images held by entering trainees. There was a strong personalistic theme: the good primary teacher is committed and caring, plays a nurturing role, and in her exemplary behaviour acts as a role model.

The teachers' personal characteristics and attitudes were foregrounded rather than their knowledge and cognitive skills. In general, the teacher's role was seen as 'restricted'. This was particularly evident in Ghana and Malawi, where tutors described the good teacher as one who delivers the curriculum efficiently by using a variety of classroom skills and techniques, that can be listed, learnt and applied. In Lesotho the discourse was more child-centred, stressing that the good teacher responds to individual needs and adjusts her approach.

In general, few tutors have well-developed or clearly articulated strategies for producing these 'good' teachers. In both Ghana and Malawi tutors seemed to have a relatively simple model of training in which both knowledge and skills are transmitted to students who will then be able to apply them routinely. In general, tutors everywhere seem ambivalent about the role of the schools in the process of learning to teach. On the one hand, many said that teaching practice was an extremely valuable part of the programme.

In Malawi most tutors held a rather closed view of knowledge as something 'out there', fixed and given, which was to be transmitted to students. Public propositional knowledge was given precedence while the student teachers' personal experiential knowledge was devalued. Most strikingly, tutors implied there is 'one right way to teach', which students must learn. In Ghana there was a similar view. Tutors supervising Teaching Practice hoped to find students doing exactly what they had been told or shown in college, rather than responding to the situations and needs found in the classrooms.

In Lesotho tutors held a relatively open view of knowledge, albeit not explicitly 'constructivist'. Although they taught propositional knowledge in the form of theory, and expected students to apply this, at least some also recognised the value of teachers' experiential and situated knowledge. In Trinidad and Tobago some tutors did indeed appear to be aware of the need for students to develop their own understanding of classrooms, and their own 'personal theories' of teaching.

However, very little of this openness was apparent - in either country - in the college curriculum documents or in the classrooms observed. It may well be that individual tutors' own 'espoused theories' could not be implemented given the different orientation of the more general educational discourse, ethos and practice. This points to the need for a much deeper epistemological change at the system level. Tutors everywhere are aware of the recommended shift to 'learner-centred' teaching, on which modern primary curricula are supposedly based.

They pay lip-service to this, in that they teach their students about participatory and active learning methods. But very few of them appeared to be able to put these into practice in the college classrooms. Training teachers is largely seen in terms of transmitting knowledge and skills which trainees will then apply. In Malawi the discourse often seemed derived from a 'behaviourist' approach to teaching, yet paradoxically even the skills element was often taught through tutors telling rather than through students practising and doing. Similar practices were observed in the Ghanaian colleges as well.

In Lesotho much of the discourse - though not the practice - was about 'child-centred pedagogy'. This seems an example of an 'applied theorist' approach, in that students were presented with the concepts as though this model of teaching could be used regardless of context, rather than being presented as a set of guiding principles or hypotheses to be tested, developed and modified in Lesotho classrooms.

There were few suggestions that learning to teach involved learning to solve problems, or to exercise informed judgement in unique, confused and difficult situations. Reflecting on practice, learning from mistakes, developing one's own personal theory of teaching and repertoires through experimenting both individually and collectively, were seldom part of the discourse. Still less was any notion that teachers might help transform society through their work.

There were, in all the countries, individuals who demonstrated a reflective attitude when talking about their practice, and clearly some of them tried to work with their students in inquiry-oriented ways. But because this was not shared by colleagues, and because the whole programme, in both structure and content, was geared toward the transmission of knowledge and skills, their efforts seemed not to reach beyond the limits of their own classroom.

As academic standards are raised, tutors need to be university graduates, and so increasingly they come up through secondary school teaching, but such people may have little understanding of, or sympathy for, primary classrooms. It is essential to select suitable primary teachers for professional upgrading so they can take on the role of tutor. Beyond that, there need to be sufficient avenues of promotion and reward structures, with clear criteria, to attract and retain quality personnel.

A key issue in all the countries studied concerned the pay and conditions of service for teacher educators. As in all teacher development and INSET work, the new ideas and skills will only be put into practice if there is opportunity and support in the home environment. Just as teacher INSET is moving towards 'whole school development' approaches, so a strategy of 'whole college development' is needed.

Such an approach would require a senior management team with a clear vision of change - and a brief from the authorities to carry it out - and groups of tutors prepared to commit themselves to professional improvement. This has implications for the ways in which the colleges are administered and managed, since such things as rigid timetables, heavy teaching loads, examinations system, and bureaucratic regulations constrain the ways in which professional teaching and learning can take place.

College management is currently given little training or support for innovations, and the system of financing often adds yet more problems. Changes in structures, as well as in the mindset of those who work within them, are equally necessary. There is a strong need for new and contextualised models of teacher preparation and development. The current variants of the 'technical rationality' model found in the colleges seem inadequate for preparing teachers to deal with the realities of primary and basic education classes in countries of the South.

Developments in understanding of professional knowledge and learning suggests more interactive and more flexible approaches would be more likely to produce teachers able to deal with the challenge of 21st century classrooms. However, these cannot be borrowed wholesale.

One major task for teacher educators in low income countries is to adapt the new approaches to local realities and cultures. Textbook knowledge about teaching - often deriving from very different cultural origins - is often seen as sacrosanct, and local contexts become forced into ideal models of teaching.

When the tutors emphasise professional attitudes and ethics, when they describe primary teachers in terms of personal characteristics and interpersonal skills rather than knowledge, when they complain they cannot work with such large groups of students, they are implicitly critiquing the 'technical rationality' model that focuses on knowledge and skill rather than on personal development. It seems plausible that this tradition, if linked to a more open and constructivist view of knowledge, would be a good foundation for developing a more reflective and more professional view of teacher education. The process of change is long and complex.

Teacher educators could be the fulcrum for raising standards among teachers and therefore in schools, but they have been neglected by policy-makers. They should be recognised as an important sub-group with particular professional needs. Among these are:

— Induction and orientation when they move from school to the college

— A career structure that offers them appropriate status, promotion opportunities and monetary rewards

— Accelerated academic development programmes for selected primary teachers to enable them to become trainers with equal status to their secondarytrained colleagues

— Continuing professional development that includes academic upgrading in their specialised area, as well as training in the theory and practice of adult development

— Opportunities to work closely with schools throughout their careers

Many colleges have a long and respected history, but they now seem to have difficulty in keeping up with developments in other parts of the education system. Reform and renewal are urgently called for. The colleges themselves need to develop stronger leadership and more effective management, together with a clearer sense of their role and mission. Policies of 'whole college development' might be one strategy for change.

In Ghana teachers for the basic education cycle are trained through a three-year postsecondary full-time programme which is offered in the 38 teacher training colleges (TTCs). With the exception of the TTC in Accra, all others are residential. All colleges currently prepare teachers for both primary and Junior Secondary (JSS) levels. The 38 TTCs are dispersed among all ten of Ghana's administrative regions and vary in size in terms of trainee enrolment.

In 1996, the smallest was Mampong Technical TTC with 241 trainees; the largest Foso with 914. Average enrolment in 1996/97 was 510 per college. The most recent data indicates there are 1,044 tutors giving an average trainee-tutor ratio in 1998 of about 19.5:1, which can be compared with a target figure of 15:1. The number of new trainees admitted each year is loosely based on a quota allocated by the MOE that does not appear to be linked to an overall analysis of teacher demand.

Total TTC output of trained teachers has been between 5,500 and 6,200 since 1995. Female enrolment as a percentage of total enrolment has increased from 33% to 38%. Total enrolment in 1998 reached 20,400 suggesting that the system has a maximum capacity using the current the current mode of training of no more than about 7,000 a year. Minimum entrance qualifications for entry are currently set at Senior Secondary School Certificate level. There is no constraint on applicants arising from a shortage of those with this level of qualification in the labour market.

Ghana allocated about 35% of recurrent expenditure to education in 1998 and nearly 4% of GNP. Expenditure on senior secondary (SSS) has been rising and now accounts for about 15% of the total despite falling enrolments - the same as tertiary level expenditure. Teacher education has seen its share rise substantially from under 3% to about 6% and this is projected to reach 6.7% in 1999. College running costs are concealed in this budgetary allocation system. Trainees do not receive the entire value of the stipends since a proportion is held back and used by the colleges for operating costs.

Increasing the college student-staff ratio would reduce costs per student. However, ratios above 20:1 might be thought to be unsuited to conventional curriculum delivery. The only large element of costs that might be reduced relates to students' stipends. Judgements would have to be made whether that proportion which is withheld is efficiently allocated, and whether the proportion of the stipend paid directly to students for living expenses is appropriate. As currently structured, most costs are variable and rise directly with the numbers of students.

Increasing average college size from current levels, which are small by international standards, would not result in large savings since it is only perhaps 10% of the costs that could be regarded as fixed within different ranges of enrolment. Currently there appears little incentive in the budgetary system at college level to increase the efficiency with which resources are used. In Ghana the college teaching year is not as it seems in the sense that the actual number of weeks of teaching delivered in the colleges is well below the theoretical maximum. Although 33 weeks are available a year for teaching, the real number of teaching weeks is much less.

Increasing active learning time could improve the quality of learning and might lower failure rates. Failure rates of 20%, an average across the colleges, increase unit costs per trained teacher by a similar amount and represent wastage, especially if failure is not retrieved by successful re-sitting. The way in which teaching is organised has important implications for curriculum delivery and costs. In the training colleges almost all the teaching is organised in a classroom and scheduled according to subject-specific contact hours with tutors. This means that often a tutor's teaching load is viewed strictly in terms of the fixed contact time with students. A common complaint from tutors is that their teaching load is already excessive and that this makes it unrealistic to provide richer quality learning experiences to smaller teaching groups.

Ghana Ministry of Education policy stipulates that staff-student ratio should be 1:15 and tutors should teach between 32 - 36 periods a week. Teaching loads expressed in student-periods should be between 480 and 540 per week. In Ghana total primary school enrolment in 1998 was 2.29 million, and 1.31 million at junior secondary (JSS).

Enrolment rates across the primary cycle averaged about 73% in 1998, having fallen from nearly 80% in the early 1990s. At JSS level, enrolment rates were stable through the 1990s at around 58%. Over the period from 1988 to 1998 the school age population of 6-14 year olds grew by nearly 4% per annum, suggesting the total number of teachers needed was doubling about every 18 years.

The total number of teachers at primary level has fallen over the last ten years, while enrolments have grown by 37%. As a result the average pupil-teacher ratio has increased from 26:1 to 36:1. Interestingly the pupil to qualified teacher ratio has remained fairly constant at about 45:1. At JSS level the number of teachers has increased by 16% and the number of students by 24%. Overall pupil-teacher ratios have increased marginally to 20:1 and the pupil per qualified teacher ratio has fallen to 23:1. 12,700 primary teachers and 5,100 JSS teachers are untrained.

Teacher attrition rates are difficult to estimate. Over the period 1988 to 1998, Mereku estimates that the rate of increase in the number of trained teachers employed was a little below 4% and the rate at which newly trained teachers were being posted was averaging about 9% of the number of trained teachers employed. The difference gives an estimate of the underlying rate of trained teacher attrition from all causes. It is now possible to estimate future demand for teacher training over a ten-year period.

In Lesotho, the National Teacher Training college was established 1974. The college is the only provider of initial training for primary school teachers in Lesotho. It also trains junior secondary school teachers and secondary school teachers of technical subjects. The college is currently consolidating the three programmes at primary level into a single Diploma of Education, Primary (DEP) course. This is of three years' duration. In 1999 the NTTC had a total enrolment of about 900 students, of whom nearly half were part-time, giving a full-time equivalent of perhaps 650 including secondary level trainees.

Many applicants apparently do not have the minimum of four credits and two passes needed at Cambridge Overseas School Certificate level (COSC) and this is one of the reasons for under-recruitment. About 2,000 students qualify at COSC each year, suggesting that at current levels of recruitment the supply side constraint is a result of small proportions opting for primary school teaching.

There are 43 teaching staff members in the primary division at NTTC. Each member of the teaching staff teaches on one or two of the primary programmes They usually take responsibility for one or two groups in a programme. Sometimes they cover all the groups depending on the numbers. The overall staff-student ratio at NTTC is 1:14 for the primary division. This should allow the convening of staff in ways that enables a rich curriculum to be delivered to groups of students that are not excessively large.

However, the teaching and groups sizes are unevenly distributed over the different programmes and this gives rise to some problems. Staff members who are teaching the diploma groups are handling smaller numbers than those who are teaching the PTC groups and this causes an imbalance in the loads in terms of student-hours. There are also differences between subjects.

Alternative patterns of organisation for teacher education are being considered as a result of dissatisfaction with some aspects of MIITEP. An illustration can be provided of the most commonly discussed alternatives. The training model could return to a pattern of one-year full-time and one-year school-based, or two years full-time with teaching practice integrated into the programmes.

3

Influence of Information Technology

The rapid infusion of technology into schools requires a new generation of leaders who are able to use the new tools to enhance their own productivity and decision-making activities and who understand the importance of integrating technology into the learning process. Leadership is often the most important factor in the successful integration of ICTs into the school's instructional practices and curriculum.

Many countries in Europe have official recommendations for ICT-related skills for future and practicing teachers. Eurydice, the information network on education in Europe, annually publishes Basic Indicators on the Incorporation of ICT into European Education Systems. In the majority of European countries, as much importance is attached to the teachers' personal command of ICTs as to mastery of ICTs for teaching purposes.

In France, the Netherlands and the United Kingdom, the content of training is determined to some extent by the mandatory standards. In the UK, there is also a detailed curriculum for the use of ICTs in teaching specific subjects. Countries and regions adopting standards for the first time may wish to do so in stages. This was the strategy taken by the UK, which currently has the most detailed standards of any country in Europe. The standards were first imposed with a relatively simple section within the mandatory standards for pre-service teachers in 1989. In particular, all courses should contain compulsory and clearly identifiable elements that enable students to make effective use of information technology (IT) in the classroom and provide a sound basis for their subsequent development in the field.

UK government developed highly detailed standards for pre-service teacher education and then also developed a nationwide strategy to train all teachers in pedagogical use of ICTs. The detailed curriculum has the following expected outcomes for teachers. The Teacher Training Agency also developed a CD to help teachers analyze their own training needs. A complementary outcomes-based curriculum has also been developed for school librarians.

An ICT training initiative funded by a charitable lottery has resulted in the creation of a large number of training organizations, many of which are public-private partnerships. A different approach has been taken in Scandinavia. A standard test was first developed that focused on ICT skills. It is known as the European Computer Driving License (ECDL) and is used in many professions and with students in schools.

More recently, a Pedagogical ICT Driving License has been developed for primary and secondary school teachers in Denmark for the integration of ICTs in education. Several countries in South America have extensive projects to develop and integrate ICTs in education, but the lack of national policies for the use of ICTs is notable. The final example provided is the generic curriculum used by the international Intel Applying Computers in Education (ACE) project. The project trains classroom teachers to integrate the use of computers into existing curriculum to increase student learning and achievement.

Role of Information and Communication Technologies

Through the ongoing use of technology in the schooling process, students should achieve important technology capabilities. The key individual in helping students achieve those capabilities is the classroom teacher. The teacher is responsible for establishing the classroom environment and preparing the learning opportunities that facilitate students' use of technology to learn, communicate, and develop knowledge products; consequently, it is critical that all classroom teachers are prepared to provide their students with these opportunities. Teacher preparation programmes must provide technology-rich experiences throughout all aspects of the training programmes.

Teachers must be prepared to empower students with the advantages technology can bring. Schools and classrooms, both real and virtual, must have teachers who are equipped with technology resources and skills and who can effectively teach the necessary subject matter content while incorporating technology concepts and skills. Real-world connections, primary source materials, and sophisticated data-gathering and analysis tools are only a few of the resources that allow teachers to provide heretofore unimaginable opportunities for developing their students' conceptual understandings. Teachers must prepare their students to apply strategies for problem solving, and to use appropriate tools for learning, calculating, collaborating, and communicating.

ICT tools and resources can contribute dramatically to establishing these new learning environments, both in P-12 schools and in colleges of education. ICT competencies must be integrated into the curricular and pedagogical content presented, preparing teacher candidates to create the new learning environments. Teacher educators must therefore model the use of these new learning environments in their own university classrooms. The curriculum for teacher educators is often rich with strategies for presenting subject matter and pedagogy; however, it may be lean in terms of integrating technological tools for supporting that learning. In an effort to implement ICT standards in a variety of coursework taken by pre-service teachers across all subject disciplines, a number of methods and strategies have been identified. Many of these strategies employ commonly used productivity tools such as word processing, database, spreadsheet, or browser applications.

With the growth of infrastructure around the world comes the ability to access others through remote connections. Students and teacher candidates can connect to experts and peers through a variety of formats, such as chat rooms, electronic bulletin boards, and email. Communicating online offers participants freedom to send and receive information efficiently across diverse geographic locations. Communication can occur asynchronously allowing time for reflection, or to compensate for varying time zones. Online discussions can provide rich learning experiences as the inter-cultural exchanges develop both linguistic skills and cultural knowledge. One successful strategy is for students to read in the target language, while writing in their native language.

The teacher education institution itself may be scrutinized along with individual programmes within the institution. The quality of the teacher education institution and its programmes is often judged by the performance of the teachers they produce and the success of their graduates in effecting improved student learning in their P-12 classrooms. Quality assurance is often determined through an accreditation process. Demonstrated competence of teacher candidates in use of ICTs in teacher education has become increasingly important in making accreditation, certification, and programme review decisions. This is particularly true in the two countries that have adopted detailed national standards, the United States and the United Kingdom.

The most critical factor in the successful integration of ICTs into teacher education is the extent to which the teacher educators have the knowledge and skills for modelling the use of ICTs in their own teaching practices. To enable them to develop these skills requires a well-conceived and sustained programme of professional development. Professional development may be provided to other small groups of faculty, thus expanding and refining the professional development efforts. The most important criterion for effective professional development is to tailor it to the learning needs and skill levels of individual teaching staff within a faculty. In structuring professional development options and resources, it is helpful to explore collaboration opportunities with partners outside the university.

The opportunities for ICTs to create new paradigms of teaching and learning will depend largely on leadership and a shared vision, and on appropriate and continuing professional development. The planning and implementation of ICT-related professional development of teacher educators should be led by a planning group that includes representation and expertise from teacher educators, programme administrators, teachers, school administrators, technology experts, and business leaders. The diverse perspectives of the group should provide an understanding of the realities of the classroom, new views of the teaching-learning process, knowledge of the array of technologies that may be used to enhance learning, and community opinions.

An important aspect of professional development is not only enabling teacher educators to understand and use ICT tools in their teaching practices, but understanding how technology coupled with new approaches to teaching and learning, may enhance student learning. Many teacher educators recognize that approaches to education are changing and that new technology has the potential to improve education and student learning. They may also recognize the implications of increasing use of technology in society and employment, including employment directly related to their own disciplines and content areas.

Less obvious are the implications for literacy and numeracy at the core of the educational process, and the need for teacher educators themselves to model good practice in their teaching so that their students can easily transfer these strategies into their own teaching practice. Teacher educators are experts in a domain, and it is important to respect this domain while helping them to revitalize and modernize their teaching with ICTs. Similarly, the risk that established teacher educators must take to develop their practice needs to be recognized and mitigated as much as possible.

The most significant change required of individuals and organizations providing teacher education is to redefine student roles and responsibilities. Both students and teachers have always had rights and responsibilities, but the redefinition of the learning environment requires a change in the balance of rights and responsibilities, with the student assuming more of both. ICTs demand this shift because technologies are constantly changing. Students need to develop the ability to think for themselves, continually learn as technologies change, and provide support to one another.

Peer teaching, is a natural product of ICTs because often the younger generations bring increasingly high levels of competence into the learning environment. This is a positive shift, and it should be noted that these strategies are also appropriate for competencies that do not involve ICTs. Teachers and teacher educators develop ICT competence in stages. Those who are fluent with technology may not appreciate how difficult it is for technology novices to appropriate ICTs into their professional practice.

Teacher educators often find this task even more difficult than teachers do, because they typically have higher levels of content and pedagogical expertise that must be respected. Teacher educators, because they have to work in multiple contexts-both the home institution and the field where students are placed to observe and practice teaching-may also be more influenced by the absence of the essential conditions for ICTs in teacher education. All the teacher educators and support staff received ICT professional development to facilitate a rich environment of good educational practice.

Students were able to practice teaching in pairs with a group of four children. This strategy may be particularly appropriate at early stages of ICT adoption in a region where there are few resources and little ICT practice in local schools. In US, the new government requirement for ICTs in pre-service teacher education provided ample justification for change and an argument for expanding resources in teacher education.

Teachers also need professional development in the pedagogical application of those skills to improve teaching and learning. Traditional one-time teacher training workshops have not been effective in helping teachers to feel comfortable using technology or to integrate it successfully into their teaching. Instead, a new paradigm is emerging that replaces training with lifelong professional preparedness and development of teachers. The importance of training additional school community members is stressed, and recommendations are offered for overcoming the persistent problem of insufficient funding for teacher professional development.

When designing or implementing any teacher professional development program for technology, it is important to situate that program within the context of a theoretical framework for adult learning. Each of the dimensions is presented as a continuum, with contrasting values at either end. Teacher professional development in the use of technology should be designed and implemented to move teachers toward the right-hand end of this continuum. This framework emphasizes the potential of Web-based instruction to contribute to pedagogical reform, rather than technology's rich multimedia features or its ability to access information resources around the world. Stated more simply, technology can promote effective instruction that is more student-centered, interdisciplinary, more closely related to real-life events and processes, and adaptive to individual learning styles.

Such instruction encourages development of higher-order thinking and information-reasoning skills (rather than memorization of facts) among students, and socially constructed (collaborative) learning, all of which are increasingly required in today's knowledge-based global economy. This potential of technology to improve instruction needs to be integrated (modeled) into the design and delivery of teacher professional development programs in the use of technology. Perhaps most important for the purpose of teachers' professional development, technology implies a shift in the teacher's role from being the sole source of knowledge and instruction to being a facilitator of students' learning, which is acquired from many sources.

More concretely, this means that teacher professional development in the use of technology needs to combine lecture/ presentation modalities with small-group and plenary discussion, individual and collaborative activities, and opportunities for teachers to reflect on their actual teaching practices and how they might do things differently with technology. Such an approach also means that learning materials need to be in several formats: print, CD-ROM, e-mail attachments, online (HTML and Java), and even DVD.

It also implies a need to develop both synchronous and asynchronous modalities, so that teachers can take advantage of training opportunities when they have the time, which is not necessarily when the trainer is available. Key to successful teacher professional development programs is a modular structure, corresponding to different levels of teacher experience and expertise using technology. Adapting materials to teachers' comfort level and starting points is essential. In this way, teachers new to technology can be exposed to the full series of professional development modules, while those further along on the learning curve can enter where their knowledge and skills stop, and help their less technology-savvy colleagues along.

The basic principles of adult learning also should be incorporated into the training program. This implies that the program should be highly social and cooperative, with opportunities to share experiences and combine instruction with discussion, reflection, application, and evaluation. In addition to these principles, technology enables an even more collaborative approach and maximizes peer-to-peer sharing of the challenges, frustrations, advantages, and successes of using technology to teach and learn.

Such an approach encourages use of illuminating failures in the use of technology in the classroom as well as examples of best practice. Finally, these principles imply the need to build ongoing community and systems of support from peers, mentors, and experts. The International Society for Technology in Education (ISTE) has produced a set of standards for teacher skills and knowledge in the use of technology, a useful guide for determining the content of teacher professional development programs. Teachers need to be encouraged by administrators, particularly their school directors, to participate in training activities.

Administrators need to ensure that teachers have adequate time to participate, and do not have to sacrifice too much personal time to do so. From an administrative perspective, this should be viewed as an investment and a contribution to the capacity building of the country's teaching force. But, in addition to time allocation, supervisors should recognize publicly teachers who successfully complete professional development courses. This provides immediate personal reward to teachers, raises their status in the eyes of their peers, and encourages others to participate. Many teachers lead an isolated professional existence, with little input from or collaboration with their peers or supervisors.

Learning new technological skills, especially if they include Internet and e-mail, allows teachers to break down the walls of their classroom and share lesson plans, evaluation strategies, student assessments, and even just the joys and frustrations of teaching. For example, more than 80% of teachers in both Africa and Latin America who responded to the survey included in the 1999 evaluation of the World Links professional development program, conducted by SRI International, gave the highest possible ranking to the program's impact on their motivation and satisfaction as teachers.

In other words, technology reduced their isolation and made them more excited about teaching. Sharing that experience should serve to motivate other teachers to participate in similar professional development programs. Technology can speed up and increase the efficiency of a range of noninstructional teacher activities such as student attendance, grading, textbook distribution, and preparation of administrative reports. It also can enhance the productivity of basic instructional tasks, such as preparing lesson plans and class outlines, developing quizzes and examinations.

More advanced applications include fast identification of educational resources (online), use of CD-ROM materials, and curriculum-linked telecollaborative programmes. In fact, there is a nearly limitless range of opportunities for teachers who develop the necessary skills and knowledge in the effective use of technology in the classroom, and who have access to technology and Internet. Teachers may be motivated to participate in professional development workshops in the use of technology because they see them as an opportunity to become a trainer/mentor for other teachers.

In many cases, becoming a trainer brings additional financial and professional opportunities (travel, participation conferences, publications, etc.). If the training workshops come with some form of official certification for successful completion, motivation is enhanced further. School directors, finance officers, and other administrative personnel also need professional development in the use of technology for noninstructional purposes. Technology can improve significantly the productivity of activities related to financial management, class scheduling, personnel management, student tracking, administrative reporting, communicating with parents, etc.

However, training of school directors should not be limited to noninstructional uses of technology. It is vital that school directors understand and support teachers' efforts to integrate technology into the classroom. Far too often, school directors minimize the time and effort required for teachers to develop the skills and knowledge required to use technology effectively, and, in many cases, directors actively oppose teachers' efforts to use technology in innovative ways. For this reason, it is strongly recommended that all school directors participate in introductory professional development workshops in the pedagogical application of technology.

If at all possible, this should be done in collaboration with teachers (even students!), so school directors understand that technology requires us to be both learners and facilitators of the learning of others. School directors need to see the potential of technology to be a catalyst for more effective learning. They also need to understand (and empathize with) the process and the time required to tap this potential.

Technology training for students has a "viral" character to it in that it tends to replicate itself spontaneously and spread among other students, many of whom have extremely strong intrinsic motivation to learn new skills. This motivation is related to youth's natural affinity for new technologies, their desire to improve their academic performance for downstream educational and economic opportunities, and their understanding that these skills are increasingly demanded in their countries' labor markets. Such motivation is not often present among teachers. Technologically savvy students can help teachers use technology in the classroom in many ways, especially when collaborative, constructivist, and authentic learning strategies are used.

At a basic level, students can provide technical support in the classroom to their peers and even to the teacher in the use of software, Internet research, leadership of small groups, and even simple computer maintenance and troubleshooting of common glitches. At a more advanced level, students often have more time and desire than teachers to develop their technological skills further. Generating parent support for technology in schools is important if technology investments are to be sustained and/or expanded. Many different technologies have been used to support or provide teacher professional development. Often grouped under the vague heading, 'distance learning,' they include basic correspondence courses, broadcast television, interactive radio, and video.

The potential of new digital technologies (the Internet, digital radio, CD-ROMs, DVDs) for teacher professional development. To begin, it is important to distinguish among different approaches or models for online professional development. Many developing countries looking to improve the quality of their preservice and/or inservice teacher professional development programs can begin here. However, this approach does not reduce costs (it increases them), nor does it replace face-to-face instructional time (the primary cost) or improve scalability of training. The online lecture model offers opportunities to reduce instructional costs and reach large numbers of teachers.

It emphasizes primarily one-way delivery of high-quality content. Considerable resources often are invested in developing online instructional resources, with personal contact provided over the Internet through instructor responses to assignments and exams, moderated discussion groups. For motivated and disciplined teachers, this model can be an effective way to provide professional development at a reasonable cost, particularly in countries where qualified teachers are in short supply. However, the loss of personal contact implied by this model typically results in extremely high dropout rates. The online correspondence model is similar to the online lecture model, but it usually invests fewer resources in content delivery in exchange for increased personal contact with the teacher through graded assignments and examinations.

Indeed, quite a few traditional correspondence training programs that used postal systems to exchange the work of participants and instructors have transferred their courses to the Internet. The cost is relatively low, but the lower quality/quantity of instruction (much of the training is actually self-paced reading) limits this model to highly motivated teachers and specialized content. The online collaborative model emphasizes the full potential of technology to enable teacher-teacher collaboration during their training course.

Teachers engage in training online on their own, at their convenience, and they can do so as often and for as long as they want. Ongoing pedagogical support and teacher networking, key ingredients of effective inservice training, are facilitated by the technology. By infusing technology into the teaching and learning process, teachers' careerlong professional development has become a continuous and planned process. Technology extends training into and beyond the classroom, no longer bound by fixed schedules or physical spaces for instruction (anytime, anywhere learning). This potential can been seen in the evaluation of the World Links Program by SRI International, in which more than 80% of teachers surveyed reported that their attitudes about teaching improved 'a lot' or 'a great deal' as a result of their involvement in the program.

The program offers access to technology and the Internet, teacher professional development, involvement in international telecollaborative projects, and development of online educational content by the teachers themselves. But perhaps more important than providing additional training opportunities, the use of the Web as the training medium exposes teachers to pedagogical practices analogous to what they may do with their own students using technology. Teachers begin to learn skills and develop new knowledge online, through interaction with instructors, mentors, peers, and subject matter experts, modeling the potential learning experience of their students after the training.

More specifically, from a pedagogical perspective, teachers working together online with their instructors, peers, and experts share and collectively construct their skills and knowledge. This replaces the traditional vertical training model of trainer imparting information 'down' to a teacher. In the corporate world, e-learning has demonstrated over the past five years that it can cut training time by one-third, increase training effectiveness by one-third, and reduce training costs by one-third. The same efficiencies need to be explored in the public sector, even if some of the costs and technology investments are different.

Traditional teacher training approaches simply are not equipped to deal with all of these new expectations. By contrast, ICTs can help teachers to meet these expectations, by providing productivity tools, access to information and colleagues, and collaboration opportunities. As teachers experience these external pressures, and realize the potential of technology to help them respond, their demand for training in the use of technology will grow. Scale and complexity exacerbate the issue of teacher motivation.

Ministries of education around the world are struggling for techniques and incentives to get beyond the 'champion teachers' and so-called early adopters to reach the average teacher. Paradoxically, there is both excess teacher demand for training (relative to capacity to provide it) and insufficient teacher demand for training (relative to the physical distribution of computer hardware in the schools). New teacher professional development methodologies are required to address this issue of motivation. In the future, ministries of education will issue new standards for teacher competencies in the use of technology, which will affect both preservice and inservice teacher training levels.

These standards are likely to be linked to official certification requirements and processes, so that education ministries can track the proportion of teachers who have the necessary skills and knowledge, and so that teachers have an incentive to participate. As the need and demand for teacher professional development increases, the key challenges will be ensuring content quality, reliable and appropriate training delivery infrastructure, follow-up support, and measurable outcomes—and all at an acceptable cost. E-learning is a way for teachers to learn new knowledge and skills using computer network technologies. The technologies provide not just text, but also sound, video, simulations, and collaboration with other learners who may be scattered around the country or the world.

Currently, most e-learning is delivered using the World Wide Web; however, future e-learning could include delivery via mobile handheld devices, cell phones, and digital video devices. The rapidly declining cost of digital video disc (DVD) production and replay offers exciting opportunities to capture the work of master teachers and trainers and share this with teachers wherever they are. Internet-enabled DVD will be available soon, so that teachers learning with a DVD will be able to access materials and resources located on the DVD itself and on the World Wide Web.

A $250 DVD player linked to a computer (and perhaps an Internet connection) would bring full video and audio capabilities to professional development, in combination with community-building tools and other resources. This will open up a whole new range of visual and audio possibilities in a distance training format, which is easily scaled. As Internet access and bandwidth improve in developing countries, additional Web-based synchronous and asynchronous teacher professional development opportunities will arise. For instance, a reliable 56 Kbps Internet connection would enable online teacher professional development that includes live voice-over-IP, file sharing, control of all participants' computer screens by the instructor-facilitator from anywhere in the world, online assessment, and many other features.

The instructor-facilitator would control the microphone, be able to 'pass' it to participants when they want to ask a question or make a comment, provide individualised evaluation and support to participants, and do this with teachers located in 25 different countries simultaneously. Professional development of teachers in the use and application of educational technology should be designed and implemented as part of a broader educational reform program that, at a minimum, combines technology access with teacher professional development and local content development.

No strategy that ignores any of these three elements is likely to succeed beyond superficial applications. Ideally, teachers' professional development should not be isolated from other elements of instructional and noninstructional educational environments, such as curriculum reform, physical/technological infrastructure, examinations, and research. Simply providing professional development for teachers in the use of computers and the Internet, in a situation with outdated curricula, traditional standardized test systems, and insufficient technology access, is unlikely to produce any systemic improvements in learning.

In fact, the high-stakes traditional examinations system frequently operates against teachers trying to incorporate technology and encourage deeper forms of learning, which frequently are not measured by standardized tests. Success in ensuring that teachers acquire the skills and knowledge they need to use technology effectively opens the door to all kinds of new educational opportunities for both teachers and students, and downstream economic opportunities for graduating youth and their countries. It is the key to participation in the global knowledge-based economy.

Accordingly, teacher professional development in the use and application of technology must be given the priority and resources it deserves, while maintaining a constructively critical eye on its costs, methodologies, and impact. Many nations are increasing their investments in education and education technology to support the transformation of teaching and learning. Yet, not enough attention is given to the development and availability of instructional content-ware that makes the investments in hardware economically useful and educationally meaningful. One possible reason is that equipping schools with radios, televisions, and computers and connecting them to the Internet is simple compared to developing corresponding instructional materials. Today multimedia as a means of learning is equated with tightly structured content built by a commercial vendor—a developer. It is a product, not a possibility. The excitement of choice, of trial, of process is absent.

Yet, multimedia in its broadest sense is among the most effective and egalitarian of computer-based resources available. By establishing the potential for the artful interaction between learners and content-intertwining information, skills, and even the synthesizing vision that is so important to comprehension-multimedia 'contentware' is effective across the wide range of circumstances. In dynamic fields, such as astrophysics, genetics, or political geography, updates to contentware can ensure that teachers and students encounter and have the chance to work with current and even cutting-edge knowledge.

Such encounters tie learning to the most important events of time and underscore the general idea that knowledge itself is not fixed and finalized, that there is a universe of discoveries and a library of analyses that can be available to students. Finally, computer-based and Web-based multimedia content-ware is itself dynamic, built of bits and bytes, using software development tools that combine, in some cases, the power to create with the simplicity of use.

Unlike textbooks or library-based resources, contentware has the potential to engage all stakeholders in the education system—from software developers to ministry personnel to education researchers to teachers and students-in the development of multimedia learning resources. A decade and more ago, national efforts to introduce ICTs in education anticipated increases in efficiency, without attending to the nature of learning and cognition, or to the distinction between skills mastered in abstraction and knowledge built to be used, expanded, and eventually transcended.

To build resources that enable learners to build knowledge, broaden perspective beyond building skills and memorizing facts in the abstract; if these are educational goals, technology will prove neither cost-effective nor effective in absolute terms. If goals include enhancing analysis, synthesis, communication, and the grasping of interrelationships in the ways in which represent world, will find that technology supports and empowers all of efforts along these lines. The use of multimedia as engines of learning is conditioned by several dynamic contexts, including evolving understanding of cognitive factors with direct bearing on learning and changes in school environment ranging from infrastructure to resources to teacher development. The emergence of technology as a change factor in education coincides with the sweeping influence of cognitive science and brain studies as a factor in the transformation of teaching and learning.

The influence of both of these forces has increased with the recognition of globalization, the concomitant demonstrations of the value of innovation, and the prevalence of strong 'knowledge-work' sectors. Advances in technology, cognitive science, and measurement also show the need to reinvent large-scale assessment, and this process of reinvention may stand to benefit from incorporation of multimedia. Dynamic stimuli, such as audio, video, and animation, may make performing such tasks as problem solving more relevant to student experience. To accomplish this objective, multimedia development must consider cognitive complexity, sensitivity to instruction, meaningfulness, reliability, fairness, and linguistic appropriateness.

Multimedia material produced for teaching and learning must be produced for assessment as well, with compatible goals, similar depth, and equal quality. When developing educational multimedia resources, it is important to take into account objectives at the level of the individual learner, the school, and the state. Each has different characteristics, expectations, and needs, and the means to fulfill them are all interrelated. For this reason, development of learning resources is linked, strategically, with processes of educational reform and the transformation of teaching and learning. They may use conceptual maps linked to Web pages that highlight different aspects of a content domain: how knowledge is acquired by experts; how problems are solved; what language is used in that domain; the current pathways of deepening knowledge; and the different possibilities of presentation for different publics of different ages.

Multimedia also can broaden the scope of school learning environments by enabling experiments that otherwise would be too dangerous, too expensive, or take too long. (There are already some excellent CD-ROMs available in this niche.) And visualization and modeling tools give students the opportunity to enter into much more complex knowledge-contexts (so many of which are now necessary in world than ever before), while continuing to build their comprehension of the core knowledge of those domains. Technology can help facilitate self-assessment and other meta-cognitive activities in students, in part by giving frequent feedback.

Collaborative tools and communication tools may promote reflection and learning as a social activity, enhancing the potential for conceptual change. Interactive multimedia can play a crucial role in helping students overcome misconceptions in other ways as well. Students can be enabled to develop their hypotheses as far as possible, aided by the capabilities of well-planned multimedia. At that extreme point of development, visual feedback can intervene, providing alternatives or deconstructing their beliefs.

It is possible to produce simulations and animations that feature embedded 'expert-systems examples,' demonstrating how experts have addressed the same problems or arrived at true conclusions, only after students tried the simulations on their own. Technology can play a crucial role in connecting schools to professionals in their communities and around the world, and by allowing the school to develop ideas and positions and make them public.

Educational publishers frequently 'bundle' CD-ROMs with textbooks, providing additional resources, updates, and other information. Interactive simulations are often 'wrapped' with text addressed directly to learners, providing contextualizing information, and with text addressed to teachers guiding them in facilitation of classroom activities, questioning strategies, and assessment.

In this sense, supporting radio broadcasts or audiocassettes with print-based workbooks comprises a multimedia combination of different instruments. In all of these combinations, not only are limitations mitigated, but the strengths of each instrument are also magnified beyond the potential of any single instrument deployed in isolation. That above characteristic implies a fundamental goal of multimedia design-to combine instruments in ways that best address the requirements of a specific content domain, the abilities and deficits of targeted learners, and the infrastructure and systemic conditions of the prospective learning environment to achieve results beyond what is possible with individual instruments and isolated media. The Internet and CD-ROMs, of course, have the potential to serve as platforms for the full range of modes-text, images, audio, video, and simulations.

To this potential, the Internet adds the possibility of frequent updates, collaborative or participatory solutions, and near-infinite scalability. Bandwidth and platform constraints, however, continue to pose limits in most circumstances. In all instances, effective design and development processes are required to arrive at a creative, effective, and appropriate implementation that addresses specific parameters. Educational gains can be maximized for every situation when the most appropriate tools are used. It is not possible, however, to give recipes for what technology tools to use or when to use them.

In addition, the explosive popularity of various techniques for exchanging music over the Internet has already led many students to explore the power of information exchange via Web-based and peer-to-peer collaboration. Many students are eager to produce and publish their own sound files. It is easy to channel such motivated activity toward production of materials that also have educational value-for the creator. Again, resource considerations may pose limitations: although software is not too expensive, it is necessary to have a good sound card, a good processor, and sufficient RAM (random access memory) and storage capacity.

ICTs have reshaped the contours of production profoundly in all sectors. Changes in the development of materials for teaching and learning have occurred most visibly in an expanded range of available modalities-with interactive CD-ROMs, Web-based simulations, and intelligent tutors among the array of new resource types presented to educators and policy makers. However, the more profound shift in creation of educational resources centers on the changing identity of the authors of learning resources, and on changes in the relationship between authoring itself and learning.

Before the widespread adoption of ICTs in universities and schools, educational resources were generated largely by private-sector publishers or centralized government-operated organizations. University faculty and, at times, schoolteachers are engaged as subject-matter and pedagogical experts. But the production, marketing, sale, and delivery of resources to the education sector generally remains solidly under the control of a single organization-whether a ministry of education or a private vendor.

For this reason, it is the organization-not the individual educators engaged by the organization-that retains ultimate control over the evolution of the learning resource. Whether the target client is seen to be a ministry-level decision maker, the head teacher of a state school, a teacher in the classroom, or the operator of a private school or tutoring business, it is most often the publisher developing a product who determines the scope of the resource, its requirements, and the kinds of learning opportunities it affords its users.

In some instances, centralized developers have achieved stunning successes, especially when their efforts are focused on innovation, and when such innovation is fueled by the results of research and experience. Institutions-universities, government- or privately funded research facilities, and international agencies-may be effective developers or sponsors of multimedia resources, initially free of cost, and market considerations that may limit development in the private sector. Successful resources or approaches may be transferred later to the private sector for support and elaboration, however.

In Turkey, for example, the technology research agency, Tubitek, successfully transferred its research results in education to a start-up private-sector company, Sebit, which has released a comprehensive set of interactive test-preparation tools, with efforts underway to localize these for schools in the United States and China. Alternatively, institution-based development may provide the benefits of scaffolding experiences and innovations. Nongovernmental and nonprofit organizations have been in the forefront in linking students in innovative and effective ways. The International Education and Resource Network began in 1988 to promote project-based collaborative learning and remains among the leaders in global, Internet-based education.

4

ICTs in Teaching and Learning

The intersection between the new technologies, and the power wielded by their combination, together with the growth of education systems, makes their application to modern education potentially a huge enterprise. The extension of universal compulsory primary and then secondary education through more and more countries is being followed by a transition from elite higher education towards mass or even universal tertiary education. New notions of lifelong learning and learning societies extend the "market" for education as a business to all age cohorts.

The new technologies offer hitherto unthought of opportunities for reaching people in their homes, communities and workplaces where they can combine learning with other roles. Old notions of boundaries lose their validity. Beyond education the major social sectors also become less sharply separated. Public and private sectors get blurred, and silo administration proves ineffectual. The very nature of the school and of education become problematic in the lifelong learning society. In this changing environment the concept of social dialogue, one of the International Labour Organisations (ILO)'s four strategic objectives, acquires if it is possible even more significance and strategic importance. Education systems and their institutions have a poor and uncertain future if they try to be closed, inward-looking and inward-referenced. They depend increasingly on more open discourse with their "client" students, parents, communities and regions, and on more effective collaboration with industry, business, local government and other communities of interest which are fellow stakeholders in their respective localities.

The notion of social dialogue, along with related ideas of joint participatory planning and development—the shared production, ownership and use of knowledge and purpose—becomes more persuasive with increasing complexity of relations and rate of change, features long ago referred to as turbulence and puzzle, and more recently as mess and super-complexity. Without collaborative planning and the sense of purposeful ownership which derives from this, the chances of successful management and development are slight. No one party, whether government (itself often complex, divided into silos and multi-layered), employers, or professional workers—teachers and other school and college staff—can alone meet the diverse and demanding learning needs of even a relatively standardized age-graded school, let alone a large complex secondary or tertiary enterprise. The means of social dialogue and the planning, ownership, implementation, evaluation and further planning which result vary between cultures and political traditions from well-developed tripartite arrangements for collective planning including bargaining to more confrontational industrial modes. It is unhelpful to prescribe one mode for all countries, even if, consensual tripartite modes can be demonstrated to be more productive and efficient. Different systems may have different, well-developed, covertly acknowledged and owned, informal means of securing common purpose through social dialogue outside the formal settings of more ritualized contest.

ICTs and Open and Distance Learning

The new technologies have a wider impact in education systems, since they are also essential to storing, handling and interrogation data in large complex systems. New ICT enables institutions to manage admissions, assessment and progression, and the transfer of student credit, in more sophisticated ways than do simpler systems. The broader curriculum, and the recording and management of learning and its outcomes, are thus enabled to operate in different ways.

Nevertheless, focus is on matters of pedagogy rather than administration and management information systems (MIS) per se. In terms of support for pedagogy, the new ICT may be regarded as an extension of earlier forms of teaching and learning aids and supports. It is, however, usually now assumed with good reason that the gain in power and sophistication represented especially by the Internet or World Wide Web is such as to represent a change of state and not merely of scale.

In particular, the access to information which this allows any user with access to search engines and data bases is of a totally different order than has hitherto been available to anyone, senior professor as well as primary school pupil. This change of state surpassing mere change of scale has aroused great hopes, ambitions for learning and for profit, and deep anxieties of a moral as well as an interested kind. The wealth of opportunity opened up is all but universally welcomed. The problems it presents for unfettered access to data include: the protection of minors from harmful material; the inability without help and guidance to discriminate and interpret, so turning information into knowledge; the loss of ownership and control of intellectual property and of a managed curriculum which facilitates deep and well ordered learning; and a further widening of the gaps between rich and poor in terms of a digital divide.

A particular sensitivity affecting higher and some other tertiary education more than school levels concerns the privatization and marketing of curriculum subject matter or courseware, and of the means to its access and use (carriers, hardware as well as software). Aspirations to great wealth by means of virtual universities and consortia teaching over the World Wide Web have been labelled cyperbole. They take the form of seeking to be first in a multi-billion dollar enterprise selling mainly post-graduate, short course and also undergraduate degree study worldwide.

The quest for new markets is sharpened as higher education institutions find themselves compelled to diversify and generate higher levels of non-government grant income. It is coming to be recognized however that the power and value of the new ICTs may have more to do with quality and choice of learning methods for existing and on-campus student clienteles. In business terms it may mean retaining or slightly extending market share, rather than winning big new markets with economies of scale and the removal of all faceto-face tuition.

The emphasis is more on computers in schools and in each classroom, and on equipping teachers to understand and use the new ICT effectively with confidence. Around the corner lurk other issues, as the power of new ICT lends itself to distance learning for school as well as for tertiary students.

Another frequently used term, to be handled with thought and care, is flexible learning and delivery. This is often used freely and interchangeably as if it means the same as distance learning. On the one hand, distance education predated these new technologies by many decades. Australian universities in that large and sparsely populated land have for decades supported external study for degrees mainly through the mail.

There is a long tradition of distance schooling, for example, using the radio. Home study was common. It is now re-emerging as a possible alternative to schooling for more young people in various countries, with benefit of the power of the Internet. London external degrees were available around the world for self-directed as well as instructed study long before the Open University was created.

On the other hand, much of what constitutes flexible learning and delivery does not use the new technologies. It has been suggested that up to four-fifths of F/L takes the form of reordering the teaching (and learning) day, week and year, and in individualizing the curriculum to meet the needs of diverse communities and types of students. Better enabled and individualized self-directed learning may include new technology, on campus in the classroom and laboratory or more remotely. Perceived thus, the new modes of the new ICTs appear to add to the battery of resources for greater customization of learning opportunity for a more diversified clientele. Greater choice of learning modes and arrangements ought to allow more people to study in ways convenient and effective for them. The impact on the roles and working conditions of teachers may be no less significant; likewise the changes brought about in the school or college as a "learning community".

Lifelong Learning and Teacher Education

Considering Lifelong Learning in the Twenty-first Century, the ILO summarized thus:

— There is a growing consensus that the ways in which we will learn in the new century will be significantly different from those that prevailed in the last one. To move steadily towards the concept of a learning society, more innovation, resourcefulness and flexibility are expected in the way formal education and training programmes are organized so as to maximize learning access and outcomes. Schools, training institutions and workplaces will need to become learning communities in their own right—places of broad-based knowledge sharing and socialization which fosters living and working together: above all places where individuals learn how to learn. The creation of such an environment will in turn require sometimes significant adaptations in the roles and responsibilities of those entrusted with organizing learning opportunities.

— Most of the concepts and insights which cluster around the terms lifelong learning and learning society were formed in a first generation of innovative thought during and just before the 1970s. Their revival in the 1990s coincided with accelerating development and application of new ICT, as well as other changes associated with globalization. They have taken hold universally in policy discourse and generated much academic literature, running ahead of and often only loosely connected with practice. Empirical research is lacking on the practical meaning and expression of lifelong learning in the life of schools and teachers, partly because the concept is large, far-reaching and variously understood. It is best understood as a paradigm shift, a wholly different way of thinking about education, schooling and learning.

— Like other paradigm shifts, this means that many of the new features and elements are already in place, some not recognized, some exaggerated. Old and new worlds coexist. Perceptions differ about the same situation. A current OECD study on the nature and future of schools has six scenarios for the future of schooling ranging from "business as normal" through degrees of incremental change to a radically different scenario. At its extreme lifelong learning in a learning society may appear to imply the end of schools and schooling. Learning takes place lifelong and life-wide. It combines "learningful work", "learningful play", and "learningful community life". Learning is no longer segregated into one age phase and one set of institutional forms called schools and colleges.

The reality will fall short of "pure deschooling", but significant changes are taking place and new ICT will help the process. This matter is about how the roles of teachers brought up over generations in what we may call a teaching and education rather than a learning paradigm are changing, and how teachers themselves take part in the processes of deciding on and implementing change. Student-centred teaching/learning is an attempt to bridge the two positions. It has had mixed fortunes, caught up in the back to basics controversy about quality, standards and intellectual authority. As learning is recognized to be universal, often better attained through life-integrated arrangements rather than as a separated "school"—based activity, the role of the teacher, and the nature of "education", might shrink to residual essentials still requiring well-bounded arrangements and traditional teacher-student roles. Or it might extend to support learning in more new ways and places.

To anticipate, new ICT does now often feature in consultations between teachers, employers and government bodies, and is a serious concern in terms of teacher updating or continuing professional development (CPD), less immediately in respect of roles and conditions of service. As to the wider scenarios for the future of teaching and schools, the picture is less well formed. The lifelong learning married to new technological possibilities has farreaching but still speculative consequences for teachers, schools and teaching.

All levels and areas at least of formal education, usually classified as primary, secondary, and tertiary or higher. After and beyond the third level and stage is the less well bounded field of adult, community and continuing education, further classified as formal, non-formal and informal. It is complicated by a distinction between informal and incidental learning, the latter often excluded from educational consideration. The recent resurgence of the concept of lifelong learning has raised new questions about this life-wide, unorganized, and hitherto barely recognized activity. One response is to exclude and ignore it. Another is to seek to "capture" it through recognition of prior and experiential learning, and by embracing community, work-based and workplace learning. A further complication concerns the dissolving boundaries of higher education, now commonly absorbed in policy discourse into tertiary education, as by the OECD and more recently the Government of New Zealand via the Tertiary Education Advisory Commission and the Tertiary Education Commission now succeeding it. The universe of post-compulsory "out-of-school" education and even learning may be included in this wide use of tertiary. The dominant typology and frame of reference reflected in the social and administrative arrangements of schools and teachers remains the three levels primary, secondary, and tertiary or higher, the latter often split between "further", "community" or "technical", and higher.

Teachers' organization largely reflects and matches these segmented levels. This may increase their difficulty in engaging with the more radical ideas of lifelong learning, and with some of the power and uses of new ICT. One question is about the amount and quality of discourse, solidarity, professional and policy development, across the different levels, among teachers and their unions. The flow of collegiality, innovation and professional development is stronger internationally and horizontally than up and down between some of these levels in at least some countries. This is most likely for higher education, but may be true more widely. It has implications for the work of the ILO and others in fostering the development of policy and good practice transnationally.

There is a separate but related question about the sources of innovation and the flows of understanding and emulation across sectors and their teachers. Paradoxically, the large but largely unorganized and non-unionized "adult education" sector has been the source of many aspects of the new pedagogy which intersects and can be amplified by the new ICTs now promising to transform pedagogy. Self-directed learning, peer learning and support, "client"—or student-centred pedagogies, critical reflective practice and experiential, grounded and applied approaches to learning which place central value on students' context, motivations and existing practical knowledge: all of these are well established in the mantra of adult educators in many societies.

In the United Kingdom, to take one example following the election to power of New Labour in 1997, there has been keen interest and sustained inquiry into the arena of informal learning abcut ways in which it might be used and linked to bring more students into recognized and accredited study to meet national education targets and standards. Meanwhile, the earlier Administration having proved inimical to most "adult education" endeavours, much of the work and the values and energy it was based on was "exploded". It found its way, fragmented yet still alive, into formal education, mainly at further and higher levels. Consequently, much of the pedagogy of lifelong learning is already seeded within older formal systems. Being weakly identified and organized, traditionally taught by casual, part-time and little protected labour, it lacks institutional identity. Thus, a growing edge of "lifelong learning" is no longer outside formal education but has nested and is nurtured through changing practice within it.

How can each school and teacher get enough of it of a quality to be useful, and how can they be guided in its effective use? There is keen concern about the ownership, control and use of knowledge in higher education where the threat of the virtual is either present or much more imminent. There is also concern about the fragmentation and decomposition—or proletarianization—through new ICT of academic and professional roles in higher education. Consultation in the two main sectors, school and tertiary, thus tends to be about different issues.

Beyond questions of financing and organization, the heart of redesigning systems for lifelong learning without doubt resides in clearly defining the profiles, roles and responsibilities, and conditions of work of the people that will teach in, manage and support the system's operation. Teacher aids and other professional support staff, notably librarians whose roles increasingly widen into information systems and technology and who serve as guides, teachers and mentors to both teachers and students, are clearly relevant. So is the tendency to involve "teacher ancillaries" or aids, whether trained at a lower level, and working in team situations, or as volunteers from the community (parents, the retired). In a parallel to the health sector and nursing this may be seen as either elevating or undermining the role of teacher. Teachers' unions must decide whether to resist or help manage such changes, and whether to widen their membership and remit to take in these new classes of workers. It is an area of conflict for the United Kingdom and the National Union of Teachers (NUT) at present.

The use of new ICT in schools and colleges goes beyond the classroom and its pedagogy. It extends to the "exploded classroom" in the community. Here, school students (as well as more obviously learning adults) can use the Internet to work at home, with WWW as the library and parents as mentors—but also the paid teacher an instant away and vulnerable to seven-day all-hours demand at the end of an email inquiry. It extends also to the principal's study and the administrator's database. Here, performance can be monitored in new, sophisticated and possibly oppressive ways. Here also, student-centred learning and progression can take the form of much more individualized curricula and pathways, between as well as within institutions. This can mean the loss of the (age) cohort and the class, and demand rethinking of notions of class size—in schools and especially in tertiary education usually represented as SSRs or staffstudent ratios, and contact hours. Like new ICT in teaching itself, it can represent extended power, choice and opportunity. It can also fundamentally threaten the rights and conditions of teachers, for which unions may have negotiated long and hard. The way these new challenges are received varies greatly with the context—the tradition and culture of industrial organization, social dialogue including collective bargaining—from country to country.

The practical manifestation also varies with traditions and changing practices of educational organization and administration: especially the tendency to devolve decision-making to more autonomous and entrepreneurial schools-as-businesses. There is then a question, again in the context of national approaches and changes, as to how far changing conditions for teachers are negotiated nationally and collectively, and how far at the local enterprise (school workplace) level. Teachers' unions may be restricted to providing frameworks of advice and attempting to set limits within which local enterprise bargaining (EB) is conducted and confined. In Australia this tendency has been evident in the confrontational approach to unions adopted by the Howard Administrations from 1996, and complicated by the federal character of government and social dialogue in that country. The main higher education union (NTEU) has sought to control the successive rounds of workplace EB university by university, while the federal (school) teachers' unions provide advice and frameworks to state branches, which have the direct involvement with local schools.

Another issue for the unions, varying with different traditions, is how to combine industrial bargaining with other action having professional identity and stature, which gives the capacity for and right to effective consultation in the policy-making arena. This calls for role differentiation and different means of participation and input in different places and ways. In these contexts new ICT raises new issues and possibilities which may need to be addressed in novel ways. Issues about the nature of education, the nature, conduct of learning and its assessment using the new media, and the ownership and use of electronically communicated knowledge, are new challenges for teachers' unions. They may also pose questions about the place of teachers' unions as education associations on the national stage and within national peak union organizations, as awareness of the demands of the knowledge society and the knowledge economy grows. Schools and colleges produce rising proportions of knowledge workers among their graduates.

Lifelong learning roots grow deeper into employer and government thinking. Education leaders may become the cutting edge for issues of new ICT and the "new economy" beyond educational institutions. This takes them beyond contact hours and class sizes, into issues of free trade in educational services and globalization. Organized mass member teachers' associations are only one way that government can consult teachers on issues raised by new ICT.

Democratically run mass-member organizations may be in weak competition with more specialized bodies, which appear easier to meet and more attractive to government and employers. The notion of employer is problematic. Vice-chancellors and rectors may be employers, or they may serve as CEOs for governing bodies as the true employers; or the State may be the true employer of those in higher education institutions. School principals and other senior staff are certainly in management roles. Like middle-level managers in tertiary education such as heads of academic departments they have to "face both ways", representing both members and senior management. Tripartite consultations may involve unions, associations of vice-chancellors or school principals, and government. Or government may stand back leaving unions and institutional heads to battle it out. In this ambiguous and unsatisfactory situation organizations of school principals and other senior staff may become a surrogate for "consultation" and even representation by government, leaving mass-member unions to a strictly industrial role. With fast-changing technology and new demands on teachers, exclusion of the mass of "chalk-face" workers with the most powerful experience of what the changes mean is unlikely to yield the best-informed outcomes.

As we examine the relationship between union consultation and new ICT in education in different countries, other features appear. Some unions, such as the NTEU in Australia, appear as more true custodians of societal and educational values than institutional heads pressed to return a positive year-end account. The longer term educational issues—the moral higher ground—may seem to belong to union forces. Concerned about the effects of globalization and new ICT combined with private venture initiatives within education as a public good, some unions are adept at using the new technologies to organize and strategize, and for purely professional development, using peer networks for mutual learning and exchange of good practice.

Schools may decide what educational structure they apply, what kind of new training programmes they launch and how they develop the pedagogical methods used in the education process. Since the relatively rapid reform process has taken place in a strongly decentralized and competitive system, a pattern of isolation in the diffusion of school – and locally based innovation has become a key feature of the Hungarian school system, including the development of ICT use.

The biggest contradiction in the reform process of the educational system is that many innovative changes have taken place at the same time as a dramatic drop in the living standards of teachers. School teachers are regarded as one of the worst paid groups even within the ranks of severely underpaid public servants. The real value of teachers' salaries decreased by approximately 40 per cent by the middle of the 1990s, leading to a significant drop in motivation. At the same time, the deteriorating social prestige of the profession has created problems with regard to recruitment. These contradictory trends reappear in strategic ICT development plans whereby teachers are expected to become disseminators of ICT culture, a role requiring expensive equipment for personal use.

The growth of professional organizations and teachers' unions accelerated in the 1990s. The number of registered teacher organizations was 117 in 1999. These organizations include subject-teacher organizations, different bodies for the separate educational levels or functions, organizations formed on ideological grounds, associations serving special student needs or special education-policy aims, movements and organizations for the education of the young, chambers, and local or regional associations.

Sixteen per cent of teachers are members of one professional organization or another, with the vast majority registered in subject-teacher associations. Forty-nine per cent of teachers are members of a trade union, with most (42 per cent) registered in the Trade Union for Teachers. Computers appeared in the schools in the early seventies but they were used to teach programming at that time. A new phase started with the national school informatization programme launched in the early 1980s at the same time as personal computers appeared.

In this period groups of teachers committed to ICT use in schools developed. In some schools, computing as a subject appeared in the curriculum, and through the appearance of the Internet the PC became an effective communication tool, representing a breakthrough in ICT use. The most intensive phase of hardware development occurred between 1995 and 1997 when the World Bank and the European Union programme PHARE launched big projects in the country. Far beyond just the purchase of up-to-date technology, these projects resulted in a fundamental modernization of vocational education and the development of distance education. The Hungarian Schoolnet project thus relied on a firm foundation with hundreds of secondary schools that already had some expertise in using ICT. In accordance with the National Core Curricula, ICT became a compulsory subject from 1998, taught both in primary and secondary schools in two periods of 45 minutes per week (on average) from age 12 to 17.

ICT access in higher education is relatively good, and the use of personal computers and the Internet have become a general requirement for students. There are also training opportunities for students to catch up with ICT skills during their studies and to be able to use the computer as a common individual working tool. The majority of training courses offered for students concern introduction to the use of PCs. Some ICT laboratories and departments operating in teacher training universities and colleges manage innovative pilot projects and participate actively in international programmes.

They offer special training courses for prospective teachers (e.g. multimedia development, specific subject-related aspects of ICT use and so on). Even though several important proposals have been put forward, the preparation for the specific use of ICT is not yet an integral part of initial teacher training. Recommendations for the training of prospective teachers specifically to teach ICT have been formulated in a comprehensive analysis prepared by experts on behalf of the Governmental Office of Informatics in 1999.

A new career scheme was developed by the former Government, and professional debates on the proposal were launched in schools at the end of 2001. The proposal aimed at enlarging teacher career opportunities, currently limited by a rather "flat" hierarchical structure. The other important aim of the proposal was to fix teachers' statutory salaries up to 2006. The draft proposed to introduce a specific salary-scheme for teachers.

A new classification for school staff was set out—beginners, candidates for master-teacher, master-teachers–each of them with different duties and additional remuneration for tasks fulfilled. The proposal contained recommendations to enlarge bonuses and allowances (e.g. for health care and retirement). Provisions for professional assistance to beginning teachers were also set out (systems for mentoring, grants for three years). The reception of the overall proposal was varied, reactions focusing mainly on the salary issues.

Since the professional skills of foreign language teachers, ICT teachers and, above all, school ICT system managers are much in demand on the labour market, the best qualified teachers are more and more attracted to the high salaries offered by private companies. This has caused increased turnover in school staff which destabilizes the provision of education.

The government proposal concluded that the problems of remuneration for these groups of teachers was impossible to solve within the framework of the new career scheme. The text assumes that the typical attitude of most teachers—who would consider it unfair to make salary differentials among teachers of different subjects—poses the main obstacle to a more diversified career structure. The Trade Union of Educators is also opposed to different treatment for certain groups of teachers.

In-service Teacher Training

More than 37 per cent of Hungarian teachers have worked for 15-20 years since they received their initial training, and this would be an important reason in itself for further training. Fundamental changes affecting public education represent other serious challenges for teachers. Some specific areas should be mentioned:

— There is an increasing demand for development work at institutional level. On the basis of the National

Core Curriculum, schools were required to prepare their own pedagogical programmes and curricula by 1998 with the help of nationally approved programme patterns. According to surveys, one-sixth of all schools introduced completely individualized, self-developed curricula, while almost 60 per cent reshaped other set curricula or took parts from additional sources to suit their specific needs. Another phase of this work was the adaptation of the school-level programme to the Framework Curriculum.

— Rapid changes in the labour market require adaptation of the training programmes and development of new ones.

— Quality assessment and quality management are a new requirement in public education. More than 1800 schools are participating in the "Comenius 2000" project launched by the Ministry of Education in 1999.

— Social changes imply pedagogical adaptations. As a result of increasing school attendance the social composition of the secondary school population has changed significantly and has become more diverse and varied. This necessitates development of particular methods, individual preparation and closer cooperation within and between teams of teachers at school level.

— The expansion of information technology and the introduction of Internet into schools mean that ICT has become a priority area for further education for teachers.

— According to the estimates of school principals, 35 per cent of teaching staff participated in training courses in 2000. Participation in other forms of professional development such as visiting other schools (30.6 per cent) or attending workshops (16.5 per cent) involves a considerable number of teachers.

In Hungary the right of teachers to participate in in-service training programmes was made statutory by the Act on Public Education in 1985. This right became an obligation and, according to statutory regulations, participation in in-service training programmes figured among criteria for employment in 1996. The regulation required teachers to take part in training programmes regularly, at least on a seven-year basis. It also compelled teachers to pass the post-professional exam (within set time limits).

The Amendment to the Public Education Act in 1999 modified certain elements of the scheme. The post-professional examination became optional, only remaining mandatory for some posts, and the Act stipulated that teachers with the post-professional exam would be placed in a higher category in the job hierarchy. The condition for fulfilling the obligation is the completion of 120 hours of accredited in-service teacher training courses by the end of the seven years.

After completing 120 hours of courses, the period of employment required to move up one civil service wage category is reduced by one year. By drawing up five-year in-service training programmes, schools assert their institutional interests with respect to their pedagogical curriculum. In-service teacher training is subsidized by the state budget and now, contrary to earlier practice, state funds for in-service training are directed to the schools instead of the institutions offering the programmes.

Following the decentralization of education management, funds from the state budget set aside for in-service training must be distributed to the institutions through their maintainers in proportion to the number of teachers. This system calls for planning in-service training at the institutional level and principals are also responsible for developing an in-service training plan on an annual basis, which is to be approved by the maintainers in accordance with the teaching staff. Considering that the division of the training subsidy among staff is a means of allotting career opportunities, it is remarkable that, according to the latest survey, 42.3 per cent of school principals participated in training programmes providing diplomas or certificates while this ratio was only 8.3 per cent among teachers.

The in-service training system is organized on market principles, a new concept to public education in Hungary. However the funds for operating the system are provided from the state budget and therefore it has become imperative to create a system which guarantees that the courses offered are all of high quality. All kinds of institutions can take part in in-service teacher training, but the regulation ensures that the standard amount to be used for in-service training can only be used to finance accredited programmes. The In-service Teacher Training Accreditation Board makes its recommendations with the assistance of experts. The request for accreditation must contain the goal of the in-service training programme, its target group, its topics, the content and formal requirements for completion of the programme, the personal and material background necessary for its implementation, and for each and every programme, the obligation to carry out quality assurance procedures required by the regulation. Accreditation as a certification of quality is valid for five years. Only modules offering at least 30 hours of courses can be accredited. The Minister of Education issues an in-service training programme register twice a year.

ICT in In-service Training

Approximately half of the teachers can be considered to be computer users. This rate differs in relation to the level of ICT skills. As data indicate, age is an important factor in ICT use, with the picture of the first school computerization cohort (in the group of 51-55 year-old teachers) particularly revealing. Increasing the present ICT skill levels of teachers requires extensive training activity. As a consequence of relatively low skill level and the compulsory participation in training, the demand for effective training programmes adapted to the timetable of teachers is growing. A training scheme developed by the Association of ICT Teachers is considered one of the more "teacher-friendly" solutions. The Association of ICT Teachers started its activity as a professional circle in the Teaching Methodological Centre of Budapest. Shortly afterwards an independent national association was organized. The number of regular members is 412. The organization comprises both regional and specialized professional units. The main objectives of the association are to participate in the development of ICT in public education, and to represent and protect the interests of ICT teachers. Other activities cover organization of professional meetings, workshops and demonstration of the use of ICT in school, competitions in ICT, curricula development and participation in definition of requirements for ICT as a subject. Several initiatives of the association were supported in different competition schemes by the Soros Foundation, the Foundation for the Modernization of Public Education (KOMA) and the Ministry of Education.

The association has been one of the major promoters of ICT teacher training since 1997. Nearly 25,000 teachers have participated in its training programmes in more than 1000 schools during this period. More than 200 teachers obtained the "ICT and Education" qualification which authorizes teachers to perform specific ICT-related tasks in the school. The main features of the training scheme developed by the ISZE are the following:

— A specific training programme prepares ICT teachers to provide ICT courses for their colleagues in school. The advantage for participants is that the time table can be adapted to their school activities.

— As a consequence there is no need for replacement staff, and this way of organizing training is good for both the school and the school management.

— The association pays the schools rent for the facilities and premises which is profitable for the school because approximately 88 per cent of the subsidy allocated for in-service training returns to the school budget as an income.

— The association provides accredited programmes in a modular system. The modules are built in a way that offers entry at different points.

Considerable efforts have been made in Hungary since the early 1990s to establish a distance education system for taking advantage of the increasing ICT use. As a promoter of the development the National Council for Distance Education coordinated large Tempus and PHARE projects aiming at the modernization of the so called traditional "evening and correspondence education". Training of experts and trainers, establishment of Regional Training Centres and their network based on higher education institutions, and the setting up of the National Methodological Centre were the main results of this activity. The development projects concerned mostly higher education. Important funds were allocated also by a Public Foundation, "Nyitszak", later "Apertus", both created in order to coordinate developing distance education programmes in the vocational training system. Proposals have been developed by different training providers in the hope that the Schoolnet project will improve considerably the ICT access of teachers and that the schools will offer the necessary infrastructure for the new type of training provision.

The National in-service teacher training centre initiated a specific training course for principals and planned to use the distance education as a tool for a larger public. All these efforts resulted in a rather modest training supply. As for the mere facts, at the present there are only two distance training courses registered on the complete list of 1700 accredited programmes. One of the two is a basic level course in quality management while the other is an introductory course for pedagogical use of the soroban. The insufficient infrastructure combined with the limited ICT skills of teachers and limited offers of accredited programmes could be identified as main reasons for the low rate of distance education (and e-learning) in teacher training. The conservative concepts of learning is considered as another important factor. Thus, distance education is spreading mostly in the higher education and the business sector in Hungary.

Teachers are concerned about ICT access as citizens on the one hand and as members of a specific ICT related profession on the other. The striking disparity of low wages and the very expensive ICT access is an important factor in the relatively low level of ICT use. Critics blame high telephone charges for the low rate of Internet usage but the unavailability of computers is considered a greater problem.

Teachers nevertheless make an effort to keep pace with other social groups in order to access the new technology. In spite of relatively low wage levels, the proportion of PC owners among teachers is higher than the national average. The home computer access rate (50-63 per cent) represents a higher level than the country average but to give a more balanced picture it is important to note that (female) teachers revealed in personal interviews that home computers are very often owned by other family members and consequently female teachers have rather limited access to it. The Internet access at home is under the national average.

ICTs in schools

Installation of complete PC-labs (in contrast to classroom-centred arrangements) has been a strategic element of the Hungarian Schoolnet project. Considering the conditions required for teaching ICT as a compulsory subject, this can be seen as a rational approach. On the other hand, this pattern limits the use of PCs for other purposes. Recognizing these constraints, the so-called "scattered computer placement system" was initiated by the system manager of one grammar school. The main feature of this approach is that computers are scattered around the whole school. Some are placed in subject rooms (spaces dedicated to the teaching of one discipline), others are in the school library or in student or teacher study areas. For the administration of access every teacher and student has an ID to enter the school network. Detailed descriptions of the system and experience have been presented in national ICT conferences and professional meetings, and published in the Hungarian Electronic Library ICT section. As a result, the scattered arrangement has been implemented in several Hungarian secondary schools with success.

Acquiring ICT skills and becoming a real user is a long and time consuming process comprising different forms of learning. Besides participation in formal training courses, individual learning and informal ways of skills development are integral parts of this process. Considering the nature of the computer skills acquisition process– and according to experience – it can be said that informal learning has a very important role in this process. As the presence of colleagues or other advanced users is a key factor in an informal process of ICT skill development, the arrangement of PCs and open access in schools becomes a crucial issue. Internet access is far from sufficient in most schools. At present, only one in every five computers in primary schools is connected to the Net. The other factor is the lack of a competent labour force, especially system managers. At present, in about 85 per cent of secondary schools and 50 per cent of primary schools an independent systems operator is employed. Employing students to act as part-time operators' assistants is also a general practice. Some schools employ young men on "civil service" (an alternative form of compulsory military service for some years) as a temporary solution.

Forty per cent of the working population claims to have computer access at their workplace and 85 per cent of Internet users have free access at school or work. The "European pattern" of Internet access, and outcomes of the Schoolnet project strategy are reflected in data concerning Internet access of teachers, and mainly in the disparities between the primary and secondary schools. The number of hours per week spent on the Internet was less than one hour among primary and two among secondary-school teachers. Twelve per cent of primary school teachers had an email address (an additional 9.6 per cent share with others); this rate was 49.1 per cent (plus 14.9 per cent with shared access) among secondary teachers in 1999. The everyday use of school computers is concentrated mostly in administrative tasks but communication is among the important functions. Open access for teachers is reported by more than half of schools but intranet as a tool of inner communication is rather limited.

Despite ambitious slogans, ICT use developed more slowly than expected in the middle of the 1990s in Hungary. In recent years the lag has increased significantly and Hungary is amongst the poorer performers in Europe. The Hungarian Government – in the framework of the Information Society Project of the "Széchenyi" National Development Plan – put out a tender for the supply of 20,000 personal computers in September 2001. The intention was to offer 10,000 public servants and 10,000 teachers the ability to purchase a computer for home use under favourable terms. That initiative was part of a wider programme to enhance the application of ICT in daily work in the public sector. The complete preferential package comprised a personal computer, free access to the Internet for two years 1 (30 hours/month), user payments only for telephone fees, and a distance learning programme. A budget of 5.5 billion HUF, approximately US$2.5 million, was allocated for the project. A special jury was established for the selection of candidates. The names of successful applicants are published officially (also on the Internet). The requirements for applicants have been the following:

— support from the employer (the school maintainer or the school management undertakes 25-50 per cent of the costs depending on the total amount);

— at least one year of employment in the school;

— the obligation to pass a PC operators' European Computer Driving Licence (ECDL) examination and payment of examination fees; and

— participation in a distance training programme.

Applicants must hold the ECDL or have completed at least four modules of the programme. Applicants who are holders of the ECDL or higher degree qualifications in informatics have to choose and accomplish one of the following tasks before the expiration of the contract:

— tasks related to development of the quality assurance system of the school (kindergarten, college) with special regard to database development;

— tasks related to enrolment, especially data provision to remote statistical databases;

— tasks related to electronic data provision for the statistical database of public education;

— tasks related to introducing the Framework Curricula, especially the electronic form of curricula development and test-bank, and use of ICT in different subjects;

— data processing tasks in the framework of an assessment and evaluation programme. If the applicant is not a holder of ECDL, he/she must obtain the certification and, after the exam, has to select a task from those listed above. In the selection process preference is given to applicants:

— with other public servants/teachers in the household;

- undertaking more than one task or more than one exam respectively;
- having a large family (four or more children in the household);
- living in a small village (with less than 10,000 inhabitants);
- demanding lower support;
- teaching in primary school;
- teaching ICT.

A second tender was put out in March 2002, immediately before the election. Altogether 30,500 persons (civil servants and educators) have obtained PCs by this programme up to now. No analyses of implementation and effects of the project have been prepared (or published), but the programme is not yet completed. Many criticisms were made – mostly in the daily newspapers and in interviews in the media – that the government was too slow to implement the programme and not careful enough in the selection of the providers of PCs. A particular criticism has been that the examination fees for the ECDL are very high compared to teachers' income and can reduce to a large extent the benefits of the support. But the sharpest criticism has been directed at the careless selection of successful applicants.

In the meantime, a new Ministry has been established – Ministry of Informatics and Communication – as a legal successor of the Governmental Office of Informatics (IKB).

The new Ministry is developing ambitious plans in cooperation with the Ministry of Education in order to increase the rate of Internet access. The Ministry inherited the PC programme and is making an effort to accelerate the implementation but in all probability the majority (an estimated 25,000) of participants have to wait until sometime in 2003 for Internet access. The Ministry also wishes to introduce a new National Information Technology Strategy. Household access to computers and the Internet will be a top priority. There are also proposals to amend the tax laws for 2003, among which: companies would be able to write off the full procurement cost of IT equipment purchased in two years instead of three; the employer would be exempted from paying personal income tax on computers provided to its employees for home use; and the fee payable for Internet use should be regarded as a business expenditure. According to a proposal by the Ministry of Education, the Government would cover the examination fee for graduating secondary school pupils acquiring their ECDL. In addition to improving home PC and Internet access there are also plans to improve what is known as communal access. Use in public institutions (e.g. libraries) represents 8 per cent of the entire group of Internet users. According to the plans, 25 terminals will be installed in Budapest public places for free Internet access (for emails and easy access to information). In the second phase of the plan a further six access points (with 100 PCs) will be provided at municipalities and at civil organizations' offices.

Foreign language skills (especially the use of English at least at an intermediate level) play an important part in learning of ICT skills and particularly in effective use of the Internet. According to different sources the Hungarian population's competence as regards foreign languages lags behind that of other European countries. Although nearly 48 per cent of non-language teachers indicated foreign language competence in a recent survey, the overall picture is rather unfavourable. Important disparities have been noted between older and younger teachers (20-29 years old: 75 per cent, 40-49 years old: 41 per cent), and between secondary (55 per cent) and primary teachers (41 per cent). The detailed analysis of figures and interviews proved that the level of "real working" skills is much lower based on several criteria – the basic level of reported language skills, those who started but gave up language learning, and the number who reported learning Russian or Latin, languages with limited everyday use for the time being.

The contrast between the gender composition of the teaching profession and "traditions" of ICT culture should be noted among the additional factors conditioning ICT skills development of teachers. The teaching profession is strongly female- dominated in most developed countries and this trend is particularly strong in Hungary, both at primary and secondary level. In contrast with this trend ICT is still considered as part of the technological culture dominated by men. This sub-cultural difference in ICT use and learning remains rather hidden, whereas important differences in learning styles of different sexes are discovered in the literature related to the pedagogical context of ICT. A Hungarian survey of 1999 also revealed important differences in ICT use patterns between male and female teachers and also between boys and girls. Yet no efforts have been made until now to adapt the style of the ICT training and methods to specific needs of mostly female participants.

Nearly half of Hungarian schools use the Web to present themselves to a larger public and, although there are few really professional school web sites, this form of information provision has become a communication interface for teachers. Electronic forums and mailing lists operate in rather limited circles but they provide a new method, increasing in importance, for professional communication and especially for the coverage of some school-related events (e.g. debate on a new salary scheme).

The organization representing school ICT system managers provides a good example of the use of the Internet in this way. The organization was established as a professional society in order to: widen the training opportunities for school-system managers; ensure that their skills and competence gained in training are acknowledged by schools; and share information and advice on different questions relating to the operation of the Hungarian Schoolnet. The latter aspect has focused especially on the work status of system managers and their working conditions, on the centrally organized purchase of equipment, including the contracts for spending public funds for ICT development, and on all kind of questions concerning the development of informatics and ICT culture in public education.

International Collaboration and Action

Teachers have a worldwide professional and industrial voice through Education International which claims to speak for many millions of teachers. They have a voice along with other professional education bodies at intergovernmental organizations (IGOs) including the ILO, OECD and UNESCO and their subsidiary and regional agencies and systems. There is a well established European tradition for tripartite representation and discussion: thus unionists including teachers have a voice in the counsels of the OECD via TUAC, the Trade Unions Advisory Council. IGOs have various means of fostering wise policies and good practice, most by persuasion and exhortation rather than being legally enforceable. These include Instruments and recommended standards which have modest force, and Declarations with still less. Conference resolutions and proceedings have only persuasive authority, though they may direct modest resources to projects combining research, analysis, and dissemination to extend good practice.

These powers of persuasion are modest beside global financial forces and global markets, including potential markets in ICT-mediated education and training. As models of social dialogue themselves, they may bring different priorities, interests and value sets into open discourse, especially to ensure that economic policies take account of possibly unrecognized social consequences. In this sense, both process and substance, the ILO has a distinctive voice to be heard in respect of the extension of new ICTs in education and their impact on the roles and work of teachers. Given the sometimes overlapping and competing sets of IGOs interests and responsibilities, and their multiple relations with international professional bodies, it is desirable to practise open collaboration between the IGOs, each of whose resources are constrained; and maximize complementarity between their efforts. The situation is made more confused in Europe, home base of the main IGOs referred to here, by the growth of an international level of government in the European Union above local, regional and national levels. Other players include the Council of Europe and the arms of European Government in Brussels. Their relationships to the ILO are complex: government in itself, another intergovernmental agency, another catalyst for research, development and enhancement of practice.

Given the complexity of the issues raised by new ICT, the rapid rate of change and the far reach of their implications, the dearth of evidence-based research and paucity of confident understanding, alongside the sparse resources and overlapping jurisdictions of the international players, anything which can add value for limited money by complementarity, cooperation, and recognition of distinctive competences is to be encouraged. This applies with equal force to monitoring, evaluation and speeding up responses to the rapid changes related to new ICT.

There are different forms and modes of democracy. Democratic practices find expression at different levels within a society, from the constitution and the conduct of national government to relations within the family. Representative democracy may be confined to the optional exercise of the right to vote once each several years. In Australia voting is mandatory and there are state as well as federal elections. Frequency and obligation do not necessarily generate active civic commitment or ward off cynicism about politics. Participatory forms of democracy imply a more sustained, widely expressed and deeply felt sense of sharing the management, from the nation down to the smallest of enterprises. Workplace democracy has to do with sharing responsibility for decisions and their implementation. Its strength derives from the probability that there is far more knowledge about the workplace, about what works, how and why than can be wielded from senior management levels even with the benefit of sophisticated management information systems. Authority derives from knowledge and experience, not just from position. Ultimate responsibility, formal decision-taking and control are exercised by management, but based on the consent and consensus that derive from shared planning, and a continuous process of evaluative review and adaptation in the light of experience and feedback.

Where there is anxiety at governance or employer level about the exercise of principles regarding management prerogatives, consultation may be token. There may be representatives of workers on governing bodies, planning committees etc., but their influence can be minimized by the way business is handled, with a tendency to keep important matters away from the formal meetings, making decisions and fixing things outside. Token representation and token consultation seldom succeed in persuading workers that they are being taken seriously. They fail to win the support and commitment which derives from felt and shared ownership coming from genuine consultation and participatory planning. They fail to tap the knowledge, expertise and special insights of workers. The policy process is necessarily an open, public and transparent one: it centres upon discourse and the accommodation of differences among legitimate participants in that process. This serves to remind us that social dialogue is a complex, continuous cycle linking policy-making to practice, that there is a subjectivity of perception as to what happened and how, and that this can objectively define and influence what can and cannot be done. These are familiar facts in the world of industrial democracy; understandings which underpin traditions of consultation where that exists. They are anchored in a strong view of human nature and of civic and employee rights, and an appreciation of the importance of the quality of working life, as well as a wish for efficiency of production processes.

They may accompany a recognition that job satisfaction based in a reality of responsible shared commitment and ownership is important for effective and productive work especially in the "knowledge industries" where high levels of professional autonomy and exercise of judgement are required. Teaching was at the heart of the "knowledge industries" before the terms knowledge worker and knowledge society were coined. Attempts to routinize teaching in tightly prescribed "bolt-down" modes have seldom worked well, though they persist and are a source of concern to teachers' unions in different countries. New information and communication technology (ICT) may appear to make routinization and tight control easier, consultation less necessary. This would be a fallacy. High levels of effective participation and consultation are necessary to foster active citizenship in a learning or knowledge society. Effective participation is important also in the less direct sense that schools and colleges are learning sites and models for individuals' civic and workforce formation, a powerful medium for young people to learn how to participate. Teachers' experience of participation or alienation in their own working conditions and practices will influence that learning environment, in respect of new ICT as in other ways. There is a sense that schools are "sacred sites" in terms of affording protection from commercializing the content of the curriculum, whereas higher education and professional updating are regarded as reasonable markets. There is a moral edge to unions' discussion about courseware production and control, but the culture of the school is also important in terms of its socialization.

Teachers' sense of control over their professional work influences this. Consultation and participation in respect of new ICT in teaching and learning is thus a sub-set of worker participation and employment relations generally; but it is especially important, given the speed and uncertainly of change, and its closeness to the heartland of the teaching task.

Confidence, high motivation and commitment derived from a sense of shared ownership and responsibility are universally important. However, the ways that consultation is practised and succeeds take various forms. Within the diversity of cultures and contexts an important common factor is what governments will allow unions to do and be. Stern resistance to labour being organized and having a voice may make professional participation well-nigh impossible. Effective professional influence and input may require unions to separate their industrial from their professional voices, perhaps expressing these through different union leaders as is the practice of the NTEU in Australia. Sometimes official consultation is reported to be zero, yet teachers are able to exercise significant influence on practical policy implementation at district or school level, as is reported from France.

The ICT-mediated knowledge society displays high complexity and rapid destabilizing change in both the inputs and the desired outputs of the school system. These trends, globally common in knowledge societies, put a higher value on effective consultation, and may push more systems in this direction. Alternatively, different means of securing continuous, effective professional input may grow up within established traditions. Where there has been a significant change of government and policy orientation the new politics do not automatically make for greater trust, confidence and successful consultation. The disjunction seems especially marked with the more radical shifts (towards a knowledge nation) in the United Kingdom. As well as broadly different planning and free market traditions and changes, there are different arrangements from country to country in both school and higher education. These give different settings for the practice of consultation. One needs to be clear who is the (formal and de facto) employer. On the labour side teachers are organized in different ways. Some kinds of bodies such as subject associations and principals' associations may be consulted at the expense of mass member unions. Or token hand-picked individuals may be selected to "represent" a sector or perspective by a non-participatory government. This may tap expertise but not win confidence and commitment. Federal systems present another set of complexities.

In Australia, there is replication of both government and union organization at two main levels. Changes in practice, for example in the direction of devolution or delegation to regions or to individual school and colleges, have had an impact in New Zealand, as in the United Kingdom. France remains highly centralized. Different Australian states have decentralized to different extents, but none, probably, to the extent of the United Kingdom and New Zealand. These diverse arrangements raise different questions about the role of central government in providing ICT infrastructural support and equipment, and in its attitude to mandatory or optional CPD and local conditions of service. In some systems governments deflect managing the consequences of new ICT onto institutional heads rather than taking responsibility themselves. In summary, new ICT raises new issues extending beyond national level investment in infrastructure. The Australian Government tends to limit itself to providing a regulatory framework within which changes can be made at state and local discretion. The United Kingdom Government is more interventionist and supportive, but not therefore necessarily more persuasive in its consultative processes. The broad political philosophy and orientation of government is important. So are micro-level factors in the local environment of action especially at school level. The quality of leadership and consultative skills of the school principal emerge as a key to CPD and impact on conditions of service, whether in France, the United Kingdom, Australia or New Zealand. What unions do and can do is only partly within their discretion. Many of these factors are in flux, oscillating on a pendulum, or cyclic. It is necessary to discern the forces at the particular time and place to understand what CPD might work, how conditions of service can be intelligently managed under the impact of new ICT, and what forms of consultation and professional input will work best for the time being.

Teachers' organizations take different forms. The higher education unions in the United Kingdom hesitate between competition and possible merger. In Australia two unions in this sector compete for membership. Sometimes education unions cooperate closely, sharing headquarters as in France and Australia, possibly co-locating and collaborating with other educational lobbyists including employer bodies such as Vice-Chancellors' Committee secretariats, as in New Zealand. Apart from mass member organizations able to exercise considerable industrial if not professional influence there are other more specialized bodies, unions or associations: of head teachers, subject heads and subject specialists, of university deans, librarians, MIS personnel and others.

There are also public and private school sector unions with somewhat different interests, for example in Australia and New Zealand. Where different interest groups are thus separated out, sometimes with multiple affiliations on the part of different individuals, there is room for teacher interests to be played off one against another. Unsympathetic governments can select who to consult, and where to seek formal committee representation. Employer and quasi-employer bodies give an opportunity to consult the sector without involving the representatives of mass grassroots membership.

The latter can be treated in narrow industrial terms. These phenomena have been evident in Australia during the recent period of industrial confrontation from 1996. Here also a state government used new technology to address the mass teachers' union members directly, rather than via the union. Two universities unsuccessfully used a similar device to bypass and break the power of the NTEU on their respective campuses during enterprise bargaining. It is possible to hire consultants on a personal basis, avoiding any representative base from teacher practitioners. "Classroom" contact to test the practicality of ICT innovation in real-life pedagogy is then lost. Regular in-house staff experts and specialists may be replaced by external consultants lacking continuing commitment and representative accountability. There is loss of institutional memory as well as long-term commitment. This was seen under the previous administration in New Zealand, and now appears in some Australian universities. Networks get broken; informal learning and social discourse are reduced. More positively, government policy bodies at different levels may be open to informal advice and input, allowing a continuous flow of discourse between expert chalkface teachers, policy-makers and administrators.

With a widespread tendency to devolution, consultative activity may take place at the enterprise level of college or school. This may also be the site for industrial negotiation, as in Australian higher education. Devolution may be a form of empowerment. Much depends on the personality and style of local school principals as leaders and managers. The institutional head, and the mode of conducting whole-school or college ICT innovation, then becomes crucial both in consulting and in implementing change. National unions can attempt to provide advice, guidelines and frameworks. It is necessary to know who is consulted, how and what about, in each instance, not only at national system level but in devolved cases down at school level.

In terms of unions' relations with their membership, it is not surprising to find union leaders ahead of their members, especially in a fast-moving field like ICT. National leaders tend to take a wider, longer and more strategic view than local branch members, and paid professional officers than elected members. In France union leaders are quite critical of the resistance to change of some members. There is a tendency in some other countries reviewed for mass union leaders to take a more protective line, appearing to wish to slow down change.

In Australia, as in France, an overriding sense of the interests of schools and an embattled public sector is a force for social discourse; the more so where popular media and even government at the political level seem to attack schools and teachers without discrimination. Unions at school and higher education levels assume a strategic and ethical responsibility for aspects of the impact of e-learning, especially over the creation, ownership, control and use of materials put on the Web. This takes the form of members' rights in terms of intellectual property, and students' rights in terms of who influences and produces the materials with which they are taught.

The power of parents with well-wired homes can be a force for change on unions and individual teachers.

Finally, there is a new twist to the use of the new ICTs in teaching as well as learning. At one extreme, they may create an entirely individualistic and individualizing medium for the student or learner—the educational ultimate in customization. This may not threaten teacher solidarity. However, the tendency in some parts of higher education towards creating global e-markets is causing speculation that leading professors will be bought and sold at the highest prices they can command in a market analogous to that of sport stars with no sustained national or club loyalty. The global virtuoso performer negotiating high individual rates sits uneasily with the tradition of solidarity and camaraderie in which labour organization is grounded. It may add to the difficulties of unions over the uses of new ICT.

Many aspects of industrial relations and collective bargaining at national and local enterprise levels are functions of the politics and culture of the society. It is important to appreciate these different contexts, and to tease out what is specific to new ICT. Its impact is complex and multi-faceted, including teaching and learning applications as well as administration. It includes classic union issues to do with conditions of service, remuneration, and support by means of staff development; and broader social and ethical issues to do with globalization and commercialization in a "public good" sense and a largely public sector setting. Some unions are treated and behave as mainly industrial. Relations may be tough, formal and conflictual. The negative effects on capacity for constructive dialogue and collaborative development such as managing the introduction of new ICT in teaching requires, may be contained by splitting the two faces of the union so that it speaks through one voice on industrial matters and another for professional consultation and development. Teachers' unions commonly feel frustrated that their professional expertise and judgement carries little weight, while others are consulted rather than the mass member bodies. Unions often hold well-developed and grounded views about key policy, strategic and ethical issues. They see themselves as custodians of the work and bearers of a professional ethic, which may appear less well nurtured and adhered to by national and institutional managers and administrators. This relates also to differences over intellectual property, where individual and institutional interests are in conflict.

In some cases the unions occupy the higher moral ground over the nature of education and the conditions required to sustain it—especially in respect of commercialization, the creation and control of electronic teaching materials, and debate over free trade and profit in educational services. There were several expressions of concern about the impact of competitive entrepreneurialism on the quality of learning and teaching. Horizontal networking and peer support emerged as a powerful and valued form of CPD, but attitudes of commercial-inconfidence secrecy threaten individuals' capacity to work freely—academic autonomy is seen at risk within the New Zealand AUS. These attitudes are seen as wasteful: raising the cost of new ICT investment by duplication, slowing down the rate of take-up in terms of school-to-school CPD and learning about successful uses of ICT. In Australia the NTEU takes a wider and more critical view of the possible deleterious economic and cultural effects of ICT and e-learning for distance or virtual university work than does the Australian Vice-Chancellors' Committee. Some unions have a firmer view about recalcitrant staff unwilling to engage with new ICT in their teaching than apparently do those in authority. Generally, unions adopt a strong line over CPD requirements, although this may take the form of protecting staff conditions of service. It may appear obstructive when argument gets bogged down over who pays for what in whose time, putting the union in an industrial "box" rather than enabling its professional contribution to be heard.

Formal and Informal Modes of Consultation

The different country sketches make clear the importance of dialogue other than the formal. This is especially marked where government makes formal representation and consultation tokenistic, taking advice and decisions in other places and ways. As new issues emerge and change is rapid and uncertain with the introduction, use and evaluation of new ICT, the agenda for consultation may shift. More open informal modes may become more important.

Many big issues of concern to teachers and their associations reach out to the nature and management of global society and its meaning for education on the one hand, and into the future role of the school and the teacher on the other. Shared speculative scenario-building—brainstorming—requires trust and openness if it is to work creatively. In examining how different countries handle participation over new ICT in education we might use a spectrum from open dialogue and high trust to tight collective bargaining and weak informality. This could also be used to see how far different countries are able to consult, plan and manage more or less desirable futures. Much important and productive consultation is at a local level.

In some systems it is essentially at school or school cluster level. Here the leadership style of the principal creates an open or closed attitude to planning and reviewing. New Zealand is a good example. The whole society is small enough and well enough networked to allow it to function almost as one increasingly electronic village. In France weak formal national consultation is compensated in some districts by good informal consultation. Some issues lend themselves to one mode and level more than another. Technical considerations (shared infrastructure investment) also come into play. On the other hand, if teachers are to be more effectively supported as professionals in this more powered pedagogic environment greater informal consultation at manageable local levels may be necessary, within a nationally negotiated framework. Some common patterns appear to emerge. A common proposition is that consultation, co-development and collaboration are easier between non-neighbouring institutions not in direct competition for markets. With the growth of electronically mediated distance learning, it has less force. It is often a powerful consideration, certainly in Australia, New Zealand (where in a small country it applies both regionally and nationally) and the United Kingdom. It contradicts the localitybased cluster and network approach which characterizes successful innovation and use of new ICT in the industrial sector.

Australia, with New Zealand, has an informal university club of "extramural" continuing education directors with a rule of only one per state to avoid local competition and protect commercial-in-confidence information. The United Kingdom universities' association overcame this issue of competition, and achieved more informal peer consultation and more significant governmental lobbying and representation as a result. The same issues apply where universities seek global markets through e-learningbased distance education, through consortia such as Universitas 21 (U21) which includes members in the United Kingdom, Australia and New Zealand. Teachers' unions represent a wider than institutional interest, and criticize secretive and competitive developments. They may use informal influence and representation to promote what they see as these wider interests. It would be useful if studies in different countries and systems could look into ways in which the new ICT agenda in teaching and learning is altering traditions and patterns of consultation

There are strongly held positions from suspicion of cost-cutting and doubts about real educational benefit on the teacher side. These issues are furthest advanced in higher education. Even here there is little evidential grounding about the pedagogy and the learning. It is desirable to share monitoring and evaluation of new ICT. A continuous feedback loop is needed, such that all parties can understand, co-own and be committed to managing together the continuous changes that ICT will continue to produce. Unions in all the countries reviewed were critical of a failure to consult over the introduction of new technologies and especially over its effectiveness. Understanding outcomes in terms of students' learning and their subsequent employability and adaptiveness—their capacity to go on learning—in an IT-mediated knowledge society calls for longitudinal as well as collaborative inquiry.

It should immediately be possible to explore what consultation modes assist the parties to step out of role and evaluate dispassionately what works, and what the different consequences are. Joint commissioning of evaluative research and shared use of results might be a main means. It would be necessary to agree on purposes, and how to measure outcomes. This need a good grounding in mutuality based on a tradition of participation.

It should not be too difficult to develop "health indicators" of the return on investment in the new ICT itself, and of the quality of participatory planning and evaluation in new ICT for teaching. A useful reference point and possible collaborative linkage is provided by a recent CERI publication, which concludes with a useful section on research and evaluation.

Training, Support and Development

In principle all new teachers should emerge from initial teacher education or training well equipped to use new technologies in the classroom and even the virtual classroom. In practice experience and opinion are less clear-cut. Generally, it seems that new teachers have the technical essentials and some confidence to use new ICT, but are less well prepared for its practical use and classroom integration. This is an important part of the ongoing reappraisal of initial teacher education (ITE) and the extent, as with other professional preparation such as in health, to which it is and should be field—and practice-based rather than mainly separated and more theoretical, in universities and colleges. This connects with a repeated question: about the linkage and contribution of university departments and schools of teacher education to ongoing innovation, R&D in schools and systems, and to supporting teachers in the use of new technologies as part of their work in regular consultative partnership.

Demography may cause problems for teachers' unions. If their membership has a high age profile, concern about professional renewal and the recruitment of younger generations can become acute when associated with questions about new ICT, given widespread ageist assumptions about this. Unions may have to choose between protecting their older membership or going along with policies which favour early retirement.

Financially stressed universities often downsize and replace staff. However, changing demography and an older population with small young-age cohorts argue in favour of continuous support and CPD to retain the commitment and experience of older teachers in the new ICT environment. Some teachers' unions offer their own ICT updating and network support, as well as lobbying for better CPD provision. Some provision, for principals to manage their roles and responsibilities with new ICT, has union support; but there may also be criticism of "principals-first" approaches especially if this does not arise from full union consultation so that the rationale is shared.

Professional Development

The biggest United Kingdom school teachers' union spells out in detail what is wanted. Some countries display serious union concern about the stress that teachers suffer with the rapid introduction of new technology. This takes the obvious form that they are not confident and well prepared for its use; not because they are technophobes but because they have not been trained, or given enough training and learning time. There is severe union criticism that the more technologically literate use their overtime and goodwill to help peers informally, adding to their own workload and stress. A less obvious source of stress and even breakdown is the effect of ill-supported teachers working with, say, year-nine boys who are more technologically literate and may have superior software at home. It needs a particular kind of CPD and confidence-building to assist teachers in such circumstances—for instance by giving such well-placed and precocious students a role as class mentors, recognized as teaching their peers and understandably ahead of the teacher in some respects.

Unions tend to seek minimum hours and days over the year guaranteed and set aside for CPD in new ICT, within or in addition to any existing right to CPD generally. This may take the form of "student-free" CPD days at school before a term starts— something which tends to get squeezed out when economies have to be made. Staff development can become the soft end of the budget where sacrifices can be made. In addition to direct CPD as a right at a guaranteed minimum level, claims take the form of minimum numbers of staff, or staff hours, and technical support both for teachers and to maintain ICT equipment for students and teachers alike. Technical breakdown is a further source of stress. Regular trouble-shooting help-line support is required and is appearing as an important union benchmark demand for indirect CPD and teacher support. Some unions seek support on a per capita basis for curriculum applications and integration as distinct from strictly technical training and support. Integration rather than technical skill attracts most attention and concern.

Another emerging emphasis which may find its way into union claims as a right is school-based CPD in ICT so that workplace and curriculum integration are built in automatically. This is most obvious where there is a high level of delegation from national or regional to school level. With the rising importance of ICT, there may be a tendency for unions, without abandoning salary claims, to write CPD in ICT into claims even at the cost of higher salaries. This seems to be more likely where the public school system is in a critical condition and its quality and acceptability, and teachers' professionalism, are significant public issues. Some union claims include a "sabbatical" right to extended periodic leave to become more competent as professionals.

Although this tends to be generalized rather than ICT specific, the rate of ICT innovation may strengthen the bid. Individual leave for ICT purposes may have more success competitively within a small school budget. Generally, time out from teaching is a central concern, and therefore less time pressure within actual teaching, to allow the adaptations required for full integration of ICT into professional practice. The big changes required to the new ICT-mediated world cannot be picked up on the side while work intensifies. Consultation and control, monitoring and feedback in CPD to assist teachers in the integrative use of new technologies are likely to become of increasing importance for collective bargaining.

In higher education where new ICT has tended to reach further and sooner than in the school, work intensification and intellectual property issues feature in industrial bargaining. As its prominence increases in the school sectors beyond the initial computers in schools phase, it seems probable that unions will want guaranteed rights of participation and formal consultation in these crucial areas of innovation and impact on teacher confidence, job satisfaction and professional competence.

A current emphasis for CPD related to new ICT concerns time to develop skills, understandings, applications and hence confidence with these new media. Technical support and training as technologies and software change are also seen as important, but best addressed through good initial teacher education and then in-school technical staff support for both CPD and trouble-shooting. These issues spill over into the changing roles of school and college libraries and their staff, to be able to support teachers and students in uses of the new ICT for searching and studying. More radical implications do not yet feature strongly in CPD claims and activities. Some unions are aware and alert to them, concerned that they be built into consultation and into CPD and other human resource policies to enable teachers to learn and adapt. This may mean preparing teachers for quite new roles in the wired or more virtual school and within the "classroom without walls".

Several factors come together to make this an emergent area of importance for wider CPD, and indeed for a continuing organizational learning agenda. Teachers and institutions need to think through and perhaps prepare for entirely new rôles in the electronically mediated knowledge society—much as e-commerce is transforming the nature of some businesses and whole business sectors. Precocious IT-literate youngsters in the classroom, and active parents from electronically well-equipped homes, may be succeeded by wired neighbourhoods and whole wired cities and societies, as in the case of Singapore.

These changes may transform notions of the role of the school into the hub of an e-learning network, with young and older student learning partly in the wired school and partly at home and in the electronically integrated community or workplace. Parents, ethnic and other community groups, employers as well as suppliers, become partners in transforming the school's roles, tasks and environment for new kinds of individual and group or institutional CPD—continuous and lifelong learning for teachers, as already for some other kinds of knowledge workers.

A simple typology for education and specifically for CPD in an ICT context appears in the recent OECD ICT and partnership study. Traditional approaches to the curriculum characterized as just-in-case (that is general and pre-service), and being succeeded in a lifelong learning and recurrent education context by just-in-time (borrowed from industrial practice). The more individualized and customized approaches enabled by ICT are then described as just-for-me. However, unions in particular are likely to become increasingly interested in just-for who. Uses of ICT in work control and production oversight—for example in call centres, but this can apply to IT-managed work process and output measurement in any setting -raise questions about the "dark side" of CPD and new media. In higher education where time zones render the Australian night someone else's day, this problem is more acute for leading distance learning providers. In several countries including some referred to here, there are new scenarios for the ICT-era university which imply total transformation of academics' roles as teachers, calling for massive CPD if teachers are to be enabled to adapt, and healthy learning environments sustained.

Impact on Jobs, Work and Employment

The terms of reference for this inquiry ask about near future outlooks as well as the state of the art, and about the organization of schools and institutions to facilitate the use of new technologies for flexible, distance and open education in lifelong learning, and the role of teachers in this. They mention spacial and time dimensions of teaching and learning related to greater use of ICT, open and distance learning. The main emphasis is on practical and operational issues about management and organization.

There are fewer speculative considerations of new scenarios and a new paradigm for education and learning in an ICT-mediated world. These adopt both incremental or radical paradigms, with varying hopes and fears. The key elements of lifelong learning, and virtual or e-learning which form the basis of most new distance learning scenarios are confused and contested. Between different interpretations, emotional orientations, and the many different operational possibilities there is room for an infinite range of combinations. Generally, union leaders and government planners show little interest in the larger possible changes. The main interest in radical scenarios seems to be contained within the university sector, where "virtual universities" excite extremes of interest, hope and fear. Otherwise, new scenarios have not crossed the threshold from theory and speculative scholarship to planners and practitioners. Despite the rhetoric of lifelong learning most of the thinking is sectoral: schools are managed with a different mindset than are tertiary and especially higher education.

Nonformal (adult and community) education, if recognized at all, is seen as a different sector or species again. The issues and priorities differ somewhat between schools and universities. The organization of the total education system, including teachers' organizations, tends to reflect historically dominant and discrete forms and levels. Changes to roles and conditions of employment have impacted harder and earlier in higher education, and are spreading back, but cross-sectoral traffic in innovation appears low.

Tertiary Trends in Higher Education

Tertiary tends to mean all post-school education, with or without the non-formal adult sector, including both higher and what is variously called community, further, technical or "tertiary non-higher". Higher education may closely approximate universities, perhaps with a small number of specialized high-level colleges, or encompass a substantial higher but non-university sector offering degree and even higher degree work. These categories and boundaries may be open and unstable.

One issue in an era approaching universal tertiary education is how far higher education and degree study should be available outside universities and the "higher" part of the tertiary sector, in the transition towards lifelong learning and a knowledge society. In this context flexible forms of learning and delivery through new ICT open new possibilities. The structures and conditions of service suitable and relevant to a more open and universal approach are diverse and confusing.

There are different traditions and service conditions within national tertiary systems. Consequently, the reception of and response to new ICT tends to vary. National reviews need to identify these factors in considering what conditions and flexibilities might be appropriate, and how they might be introduced where there are new alliances and structures. Another difference is that tertiary education, being beyond the compulsory pre-adult age and level, is a less "sacred site" than schooling.

There is less of a sense that it is taboo to introduce private sector partners and to seek profit. Some in higher-education teachers' associations are wary of the consequences of pressures to be entrepreneurial. Since new ICT lends itself to seeking new markets using distance modes, it is a site for philosophical differences. It features in social dialogue, sometimes in collective bargaining and union demands. Generally, however, these are concerned with protecting intellectual property rights, and with work intensification, job fragmentation, and insecurity occasioned by various forms of partnership and outsourcing.

The non-higher sector in the United Kingdom has been fighting to retain conditions, especially an extended period of vacation outside teaching periods. Management has sought to tighten up and require physical appearance, work output and accountability during some of these vacation or non-teaching weeks. The current emphasis on working hours in contact with students, and working weeks in the year is proving inappropriate to the new ICT opportunities.

Students in increasingly greater numbers, both as cohorts and as individuals, can study at all times of the day, week and year, and seek staff teaching support or mentoring. The tendency towards contractual and competency-based work in the non-higher sector generally has already alerted teachers' associations to the changing conditions which such diversification implies. On top of this, ICT adds a new set of possibilities for "flexibilization". It is useful to ask in each national system with its particular traditions of administration and social dialogue how far the change is being managed within an old industrial paradigm and how far more radical alternatives are being developed between the parties.

Because of traditions of institutional autonomy and academic freedom, and because they are often seen as carrying a particular responsibility for critiquing social trends as a "conscience of society", universities and their unions and staff associations are exposed and sensitive to issues of intellectual property, and to its free use as well as ownership. The energy with which teaching materials are put onto the World Wide Web and institutions are entering global consortia with diverse commercial and academic partners to take up opportunities for e-learning has thrust issues of free trade in educational services as well as staff rights to intellectual property into public discourse and sometimes onto the collective bargaining agenda.

There is less evidence that ICT has altered dialogue and bargaining in relation to changing roles and conditions, and intensification. Again, the university sector appears to lead the way. This may be because of an earlier concern about a tendency to separate the roles of teacher from researcher, and to vary academic contracts to reflect these roles separately and in different proportions, with more teaching-only and research-only contracts. Further role differentiation within teaching is beginning to cause concern.

A sharper concern is about loss not only of control of teaching through the Web but of employment opportunities if the shift to flexible, distance- and Web-based delivery is seen as an economy to reduce face-to-face teaching and mentoring, and to casualize the teaching workforce. A dialogue is forming around higher level pedagogic issues about the nature of teaching and learning, about deep rather than surface learning, collaborative, team and peer learning, and about quality generally.

The position taken by teachers' representatives, also at school level where this issue has surfaced, is that high-quality education requires a face-to-face component. New ICT is a form of quality enhancement rather than cost reduction and labour-saving. At the sharper industrial edge, this begins to take the form of arguments about staffstudent contact load including measures of email and other distance modes in workload agreements along with the more familiar load measures of class sizes and contact hours.

Adult, Community and Informal Education

With adult, community and informal education, educational provision shades into unrecognized and educationally unsupported incidental learning, some using new ICT in an entirely individual or interest group and private or social way unrecorded as learning, much less education. This aggregation of supported activities can scarcely be called a third sector, though it is tempting to call it a third way since it represents potentially significant development towards more universally embedded lifelong (and life-wide) learning.

The more radical "death of schooling" scenarios see the future as lying in this direction, initially for adults but increasingly for younger learners also. The "sector" is essentially unorganized, casualized, and without firm identity. It has been conceptualized and drawn together in at least loose professional form most effectively, among countries considered here, in England and Wales where the National Institute of Adult Continuing Education (NIACE) lobbies for adults' learning and recognises a very broad church of adult, community and non-formal educational practice. It is tempting to exclude the sector entirely but that would be unwise, given that it sits so naturally with future scenarios based on lifelong learning.

Moreover, noticeably in the United Kingdom which was examined more closely than other systems on this issue, the break-up and reconstitution of the older adult education tradition and community of practice, has been followed not by the demise of distinctive pedagogy and practice but by the reappearance of many of these approaches within the formal sectors, especially further and higher education. Recently, the Blair Administration has worked vigorously at comprehending and seeking to capture and channel adults' informal learning in ways which will enhance the participation of underrepresented groups, mainly those with low socio-economic status (SES). This is being attempted in diverse ways, many of them relying on new ICT in learning and teaching or self-teaching.

In the United Kingdom, the Economic and Social Research Council commissioned in 2001 a review of post-school learning and teaching intended to identify areas for research priority which would enhance quality of learning outcomes. Its four-way typology of sectors for this purpose was: further and higher; work-based learning; continuing professional development; and adult, community and non-formal education. That is to say, three of the four areas sit at least partly outside the mainstream formal sectors. Work on the impact of new ICT on teaching conditions will in future need to come to terms with the ill-defined and marginal adult community area as a growing edge of teaching/learning in a knowledge or lifelong learning society.

No clear picture emerges here of the way that educational institutions are being reorganized around the potential of the new technologies to enhance flexible, distance and lifelong learning, and widen access. Access and flexibility relate to time, place and mode of delivery and educational support for learning, including assessment. There is little evidence of shared thinking about new roles of teachers as facilitators, mentors, etc., or of new scenarios for change in the established institutional learning sites. It is more a matter of adding on some new functions and options than wholesale transformation, although some institutions seek redefinition and repositioning. There is a time-lag between theoretical and scholarly scenario-building and the translation of scenarios into prototypes that can be tested.

On the other hand, close monitoring of piecemeal changes system by system in different places may show that cumulatively the change is more significant than different elements alone suggest, and that transformation of institutions and roles is under way. It may then be a question how far the more innovative institutions and practices prove to be models for generalization—early adopters followed by increasing numbers of schools, colleges and professional groups. The following are areas for monitoring and comparison.

Libraries, information technology and information services are undergoing major changes towards electronic storage and delivery. Libraries are becoming portals to "world libraries" rather than mainly hard-copy collections. Library staff are becoming more active supporters of search and interrogation processes. In terms of IT support, a concern is for adequate technical support so that teaching staff do not find themselves compromised in their use of new ICT. It is widely held that computing and e-learning should become a normal embedded skill acquired by all school students throughout the curriculum rather than an additional subject, other than for computing specialists. Other disaggregations of teaching and academic roles are a source of more serious concern in the tertiary and especially the higher education sector. Within the university, it is recognized that more functional specialization is likely and indeed necessary. There are concerns about its impact on the academic and teaching role, and on the integrative professional task of the teacher vis-à-vis the "whole student".

Some shift in emphasis from content to process specialist is recognized as likely, and not a source of wide concern. A teaching agenda around "learning to learn" and understanding the discipline or field rather than "knowing the facts" causes little obvious worry about teachers' role displacement. The worry is with disaggregation and loss of span of control, especially where functions such as the production and deployment of courseware, are given over to commercial suppliers and carriers. This is in a context of existing work intensification and entrepreneurial pressures, and sometimes deep concerns about the changing roles of universities and nature of higher education. New ICT is seen as having two faces: a means of widening access and enhancing flexibility, and a means of stripping authority and intellectual property from the teacher. In a context of reducing the proportion of continuing (tenured) staff, and treating research as a distinct activity supported for only a minority of academic staff, the motives and consequences of shifting to Web-based distance teaching for a larger market attract suspicion.

More positively, new mentoring roles and opportunities are seen favourably. There is strong professional (re-)assertion of the importance of face-to-face (dialogic) teaching, and of fostering a learning culture, community and environment in physical and human senses, including team and peer learning. Outside the immediate pedagogic setting, there are issues about the way new technology is changing administrative roles and power. Many student processes from marketing and recruitment through admission to assessment and academic progression can be electronically automated, the work delegated to technical support staff or to the students themselves. The saving in time and enhancement in efficiency are welcomed. There is also fear of technological determinism, that system convenience may displace professional judgement. Cheap and "reliable" assessment may mean loss of depth in what can be assessed, the influence driving back into the curriculum and attitudes of students as to what is worth learning. The more sinister aspects of performance measurement and control which IT can also represent do not seem to be of the same concern.

The patrimony of schooling and strong tradition of one-teacher one-class in face-to-face mode shows no signs of being dislodged in these several countries, although changes on the margin are seen and often welcomed. Parents have long been more or less involved in schools, depending on the national and local tradition. Students may have had projects in and engaging the community before the arrival of the newer technologies.

Likewise with the opened up classroom, individual teaching and teaching in teams. The classroom has become a less private place as more new technology is used for teaching, reporting and assessment, and as different kinds of ancillary staff become involved—IT technical and curriculum support staff, mentors and tutors especially at higher levels, even students with teacher and mentor roles in the use of new IT if their expertise is thus managed.

There is probably a subtle shift going on which may come to represent a major change, but it is low-profile and gradual rather than cathartic. These changes are more evident and openly contested at university level than in the more bounded and socially monitored primary and secondary school setting. Here the teaching of subjects and specializations within disciplines remains the norm, although a worldwide debate about quality and standards is pushing teaching itself as a professional practice up the agenda. New ICT is prominent in this. There is in this sector more sustained dialogue about where the changes are taking professional standing and practice. The quality debate is fuelled by the potential for distance education and accreditation by virtual universities and global consortia. A newly energized dialogue about what constitutes higher education and the role of teacher (teaching students as well as subjects) is fed by hopes and fears about new teaching and learning technologies. The disaggregation of roles in the interest of specialization and efficiency in higher education for a mass market is linked with work intensification and proletarianization.

The traditional rhythm of teaching terms or semesters with "research time" in between, already broken by yearround teaching and more intensive use of campus infrastructure, is further broken up by ICT-enabled distance modes. Teachers' unions are pulled between support for its "learnercentred" responsiveness and flexibility, allowing access to be widened, and the impact on work and roles that may go with it. Specific measures could be generated for this purpose, such as the use of staff-student ratios or class size and the incorporation of new measures for distant and periodic students into such a calculus, as well work intensification and fragmentation which such indicators should reveal. Another area to monitor is the withdrawal and outsourcing of functions which have belonged within the school or college and within the older role of the teacher or academic. Often, this is in the context of partnerships with other public and private sector interests, and suppliers and distributors of various kinds; the subtitle of the recent OECD monograph on e-learning is the partnership challenge. Ownership and benefit from intellectual property as between the institution and the rootless scholar is another issue, with a significant latent change in identity and loyalty as well as role.

Cutting across all these aspects of the teacher's changing role and conditions are less tangible matters of self-confidence, identity, and psychological security within the new ICT-enabled lifelong learning paradigm. Because it is an emergent paradigm generated by the confluence of disconnected forces, needs and possibilities—lifelong learning, the knowledge society, obsolescence, new ICT—it is hard to pin down and get into focus. Drawn together, these trends may be addressed more holistically as quality of working life (QWL) and the satisfaction people derive from their work. Managerial tendencies within education, especially in the tertiary sector under intense pressure to universalize provision, run counter to essential conditions for the effective employment of knowledge workers generally, which can be profiled in terms of job satisfaction and enhanced QWL. Although this appears as an individualized approach, it can also be used to monitor whole-school settings. The quality of leadership in the creation of an open, supportive learning environment is a key to much QWL.

Important elements include a sense of freedom and control over one's work, and elbow-room to operate with enough space and to make decisions. On the other hand, an adequate framework is needed for the security and confidence to operate professionally and make judgements. Optimal variety allows a balance between the routine and the less familiar which does not engender boredom, and allows for change of activities of different orders and kinds. A sense of being in control rather than driven by ungovernable and random forces, and a sense that the job is meaningful and worth doing, with peer and community respect, are also important. Having responsibility for one's own quality of work with self-evaluation, with managerial supervision pulled back rather than oppressively tight, let alone IT-generated and "absolute", is also part of a sense of professional self-worth and desirable (not unaccountable) autonomy. Peer support and the capacity for open teamwork also matter.

Self-confidence and self-respect, the respect of peers and significant others; community standing and valuing; an optimal degree of freedom and control over the nature of the job and how it is done; the capacity for self-learning and assessment, learning on the job, professional and career development, these are dimensions of job satisfaction and QWL which can be operationalized and used to monitor and compare the impact of technological innovation on teachers' work and lives. On the negative side there are measures of sickness, absenteeism, resignation and staff turnover which suggest failures in the management of change from a human perspective. Probably these will be reflected in the quality of student learning outcomes as well.

5

Multi Objective Teaching

Multi-site Teacher Education Research (MUSTER) project

The Multi-site Teacher Education Research (MUSTER) project grew from several roots. During the early 1990s the Centre for International Education (CIE) at the University of Sussex Institute of Education built up links with Universities in a number of low and middle income countries. Teacher education emerged as a common focus of interest. The consensus was that teacher education in many countries was under-theorised, practice was often not demonstrably effective, and existing systems were unable to deliver the numbers of qualified teachers needed at sustainable levels of cost to meet the demands imposed by commitments to Education for All.

Consequently, in 1997 the CIE approached the UK Department for International Development (DFID) with a proposal for a collaborative multi-country programme of research into teacher education. The original proposal for the research identified two separate sets of reasons for such research into teacher education. One set was policy-related, the other was concerned with insights into the nature of teacher education.

On policy MUSTER noted that: All countries have systematic arrangements in place for teacher education and allocate substantial resources to initial training in the belief that it enhances the quality of teaching and student achievement.

Despite this there is widespread evidence that achievement of students is unsatisfactory, and that teaching methods in schools are slow to change in ways that reflect approaches deemed to be effective. Though many factors are involved in low school achievement, one strategy is to improve the quality of training given to teachers before they begin teaching and enhance the support available for the development of professional skills in the first years of employment.

Little research has been carried out into the effectiveness of teacher education in most low income countries. Training programmes persist which are based on models developed by the former colonial powers. More recently contemporary models from the UK, USA, Australia and New Zealand have been influential, though their impact and feasibility is largely untested in low income countries. Ministries and development agencies trying to devise more efficient and effective programmes have few locally-based research findings to guide them; nor do they have the capacity to assess formatively which strategies are working in the manner intended.

In high income countries, where teachers have to be qualified before their first employment, there are clear conceptual and practice differences between pre-service (PRESET) and in-service (INSET). In many low income countries teachers begin working in classrooms with no training, and gain initial professional qualifications much later, if at all. In several Commonwealth Caribbean countries this pattern is effectively a policy. By default it is also the case in many African systems.

The curriculum in many Teacher Training Colleges (TTCs) and University Departments of Education (UDEs) in these countries often does not recognise and build on the prior teaching experience trainees possess. It is extremely rare for the responsibilities for training to be shared with schools in which new teachers work in many parts of Africa. Teacher education budgets in most low income countries are heavily constrained. There are indications that costs can be very high relative to other forms of education and training.

It is therefore important to generate indications of the costs of different patterns of initial teacher education and identify any areas where more can be achieved within sustainable budgets. The actual ways in which teachers acquire and use professional knowledge are not well understood. Over the last 15 years these have been conceptualised and discussed within a rapidly growing literature grounded in the experience of high income countries.

Superficially teacher education programmes in many low income countries have remained substantially unchanged since their development under colonial administrations. This is despite radically changed demands from school systems on teachers, often arising from Universal Primary Education (UPE), the commitments to Education for All, and related reforms of the school curricula. In addition, the work of teaching is intimately bound up both with the teacher's identity and sense of self and with the norms, values and expectations of the communities they serve. When these things change, some fundamental reappraisal grounded in context is needed.

Though attempts have been made to reform teacher education the limited evidence suggests that much has remained at the level of rhetoric rather than being implemented in teacher education institutions. The general theorising which can provide models and concepts for new practice has frequently not found its way into national teacher education curricula. The reasons for this need to be identified in advance of further efforts to promote more effective practice. These may differ from system to system.

Once consequence is that there is a need to identify which aspects of teacher education theory and practice developed in high income countries might be transportable, and which carry assumptions about the cultural roles of the teacher, pedagogic preferences, and infrastructure availability that compromise their value and restrict their relevance. In short MUSTER had ambitions to:

— enhance understanding of how new teachers acquire the knowledge, skills and attitudes needed to teach in different systems, and identify the professional learning experiences, including teaching practice, which are most useful and valuable to new teachers given the qualities that they bring with them to initial teacher education.

— categorise different types of pre-service provision leading to initial qualification in each system and profile their institutional bases, identify patterns of overall costs and costs per qualified teacher, and consider implications for efficiency, effectiveness and the prospects of meeting demand in sustainable ways.

— build research capacity in-country focused on issues in teacher education using both quantitative and qualitative techniques, and strengthen the resource base of young researchers with field experience through in-project training.

Ghana, Lesotho, Malawi, and Trinidad and Tobago all have single national teacher education systems that are centrally controlled and relatively homogenous. In these locations it was possible to undertake studies within a common framework with some comparative elements. In South Africa the 1990s were a period of dramatic transition.

Teacher education was diverse, fragmented, and undergoing radical change. For these reasons it became clear that MUSTER research needed to take a different form. The scope of the research was broadened to capture some of the diversity that existed and a network of researchers was convened from other institutions including the Universities of the Western Cape, Witwatersrand, and Pretoria.

MUSTER was conceived as a collaborative multi-site research project that would maintain a core agenda of common research themes. It was also designed to allow the special circumstances and concerns of national researchers to be reflected in variations to a common design and extension into themes specific to particular countries.

MUSTER developed a grid of core research questions around which there was a consensus. This two-dimensional grid identified four strands and three arenas. MUSTER used a wide range of research methods, drawing on both quantitative and qualitative techniques of data collection and analysis. This was designed to gain as full a picture as possible of the complex issues. There were also cultural reasons for using a variety of approaches.

MUSTER established an email network for communication early in its life. At first communications developed with most information flowing outwards from the centre. This generated a reciprocal flow of responses back to the centre. News from the remote sites was passed on to other sites, with limited communication along the 'rim' of the network. The notable exceptions occurred at the annual workshops where face-to-face interaction was possible. To enhance the flow of ideas among the researchers, drafts from the different sites were made available electronically, and each site was provided with a laptop computer. Facility with new technology varied, as did infrastructure and back-up services, with the result that sometimes communication failed for significant periods.

The teacher education systems in the MUSTER countries differ for complex historical, political, cultural and demographic reasons. All share influences that arise from the activities of missionaries and colonial governments in the formative stages of teacher education in each country. In all cases the systems are now government-controlled, with varying degrees of residual relationships with groups who played a role in the founding of different training colleges.

The training institutions exist within different policy and curriculum regimes, and have been subject to more or less developmental support since being assimilated into state education systems. It is the national contexts that determine the level of supply and demand for new teachers, and the nature of new entrants recruited into training.

The training systems in Ghana, Lesotho, Malawi and Trinidad and Tobago vary in terms of the entry level qualifications required, the length and location of training, the type of certification, and the mode of delivery. Ghana has only one mode of initial teacher education. Thirty-eight colleges (seven male, one female, and the rest mixed) provide three-year full-time post-secondary training. All the colleges except one are residential and all prepare teachers for primary and junior secondary level with options to specialise.

Some trainees with the minimum requirements may enter college via 'protocol' arrangements that may circumvent normal entrance requirements. A recent reform of the teacher education system has introduced an 'In-In-Out' system whereby the third year of training will be located in schools rather than in the Colleges. This is in the early stages of implementation. Ghana is committed to universalising primary education and enrolments have been increasing. Primary gross enrolment rates appear to be around 79%. The proportion of untrained teachers has been falling to below 20%, with large regional variations.

There is widespread concern with low levels of pupil achievement that are partly attributed to the poor quality of teacher education. Expenditure on teacher education has been rising and now accounts for about 6% of total recurrent expenditure on education which itself is about 35% of all government spending. The cost per trained teacher is about five times GNP per capita. There is an on-going debate in Ghana about the most suitable course structure and curriculum for preparing teachers for primary schools, and in particular how such schools can be used as training sites. There are also concerns about the colleges and the professional development of their staff.

The National Teacher Training College (NTTC) is the only teacher education college in Lesotho. It trains primary and junior secondary level teachers on different courses. Initial training has evolved through a variety of programmes but is being consolidated into a three and a half year residential programme, the Diploma in Education, Primary (DEP). The proportion of untrained teachers in primary schools has remained around 25% over the last five years. The college output of less than 150 new teachers a year has been insufficient to reduce this proportion.

The introduction of free primary schooling from 2000 is increasing enrolments thereby increasing demand for teachers. Lesotho allocates between 2% and 3% of the recurrent education budget to NTTC and commits over 30% of government resources to education as a whole. The cost per trained teacher is over ten times GNP per capita. Major issues in Lesotho concern the status and characteristics of the NTTC as the only teaching training college, how the college curriculum can be rationalised and upgraded, how teacher quality can be enhanced, and how output can be increased.

Since 1997 pre-service college-based training for primary level in Malawi has been suspended to allow for large numbers of untrained teachers to be trained through the Malawi Integrated Teacher Education Programme (MIITEP). This system provides for one term in College, four terms in supervised teaching practice, and most of a term in College preparing for and taking final examinations. The programme is run in all six primary colleges which together enrol cohorts of about 2,500 students at a time, three times a year when fully operating.

Six cohorts were enrolled between 1997 and 1999 with each college taking between about 400 and 600 students per cohort three times a year. About 42% of MIITEP trainees are female. Nominal staff-student ratios vary between 1:11 and 1:21. About a quarter of staff appear to be graduates and about 35% are female. MIITEP trainees are drawn from the ranks of untrained teachers who constitute perhaps half of all teachers. The MIITEP programme was suspended in 1999 for nearly two years whilst negotiations took place concerning continued external support.

Malawi implemented Free Primary Education (FPE) in 1994 resulting in an increase in enrolments from about 1.8 million to 3 million primary pupils. Currently Malawi allocates about 4% of its educational expenditure to teacher education and about 30% to education as a whole. The cost per trained teacher in MIITEP is about three times the GNP per capita. Important issues in Malawi are concerned with training and upgrading enough teachers to meet the needs created by FPE for more teachers.

The MIITEP school-based system seeks to share training between the colleges and the schools but this is problematic given the poor infrastructure, stringent resource constraints, and volume of demand. Challenges for training include the extent to which it can prepare trainees for very large classes which can exceed 100 in the lower grades of primary schools, and whether the MIITEP system can be refined to make it more efficient and effective at sustainable levels of cost.

Trinidad and Tobago has two government colleges where most primary initial teacher education takes place. The Teacher's Diploma is awarded after two years full-time study including periods of teaching practice. Total enrolments average between 700 and 800, split evenly between the colleges. About 30% of trainees are male. Staff-student ratios are about 1:13 and 55% of the tutors are female. Selection into the colleges is made from untrained teachers who have been working in schools for two to five years, most of entered teaching via the 'On the Job Training' apprenticeship programme.

Ghana and Malawi have relatively large populations and teacher education systems compared to Lesotho and Trinidad and Tobago. The latter is a middle-income country whereas the others are much poorer in terms of GNP per capita. Demand for new teachers is high in three of the countries, but for different reasons. In Ghana the GER at primary is still well below 100% and more teachers are needed to achieve Education for All (EFA) targets for universal enrolment. It also has a high rate of growth in the school age cohort, and teacher output must grow at least at this rate to maintain the current pupil-teacher ratio, and more if untrained teachers are to be trained.

In Malawi demand arises mostly from the growth in primary numbers, the need to reduce very high pupil-teacher ratios and proportions of untrained teachers, and the very high rates of teacher attrition. During the four years MITTEP was in progress, the ratio of teachers in post to newly trained teachers was low indicating a high level of effort in training. Lesotho is different. It has high enrolment rates and low or negative cohort growth. Its primary pupil-teacher ratio is high, but not excessive, and about a quarter of teachers are untrained. The main factor creating demand for new teachers appears to be the very low output of the training system.

The ratio of 65:1 teachers in post to output is insufficient to maintain the pupil-teacher ratio at current levels, and replace teachers who leave. This situation is deteriorating as enrolments increase and drop out declines as a result of FPE. Trinidad and Tobago also has a negative rate of growth in the school age cohort. In this case pupil-teacher ratios and teacher attrition are low, and the output ratio of the teacher education system is more than sufficient to maintain enrolment rates at current pupil-teacher ratios.

Primary teacher training in anglophone Africa and the Caribbean mostly takes place in Teacher Training Colleges (TTCs), while most secondary teacher education is in University Departments of Education (UDEs). In Africa, colleges usually grew out of missionary-run education, though generally with national independence they came under government control. These colleges usually occupy an intermediate position between schools and higher education.

They are often more like 'glorified high schools' than universities in their organisation, teaching environment and culture. Their physical location, layout and buildings place constraints on their operation and the opportunities to innovate. Colleges are mostly residential and are often situated away from towns. As a result there may be few schools nearby which can be used for teaching practice.

These teacher education institutions have their own history, culture, ethos, practices, etc. and any programme of change must recognise these as a starting point. The first TTC in Ghana was founded in 1848 by the Basel Mission and many of the colleges still have church affiliations. Others grew out of secondary schools; all are now governmentfunded and have a common curriculum.

Training colleges in Ghana have the appearance of traditional secondary schools from the way they were built and their way of operating. Many of them were started as missionary institutions to train ministers, catechists and later teachers. Some of them were built as traditional secondary schools and were later converted into colleges for training teachers. Their characteristic features include residential boarding facilities, a dining hall, a daily timetable divided into periods of 40 minutes, classrooms with seats arranged in rows and columns facing a chalkboard, a small library, staff bungalows, an administrative block and playing grounds for sports activities. Those with strong missionary roots have a chapel.

Classrooms have no visual aids or storage facilities for keeping teaching and learning materials. Their science laboratories appear to be poorly equipped and are too small. In one of the colleges studied, there was only one laboratory for practical work in physics, chemistry and biology which could only seat about fifty students. College libraries tended to be small and in one college it was estimated that it could seat about 30 students at a time. In the colleges there is an emphasis on discipline and moral training, often with daily worship.

The curriculum is developed and assessed by the Institute of Education at the University of Cape Coast, under direction from the Teacher Education Directorate of the Ministry of Education. College lecturers are involved to the extent that they sit on subject panels and help mark the exams, but otherwise exercise little control, and are reported to see their role simply as teaching what they are given.

The three main churches in Lesotho - Evangelical, Anglican and Catholic - all developed their own TTCs for primary teachers which were located around the country.

This continued until 1975 when all primary and junior secondary training was centralised in a new, secular, National Teacher Training College (NTTC) in Maseru. The NTTC aims were, inter alia, to enhance national unity, modernise the curriculum and effect economies of scale in training.

In Malawi a number of small TTCs were also originally established by the missionaries. The first government college was established in 1962; this became Blantyre TTC. After 1973 the government took control over teacher education and through a process of amalgamation 13 colleges were reduced to six, of which two are still owned by the Catholic Church.

The teaching day is divided into six one-hour periods, with study time in the evenings, though lack of electricity in BTC prevented students from doing this. In both colleges, classrooms typically are set out in traditional style, with heavy wooden seat-desks that are difficult to move. The few displays were tatty, with no evidence of student work. The total absence of equipment and consumables made the labs inoperable.

The teacher education curriculum is laid down by the Malawi Institute of Education, which is a part of the Ministry. Examinations are set and marked by the Malawi National Examination Board, with the college tutors acting as markers. The MIITEP curriculum resonates with that of previous full-time residential programmes and dates back to reforms carried out in the 1980s with only minor adjustments to the aims to reflect recent social changes. It is skills-based, aiming to produce teachers who can deliver the curriculum effectively and obtain high levels of examination achievement from pupils.

Primary Teacher Education in Trinidad and Tobago started with government and charitable initiatives dating back to the nineteenth century which first set up 'normal' schools and then a government teacher training college (TTC). Later denominational TTCs were set up, but the colonial government retained a measure of control. Alongside the colleges, for nearly 100 years there was a system of school-based apprenticeship training, by which pupil-teachers gradually acquired qualifications while teaching.

In the 1970s all the old TTCs were replaced with two government non-residential colleges, one in the north of the island and the other in the south. The campuses are spacious, with adequate buildings and reasonable resources, though the time-table and organisation are similar to those of a high school, with seven 45-minute periods per day and little free study time. The Board of Teacher Training is responsible for the curriculum, sets the exams in consultation with the college tutors, and moderates the results; there is, strangely, no link with the University of the West Indies. The college tutors, many of whom hold Masters degrees from the UWI, have been active in gradually altering and adapting the curriculum to suit new circumstances.

Malawi has very high teacher attrition rates which create a large demand which, it appears, can only be satisfied by a large scale, mixed-mode teacher education programme based in schools rather than colleges for much of the training period. Lesotho trains small numbers of teachers at relatively high costs which would be difficult to sustain if the current system were expanded to meet projected demand.

Ghana has a large system with considerable variation, and MUSTER therefore could only research specific aspects in an illustrative way. The teaching profession no longer enjoys the status it once had, salaries are relatively low, and conditions of service perceived as poor. Young people apply to training colleges often as a last resort, lacking the academic qualifications for university, and perhaps seeing it as a stepping stone to other careers.

Their characteristics, and the interaction between them and the training process, are core concerns for the reform of teacher education systems. They are a reminder of starting points for more effective training, building from the qualities, perceptions and commitment of those available and willing to train as teachers.

In Lesotho much recruitment is through the Education Secretariats of the various churches. In all cases colleges appear to have little influence over the first appointment and little systematic knowledge of where their graduates teach. . Various changes, notably greatly increased enrolments in most of the countries as a result of Education for All commitments, and curriculum reform at school level to develop improved materials and promote more effective teaching methods, have created new challenges for teacher education.

Teacher education curricula have been much slower to change than school curricula. College-based systems predominate across the MUSTER countries. History, both colonial and post-colonial, has shaped the institutions that provide teacher education, leaving them poised somewhat anomalously between the secondary and higher education sectors. The college sector, often isolated both professionally and geographically from other parts of the system, has been neglected, and teacher educators have generally not been recognised as a separate group in need of professional development.

Practice has changed, or persisted, through interactions between piecemeal government policy initiatives, institutional traditions, and the qualities and motivation of teacher trainers. The content, quality and outcomes of teacher education are in significant part determined by the resources that can be mobilised. There are wide variations across the countries in the levels of allocation to teacher education. Though some of the reasons reflect underlying structural differences, others are not so easily explained.

There may be scope for increases in efficiency and effectiveness that make it easier to sustain teacher education systems which more closely approach satisfying demand for new teachers than is the case in several of the countries. Where demand greatly outstrips supply it may be that more radical alternatives to conventional college-based programmes have to be considered.

Teacher education is a large and complicated enterprise in Australia. Its complexity arises out of a history of amalgamation of a very large number of institutions, and the current context of teacher education. In the late 1970s there were around 50,000 teacher education students in more than 30 Colleges of Advanced Education (CAEs) and several small private institutions, and several thousand more in 18 universities, almost all of which offered at least a graduate Diploma in Education.

There are now only 38 institutions offering initial teacher education, including several small private institutions. While institutions have rationalised, it has taken time to rationalise individual courses. Many institutions still have a complexity of provision that would not exist if their institutional history had not been so complex. Within about three years most of this historically based complexity should be simplified. There are other reasons for complexity in teacher education provision.

Sharp fluctuations in demand for initial teacher education, changes in school authority requirements, shifting pressures within institutions regarding total student load and financial provisions, and, not least, course innovation seeking the very best quality outcomes, have resulted in programmes with diverse structures and course length. The external agencies to the higher education sector are those at a State level seeking information on the future supply of teacher education graduates with particular specialist qualifications to inform their staffing and recruitment strategies, and their consultations with universities regarding future intakes and course development.

Each of those stakeholders may have, from time to time, a need for data of adequate quality and appropriate detail to inform policyuseful labour market analyses. There has been a lack of such quality data that is also accessible and credible to all parties. For the majority of major courses, classification as to whether or not they provide initial teacher education should not be a problem. However, there are some misclassifications and problems of long standing, and there are recent developments that create some new difficulties.

The appropriate classification of courses is important for general level teaching labour market analyses as well as consideration of particular actual or potential shortage specialisations. All institutions in Australia providing recognised initial teacher education are included in the database. However, in some cases, especially regarding double degree programmes, data for individual courses are not available, and they are aggregated under the teacher education component of the double degree programme, or a simple listing of all the separate double degree courses.

The Australian Catholic University campuses are listed according to the States in which they are located. The comments on completions are to give an indication of the size of courses, and are based on 2001 expected completions, qualified by completions in previous years, plans for the future, and information from other sources, if appropriate.

Key issues are the minimum length of the initial teacher education programme as a whole, and the minimum length of the actual 'professional preparation' aspects of the programme. In Queensland the Board of Teacher Registration requires a minimum of four years higher education in the total programme, and a minimum of two years of professional preparation. This is consistent with the broad professional consensus among teacher educators and other stakeholders expressed in Preparing a Profession, the report of the National Standards and Guidelines for Initial Teacher Education Project.

New South Wales is the only large jurisdiction that does not generally require at least four years of initial teacher education. Support for a minimum of two years of professional preparation is more recent and more contested. The main focus is a critique of one year, end-on graduate DipEd programmes.

The main alternatives developed have been two year graduate programmes, and a great deal has been invested in the development of such courses at institutions such as the Universities of Sydney and Melbourne. The two-year graduate programmes were not only a response to the perceived inadequacy of professional preparation in traditional DipEd courses, but also to the perceived inadequacy of discipline (subject content) preparation in many traditional four year secondary Bachelor of Education (BEd) programmes.

In the mid to late 1990s many institutions in NSW (and some elsewhere) planned to phase out three-year programmes and the three-year exit point in four year programmes. This was because of the belief in the inadequacy of the three-year programme of professional preparation, and because graduates of three-year programmes had at that time some difficulty gaining employment in the generally over-supplied teaching labour market, and so there appeared to be strong potential student demand for the extended programmes.

However, since then, the increasing demand for teachers has resulted in those with three-year qualifications more readily gaining employment, so the three-year qualifications have been retained in a number of institutions in response to student demand. Similar dynamics have occurred in relation to two-year graduate programmes and other longer courses. Plans to replace graduate DipEd and undergraduate BEd programmes with two-year graduate programmes have been scaled down or shelved as student demand has focussed on minimum length courses more than anticipated by teacher educators.

Thus the situation developed of continuation of the administratively difficult four year programmes with a threeyear exit point. The one year graduate programmes have continued, and the two-year programmes now often have an early exit point after one year or 18 months-resulting in the same administrative difficulties as the four year courses with an early exit point.

New structures for initial teacher education, such as double degree programmes, have now been developing in response to this and to new thinking about how to achieve the best quality professional preparation of teachers. In many institutions this has only been possible because of the stronger negotiating position that many faculties or schools of education now have within universities.

A four year teacher education programme is required for teaching in government schools in the ACT. There is no qualification barrier regarding whether a teacher can teach in primary or secondary schools-in fact the Department of Education and Community Service sees advantages in planned teacher exchanges between primary and secondary schools. The Australian Catholic University's Signadou campus, in the northern Canberra suburb of Watson, has only one initial teacher education programme.

The University of Canberra, in the north-western Canberra area of Belconnen, has early childhood, primary and secondary teacher education programmes. The four year undergraduate BEd in early childhood teaching has 29 completions anticipated for 2001. The four year degree is now a joint course with Canberra Institute of Technology (CIT) whereby early childhood students subsume the Diploma of Community Services (Children's Services) after two years. The course as now structured with CIT commenced in 1998, and 2001 is the first year of graduates.

In California, the design of a two-tier credentialing system that calls for the completion of a beginning-teacher induction program to earn a professional credential.

Expansion and strengthening of the state's support for professional development through summer institutes, subject-matter specific professional development, and funds to local districts to help teachers learn to use new curricula. The number of newly prepared teachers increased, more teachers in their first years were given induction support, more underprepared teachers were receiving structured support, and content-focused professional development reached greater numbers of teachers.

Overall, the number of underprepared teachers in the state's classrooms finally began to decline in 2001-02. The state is struggling with a weak economy, state revenues are down considerably, and the budget deficit is soaring. As a result, many of the recent policy initiatives have been undermined: there is no longer support for teacher recruitment efforts, teacher education programs are facing enforced limits on enrollment, and state-sponsored professional development has been dramatically reduced. Ironically, the same forces that threaten the state's progress in strengthening the system of teacher development may have some positive impacts: as the state economy weakens, private-sector jobs are in short supply, making teaching a more attractive profession for recent graduates.

Over the past 6 years, as California has struggled through these economic and policy shifts, the Teaching and California's Future initiative has worked to highlight the strengths and weaknesses of the system of teacher development in the state and to provide policy-makers with the data they seek to inform their decisions to strengthen schools. Led by the Center for the Future of Teaching and Learning and cosponsors-California State University Institute for Educational Reform, Policy Analysis for California Education (PACE), University of

California Office of the President, and WestEd-the initiative has brought together a group of policy-makers and practitioners to seek common ground in strengthening the skills and knowledge of the state's teacher workforce. Teaching and California's Future involves a twofold strategy:

1) support for an ongoing comprehensive study of the conditions of teacher development in the state and
2) convening a task force of key policy-makers, practitioners, and representatives of institutions of higher education and professional organizations to use this information to improve the public education system.

In the wake of class size reduction and a steady rise in student enrollment during the 1990s, the demand for teachers in California public schools skyrocketed. At a time when the California economy was growing rapidly, schools and districts struggled to find enough qualified candidates to fill the growing number of classrooms. The Teaching and California's Future initiative has been tracking the status of the teaching profession since 1999.

When local educators are not able to find an individual who has met the state's minimum requirements for becoming a teacher-the completion of a teacher preparation program and attainment of a state credential-they may hire someone who falls into one of four categories:

— Pre-interns, who have not yet demonstrated subject matter competency and who are participating in a program to help them acquire such competency. Emergency-permit holders, who may or may not have demonstrated subject matter competency and may or may not be enrolled in teacher preparation classes.

— Interns, who have demonstrated subject matter competency and are enrolled in an intern teacher preparation program.

Teachers with waivers, for whom one or more requirements for certification have temporarily been waived and who may or may not have demonstrated subject matter competency or be enrolled in teacher preparation classes. In response to the growing number of underprepared teachers in the late 1990s, particularly in schools serving high proportions of poor, minority, and low-achieving students, California policy-makers acted aggressively. In the span of just a few years, new funds were allotted for teacher preparation and recruitment to increase the supply of teachers to meet the state's need. More money was also invested in induction efforts to retain those teachers who had already entered the profession. In addition, extra funds were set aside for "hard-to-staff" schools-those with 20% or more underprepared teachers-to assist them in attracting and retaining fully credentialed teachers.

These investments led to an increase in the number of teacher credentials issued and greater activity in teacher recruitment and induction throughout the state. Today, California is in a different position than it was in the late 1990s. The state is now struggling with a weak economy. Many of the teacher recruitment programs that were begun a few years ago have seen their budgets cut entirely. The university systems that are responsible for preparing most of the state's new teachers are also facing budget reductions. The labor market has also changed.

Unemployment is up, and many of the once desirable jobs in the private sector are gone. On one hand, this change could be good for the teaching profession, since more people might enter or return to what they see as a more stable profession. On the other hand, the state's severe budget crisis is threatening school budgets, and job security for teachers is less certain now, potentially detracting from the appeal of the profession. Given these rapid changes, it is difficult to determine whether California is still facing the same challenges.

The mid-1990s saw significant growth in the size of the teacher workforce. Between 1995-96 and 1998-99, the workforce grew by more than 50,000 teachers, an average increase of about 16,500 teachers per year, or about 7% annually. This change was primarily the result of increased demand generated by the state's class size reduction (CSR) program in grades K-3. This growth slowed considerably in the early 2000s as CSR reached full implementation and the state economy slowed.

In 2003, only about 2,800 teachers were added to the workforce from the previous year, reaching a statewide total of 309,773 teachers. This represents about 1% growth, closer to the annual growth rates seen in the early 1990s, before CSR. The recent slower growth of the overall workforce is reflected in the declining numbers of first-year teachers. In the Los Angeles Unified School District (LAUSD), the state's largest school district, the number of underprepared teachers has dropped substantially in the past 2 years, from a high of 10,000 in 2001-02 to about 8,000 in 2002-03 and about 6,000 in 2003-04. On a smaller scale, similar trends can also be found in other large districts. A number of factors may be responsible for the recent decline in the number of underprepared teachers.

First, teacher hiring is down overall. As a result, the number of underprepared teachers hired has declined, as well as the percentage of new hires who are underprepared, presumably because districts have greater choice among candidates.

The numbers of underprepared teachers may also be declining because of increased state efforts to repair and strengthen the teacher preparation "pipeline." In the late 1990s, state policy-makers responded to the teacher shortage by stepping up efforts to prepare teachers, and credential production increased as a result. In addition, funding was increased for programs aimed at attracting more fully credentialed teachers and retaining them in the profession. These efforts led to an increase in teacher recruitment and induction activity across the state and may have played a part in decreasing the number of underprepared teachers in the state as a whole.

The economy may also be a key factor in the decrease in the numbers of underprepared teachers. As job opportunities in the private sector shrank, the teacher workforce may have benefited if displaced workers became teachers or entered teacher preparation programs. Additionally, the poor economy may have kept more teachers in the profession, reducing the annual number of new hires. Intern programs are teacher preparation programs for individuals who are already teaching. Now the intern program has become a major component of California's response to the requirements of NCLB, and intern numbers are expected to grow still more in the 2003-04 school year.

The teacher shortage has affected California schools differentially. For several years, we have tracked how some schools struggle to find and hire fully credentialed teacher candidates. At the same time, we have shown that some schools have never been affected by the teacher shortage, even when it was most severe. In 2002-03, the last year for which state data are available, the inequitable distribution of underprepared teachers remained. Eighteen percent of California schools had 20% or more underprepared teachers and were likely to face serious problems as a result.

For example, these schools probably had to spend disproportionate amounts of time and human resources to recruit, hire, and induct new teachers every year. They also bear the burden of training teachers on the job, usually without adequate resources to do so. Providing professional development is also a challenge in schools where more than a fifth of teachers lack even basic training. These and other issues take time and energy away from the already difficult task of focusing on highquality instruction and student learning.

In 2002-03, 12% of districts had an average of 20% or more underprepared teachers in their schools. Fortunately, the number of schools with such high concentrations of underprepared teachers has declined and is likely to decline even more. In 2000-01, more than 1,800 California schools had 20% or more underprepared teachers; in 2002-03, that number had decreased to about 1,400. Although the trends are promising, the historical maldistribution points to an important problem. The severity of the teacher shortage in future years is not known, but it is sure to be inequitably distributed across California's schools.

Teacher qualifications may be improving for the whole state, but it is certain that, without intervention, some schools will continue to have problems finding and keeping fully credentialed teachers. Left to fend for themselves in a free market for teachers, these schools simply cannot compete for the most qualified teachers. In the worst cases, schools end up hiring many teachers with little experience and few qualifications, putting their students at a serious disadvantage year after year. As in past years, underprepared teachers are still found in disproportionate numbers in urban schools, low-performing schools, and schools serving high numbers of poor and minority students or English language learners. The situation is improving, but the most recent data still show a troubling discrepancy.

Overall, urban districts are more likely to have high concentrations of underprepared teachers, although this disparity has been improving somewhat over the past few years. In 2002-03, urban schools had an average of 12% underprepared teachers on staff, compared with 10% in suburban schools and 7% in rural schools. Over time, schools serving high proportions of minority students have seen a decrease in the percentage of underprepared teachers. However, the most recent numbers still show a substantial maldistribution: in 2002-03, high-minority schools had an average of 20% underprepared teachers on staff, while low-minority schools had an average of only 4%.

This trend is encouraging, but policy-makers must still take note of the implications of the historical pattern: those schools that are most in need of well-trained, effective teachers have chronically also had the greatest percentages of teachers who do not meet the state's minimum requirements for even a preliminary credential. In this era of high standards and high stakes for all students, this pattern hardly indicates a level playing field.

Fully credentialed elementary teachers, in especially short supply during the years in which CSR was implemented, seem to be increasing gradually in number. In recent years, however, the state has seen increased shortages of math and science teachers. Fully credentialed special education teachers have for many years been in very short supply, and the situation shows no signs of improvement.

The state funds went to a variety of programs, each targeting different aspects of the recruitment and hiring process. Some funds targeted expanding and enhancing statewide and local teacher recruitment efforts. For example, the Teaching as a Priority Block Grant Program (TAP) provided block grants to districts with API rankings of 1 to 5 to implement recruitment strategies for hiring more credentialed teachers. The Teacher Recruitment Incentive Program (TRIP) opened six regional teacher recruitment centers whose services were available to all districts.

The California Center for Teaching Careers (CalTeach) provided outreach and advertising at a statewide level. Other state funds went to easing the financial burden of teacher preparation: the Cal Grant T and the Governor's Teaching Fellowship provided financial assistance to students in teacher preparation programs, while the Assumption Program of Loans for Education (APLE) assumed student loans for teachers in shortage areas at designated schools. APLE is the only recruitment program that has not been touched by the state's financial problems. From 2001 to 2003, 13,000 awards were allotted, and the state authorized another 7,700 loans in the 2003-04 budget.

The Governor's Teaching Fellowship has been folded into the APLE program, and APLE may also assume some of the burden from the now-defunct Cal Grant T program. Given the scant reporting requirements of some of these programs, it is difficult even to ascertain exactly how much of the money was spent. It is clear, however, that these programs did generate recruitment activity during their time. In 2002-03, the block-granted TAP funds reached nearly 60% of the eligible districts and charter schools. TAP has also been employed to recruit teachers with specific credentials, such as CLAD and special education, to work in hard-to-staff schools.

One large urban district used funds to increase the capacity of its human resources department, facilitating more efficient processing of applicants and reducing the number of frustrated job seekers. In some smaller districts, TAP money was used to expand the role of central district officials in recruitment efforts, funding travel to locate and interview candidates and creating local pipelines through the development of relationships with teacher education programs.

These changes have eliminated duplication of efforts by multiple schools in the same district, freeing up time that principals and other site administrators must ordinarily dedicate to recruiting new staff. Although TRIP's services were available to all districts, it appears that hard-to-staff districts sought their assistance more often for help with substantial challenges, while more desirable districts tended to use the centers only to fill particular positions.

One large urban district used the recruitment centers to find enough applicants for its openings, while another smaller, hard-to-staff district employed the resources to gain more visibility. The recruitment centers have also assisted some districts by centralizing several key recruitment needs for districts strapped for time, funds, and personnel. Cost-intensive efforts, such as media advertising, Web site development, and job fairs, were also assumed by the recruitment centers.

California is in flux with regard to teacher supply and demand. New state and federal policies, economic problems, and changing demographics all have contributed to shifts in the numbers of teachers needed and hired, and subsequently to changes in the qualifications and distribution of teachers in the state. Looking ahead, these same factors will continue to play a role in the demand for teachers and will need to be considered by policy-makers as they seek to ensure that adequate numbers of teachers are available to staff California's schools.

Of course, even if the number of fully credentialed teachers grows, such growth does not ensure parity in teacher quality across all classrooms. As we have seen, teachers do not distribute themselves evenly across California's schools. Rather, some schools have great difficulty attracting fully credentialed teachers, and many teachers would probably choose no job at all over a job in what they perceive as a highly undesirable school. In certain key areas-mathematics, science, and special education-severe shortages remain. To have the best chance at staffing all classrooms with a competent teacher, the state as a whole needs a supply of teachers that exceeds the total number of available teaching positions each year.

In this era of increased state, federal, and public pressure to improve student achievement, only an oversupply of teachers can ensure that the best teachers are recruited into the classroom to help all students perform up to California's world-class standards. To accomplish these daunting goals, California policy-makers have a difficult job ahead of them. A critical lesson of the late 1990s is that, if untracked and unplanned, the supply of teachers can drop far below what is needed to meet the demand in the state's schools and lead to the hiring of thousands of teachers who are not fully prepared to meet the needs of their students.

Although the supply of qualified teachers now appears to be somewhat closer to the demand, and despite the state's current economic crisis, the issues of teacher demand and distribution must not be neglected again. The state's recent investments in growing the teacher workforce provided some promising returns, but that progress is now threatened as the budget crunch has forced the state to reverse its teacher recruitment strategy. These decisions could be errors with repercussions that are felt long after the state rebounds, especially given the high number of teachers that are expected to retire in the next 10 years.

Many preparation programs were flooded with candidates who were already classroom teachers and who were looking for assistance on how to teach tomorrow. Incentives for students to complete their programs before entering the profession simply disappeared on many campuses as job offers came flooding in from local district administrators desperate to find an adult to head each classroom.

On the policy front, institutions of higher education came under pressure to increase the number of new credential recipients and to increase the quality of their preparation programs. In response, teacher preparation programs across the state, especially those in the California State University System, increased the production of candidates, made programs more flexible, developed "blended" undergraduate preparation programs, increased opportunities for undergraduates to enter the teacher pipeline, and began to pilot performance assessments for their candidates. The state also invested in the expansion of alternative routes into the profession in the form of intern and pre-intern programs to support working teachers without full credentials and assist them in taking the steps to complete their preparation.

Within the current changing political and economic contexts, teacher preparation programs are facing a series of conflicting challenges. The federal No Child Left Behind (NCLB) provisions may be increasing pressure for underprepared teachers to complete their programs. NCLB seeks to ensure that all children are taught by a "highly qualified" teacher. Generally, all teachers in core subject areas (English, mathematics, science, foreign language, social science, and arts) are required to have a full credential or be working to obtain a full credential while participating in a structured intern program by the year 2005-06.

In addition, the private sector has increased its production of newly credentialed teachers at about the same rate as the CSU system. However, the University of California campuses have continued to produce roughly the same small number of newly credentialed teachers. Figure 3-1 shows the trends over time. Over the past decade, the growth in production has been fairly steady among campuses serving high-need districts, with a dramatic increase in recent years. CSU campuses in the Los Angeles basin and the San Francisco Bay Area increased their production by more than 33% from 2000-01 to 2001-02.

Much of the increase in the production of newly credentialed teachers in the private sector came from the expansion of the programs at National University and Chapman University. The growth of the National and Chapman teacher education programs appears to be a result of their responsiveness to the needs of career changers and emergency-permit holders who work full-time while earning their credentials. Although comparatively expensive, these independent programs are considered more "user friendly," offering classes at many locations at convenient times.

The trend in the production of special education teachers has not matched the growth of single- and multiple-subject credentials. The growth in special education credentials has been largely in intern credentials. In fact, the production of fully credentialed special education teachers has actually decreased over the past few years as demand has risen. The fact that almost one in five special education teachers do not hold at least a preliminary special education credential is critical because of the specialized knowledge and skills needed to work with this population of students.

Specifically, special education teachers need to be aware of legal issues surrounding the federal Individuals with Disabilities Education Act (IDEA), which requires that special education students' needs be met through an individualized education program (IEP). Special education teachers also need a wide repertoire of instructional strategies through which to meet IEP goals. In addition, general education teachers frequently rely on special education teachers as a source of information on how to assist students in meeting IEP goals.

Pre-interns are working teachers who participate in programs designed to help them meet the requirements for entering an intern program. They are not yet enrolled in a teacher preparation program. Starting in 1998, the number of pre-intern programs and participants grew rapidly for four consecutive years, with more than 10,000 participants during the 2001-02 school year. However, during the 2002-03 school year, both the number of participants and the number of programs shrank.

There are many routes into the teaching profession in California. The so-called traditional route has historically been the most common path: after earning an undergraduate degree, prospective teachers complete a year of coursework, student teach, and then earn a credential. Some progress through their program full-time, while others go part-time, often taking convenient nighttime classes. "Alternative-route" is a term coined to describe a variety of routes into the profession that share the common experience that participants begin to teach before they earn a credential.

The intern route is for individuals who have demonstrated subject matter competency. The program typically involves prescribed coursework, as in the traditional program, along with some support through a mentor and sometimes collaborative meetings. Pre-intern programs serve not fully credentialed teachers who have not yet demonstrated subject matter competency. Typically, these programs aim to help teachers prepare to pass subject matter competency tests. Some programs also require that pre-interns attend a certain series of workshops covering topics outside of test preparation, such as classroom management.

Other programs have a mentoring component designed to provide pre-interns with support at their school site. The emergency "route" is not a route at all-it is an ad hoc and individual arrangement in which classroom teachers without credentials need do no more than show they have pursued minimal coursework requirements each year. Regardless of whether teachers take a traditional, an alternative, or an emergency route into teaching, they need to meet the same basic requirements for a preliminary credential. They must complete a series of courses in pedagogy and must demonstrate mastery of the subject matter they are planning to teach. They must complete a period of student teaching, during which time they are observed in the classroom. In addition, they must pass a battery of tests required by the state.

Moreover, there can be great variation within each route because prospective teachers' experiences can vary dramatically. Their courses may be demanding or not, field experiences may be valuable or not, and the teacher candidates may or may not take full advantage of their opportunities to learn. Teacher candidates may complete the program in a year, or they may be enrolled in the program part-time, just take a course or two at a time, and stretch their preparation out over many years. Not surprisingly, teacher reports on the effectiveness of their coursework vary from program to program, and even within programs, from class to class. Harold, a teacher prepared through a traditional route; Jane, an intern; and Jose, a teacher on an emergency permit who is taking some teacher preparation classes-all give mixed reviews of their coursework.

Teachers, regardless of route, seem to share a perception about one factor that lends quality to a preparation course: a faculty member with recent experience in K-12 schools. Interns and others who are teaching while taking teacher preparation courses can face extremely burdensome schedules. Student teaching is considered by many to be a particularly important part of teacher preparation. In a traditional program, student teaching ideally involves many hours of observing in an experienced teacher's classroom and gradually assuming more responsibility for instruction. The student teacher's first attempts at teaching are typically all under the guidance of the more experienced teacher, who can then provide feedback on the strengths and weaknesses of the student teacher's performance.

In alternative programs, the "student teacher" is already teaching and thus does not have as much time to observe veterans. Student teaching is the culminating experience in the program-so those who entered teaching as an intern would not typically student teach until their fourth semester as a classroom teacher. For the three semesters prior to student teaching, the nontraditional student may receive some support from a mentor, but not the amount of time observing and being coached that is possible in the traditional model.

A few intern programs require interns to student teach during their summer break or when they are off-track, so that, in a sense, they complete "traditional" student teaching as the final requirement in their credential program. However, in the majority of programs, teachers "student teach" in their own classrooms with a university or district supervising teacher completing a required number of observations. Given the differences in what it means to "student teach" in traditional and nontraditional programs, it is not surprising that traditional- and nontraditional-route teachers report different student teaching experiences.

Traditionally prepared teachers complete their coursework, earn their credentials, and then begin to teach.

At this point, they are eligible to participate in the state's Beginning Teacher Support and Assessment (BTSA) program, which provides them with, among other things, support from an experienced mentor. Interns also typically receive some type of formal on-the-job support from their programs. This is one of the major strengths of such programs and, when well implemented, can provide teachers the practical assistance they need to succeed while they are completing their preparation.

In contrast, teachers on emergency permits often do not receive formal mentoring or on-the-job support. Pre-interns may or may not receive mentoring or other support for teaching, and the mentoring they receive, if any, appears to be of mixed quality. One explanation for the low intensity of pre-intern mentoring is insufficient funding. Pre-interns, like teachers on emergency-permits, often have to rely on their own initiative to access informal supports.

Teaching full-time and earning a credential at the same time is difficult, whether the teacher holds an emergency permit or is enrolled in a pre-intern or intern program. When asked why they chose to enter teaching through a nontraditional route, teachers cited financial concerns and their previous experience most frequently. The majority of alternative-route teachers said they entered teaching without completing preparation programs because a teaching opportunity came up, they could not afford a full-time program, they already had some form of teaching experience, or they did not want to give up income while attending a preparation program.

Very few teachers decided to begin teaching without completing a credential because they felt that preparation was "basically a formality" that would not improve their job performance. Teacher preparation in California is in the midst of period of reform and change. Numerous research studies have documented the importance of support networks and opportunities for professional growth in the early years of teachers' careers. Such supports are key to improving new teachers' skills, knowledge, and retention. In a profession in which individuals typically work in isolation, new teachers face numerous challenges in managing a classroom and organizing instruction in what easily can become a "sink or swim" environment.

Teachers' experiences during these beginning years influence whether they will remain in the profession and, if they do, what kinds of teachers they become. To build and retain a high-quality teaching force and ensure that teachers have the skills and knowledge to prepare a diverse student body to meet tough content standards, California has invested heavily in induction support for beginning teachers. For beginning teachers who have completed a preparation program and have a preliminary or professional clear credential, the state funds a formal induction program, Beginning Teacher Support and Assessment (BTSA). The state's pre-intern and intern programs, although not typically referred to as induction programs, also work with teachers in their first years in the profession, simultaneously preparing them as teachers and supporting them to become better teachers.

Because beginning teachers in California are in various stages of completing their preparation and credentialing programs, the support they receive during their initial years varies considerably. Since the early 1990s, California has supported a formal induction program, the Beginning Teacher Support and Assessment program, to serve primarily first- and second-year teachers who hold preliminary and professional clear credentials.

The BTSA Interagency Task Force, which consists of members of the California Commission on Teacher Credentialing (CTC) and the California Department of Education (CDE), subsequently developed the California Formative Assessment and Support System for Teachers (CFASST), which is used by all but a handful of local BTSA programs. In addition to formative assessments of teacher practice, BTSA also provides beginning teachers with individualized induction support from experienced teachers and with professional development workshops and seminars on classroom management and instruction.

Nearly all new teachers in California-both those with credentials and those who are underprepared-receive some type of induction support. Sometimes this support comes through formal programs, such as BTSA; in other cases, it comes via informal means. Induction serves to integrate new teachers into the professional community and life of a school and supports a smooth transition into the profession. If new teachers are to be retained in the profession and become more effective educators, they need support and guidance from colleagues and administrators around their teaching practice.

Induction can provide this support in many ways, including providing opportunities for new teachers to collaborate and interact with colleagues around classroom management and instructional issues, providing occasions to observe the classroom practices of experienced teachers and learn best practices, and offering opportunities for feedback on their own practice. Teachers in California, regardless of whether or not they participated in BTSA, reported receiving a broad range of induction-related support. The most prevalent forms of induction support, received by nearly three-quarters of new teachers, were formal assignment of a mentor, being observed by nonadministrators, and receiving release time to observe other teachers.

Schools and districts vary in their capacity to provide high-quality mentor support. A key indicator of local capacity is the presence of a sufficient number of experienced teachers to serve as support providers. Districts with large numbers of experienced, accomplished teachers have a sufficient pool from which to draw BTSA support providers, as well as mentors and coaches for underprepared teachers. In these districts, the selection processes for support providers can be more rigorous and mentors can be more closely matched with new teachers, each of which can affect the nature, intensity, and quality of support.

Experienced teachers are distributed unevenly across California schools. There are fewer experienced teachers in schools serving poor, minority, and low-performing students. In the state's highest-poverty schools, the ratio of experienced to new teachers is 4:1, compared with a ratio of 7:1 in low-poverty schools. In the short term, as a result of fewer new teachers being hired, the ratios of experienced to new teachers have improved. However, the shortage of mentors in certain districts threatens the promise of high-quality induction support for all new teachers. Further, as retirement rates increase in the coming years and demand for new teachers subsequently increases, the ratios of potential mentors to new teachers may worsen. An inadequate supply of experienced teachers has implications beyond finding mentors to work with new teachers; it can also affect decisions about who can serve as a mentor. When there are few experienced teachers relative to new teachers in schools and districts, it is difficult for administrators to find people willing to take on the mentor role, much less be selective in whom they choose for this role. As a result, districts with shortages of experienced teachers sometimes resort to using fairly inexperienced teachers to serve as mentors.

Professional development for support providers. It is not enough for beginning teachers to be paired with mentors; mentors' skills and knowledge also matter. All BTSA support providers receive some training in the formative assessment process, the state's standards for the teaching profession, and coaching and observing. Local BTSA programs, however, determine the extent of the initial and ongoing training BTSA support providers receive. Incentives can encourage experienced teachers to serve as mentors. All BTSA support providers are paid, but some feel that the pay is not enough.

New teachers, on the other hand, have not accumulated such resources; yet many reported that they were not provided with any materials, the materials they were given were not appropriate to their teaching assignment, or they simply were not oriented to the available materials. As a result, new teachers often need to spend significant amounts of time locating and organizing materials for instruction. These problems were particularly acute for new teachers working with some of the state's more challenging student populations-English language learners and special education students.

During the 2001-02 school year, teachers remained engaged in many different types of professional development, ranging from workshops offered in their schools or districts to professional conferences and summer institutes. Because districts and schools rely on many sources of funding for their professional development, not just the state, the amount and type of professional development available vary considerably across districts and schools. Part of the variation can be explained by the amount of special funding schools receive to support professional development activities. Each funding source provides money with restrictions on how and for what purposes it can be spent.

Learning and applying new instructional strategies is most effective when teachers understand their students' needs. A suburban elementary school teacher worked with a coach to learn how to tailor instruction to meet the disparate educational needs of his students. Teachers in schools without a separate special education department and who work with students from multiple grade levels find it difficult to participate in standardsfocused professional development activities. Because the curriculum alignment activities are conducted by grade level and subject cohorts, special education teachers are at a distinct disadvantage because they are responsible for students from a range of grades and subjects.

6

Profile of Teaching Profession

Teaching is one of the most influential professions in society. In their day-to-day work, teachers can and do make huge differences to children's lives: directly, through the curriculum they teach, and indirectly, through their behaviour, attitudes, values, relationships with and interest in pupils. Good teachers are always optimistic about what their pupils can achieve, whatever their background or circumstances. They know from experience how pupils respond to success by succeeding further. They understand that all their pupils are capable of significant progress and that their potential for learning is unlimited.

But teaching involves more than care, mutual respect and wellplaced optimism. It demands knowledge and practical skills, the ability to make informed judgements, and to balance pressures and challenges, practice and creativity, interest and effort, as well as an understanding of how children learn and develop. It recognises the important part other people play in pupils' learning: in the classroom, the home and the local community. Just as teachers must have high expectations of their pupils, so pupils, parents and carers are entitled to have high expectations of teachers.

Teaching is a creative, intellectually demanding and rewarding job, so the standards for joining the profession must be high too. Skilled practitioners can make teaching look easy but they have learned their skills and improved them through training, practice, evaluation and by learning from other colleagues. Qualified teacher status is the first stage in a continuum of professional development that will continue through the induction period and throughout a teacher's career. Initial training lays the foundation for subsequent professional and career development.

During the induction period, newly qualified teachers can build on the strengths identified in their initial teacher training, and work on the areas which they and those working with them have highlighted as priorities for future professional development. This should help them to play an active role in their early professional development and performance management, and that of their colleagues.

The Standards for the award of Qualified Teacher Status are outcome statements that set out what a trainee teacher must know, understand and be able to do to be awarded Qualified Teacher Status (QTS). The Standards are organised in three inter-related sections which describe the criteria for the award:

— *Professional values and practice:* these standards outline the attitudes and commitment to be expected of anyone qualifying to be a teacher, and are derived from the Professional Code of the General Teaching Council for England

— *Knowledge and understanding:* these standards require newly qualified teachers to be confident and authoritative in the subjects they teach and to have a clear understanding of how all pupils should progress and what teachers should expect them to achieve

— *Teaching:* these standards relate to skills of planning, monitoring and assessment, and teaching and class management. They are underpinned by the values and knowledge covered in the first two sections.

The Standards apply to all trainee teachers, whatever route they take to Qualified Teacher Status. They allow providers autonomy in deciding how they will organise their training and respond to individual trainee teachers' needs. They do not set a curriculum, nor do they specify how training should be organised or run.

These standards are a rigorous set of expectations and set out the minimum legal requirement. Many primary teacher trainers will choose to supplement this minimum by continuing to offer a subject or phase specialism. Other trainers may choose to provide additional training which develops trainee teachers' knowledge and skills, for instance by offering:

— A specialist area of study such as the teaching of children with special education needs, or gifted and more able pupils, or a curriculum area such as personal, social and health education and citizenship

— A non-national curriculum subject specialism training to meet the standards for teaching and supporting learning in further education

— an area of training relevant to the traditions or needs of a region, such as training to work in multilingual classrooms.

Initial Teacher Training

The requirements for the provision of initial teacher training specify what providers of Initial Teacher Training (ITT) must do. They are organised in four sections are given below:

— trainee entry requirements
— training and assessment
— management of the ITT partnership
— quality assurance.

They underline the essential contribution that schools and other settings make to initial teacher training.

Knowledge and understanding

They have a secure knowledge and understanding of the subjects they are trained to teach. For those qualifying to teach secondary pupils this knowledge and understanding should be at a standard equivalent to degree level. In relation to specific phases, this includes:

a. For the foundation stage, they know and understand the aims, principles, six areas of learning and early learning goals described in the QCA/DfEE Curriculum Guidance for the foundation stage and, for reception children, the frameworks, methods and expectations set out in the National Numeracy and Literacy Strategies.

b. They know and understand the curriculum for each of the national curriculum core subjects, and the frameworks, methods and expectations set out in the national literacy and numeracy strategies. They have sufficient understanding of a range of work across the following subjects:

— history or geography

— physical education

— ICT

— art and design or design and technology

— performing arts, and

— religious education

They know and understand the values, aims and purposes and the general teaching requirements set out in the national curriculum handbook. As relevant to the age range they are trained to teach, they are familiar with the programme of study for citizenship and the national curriculum framework for Personal, Social and Health Education.

— They are aware of expectations, typical curricula and teaching arrangements in the Key Stages or phases before and after the ones they are trained to teach.

— They understand how pupils' learning can be affected by their physical, intellectual, linguistic, social, cultural and emotional development.

— They know how to use ICT effectively, both to teach their subject and to support their wider professional role.

— They understand their responsibilities under the SEN Code of Practice, and know how to seek advice from specialists on less common types of special educational needs.

— They know a range of strategies to promote good behaviour and establish a purposeful learning environment.

— They have passed the Qualified Teacher Status skills tests in numeracy, literacy and ICT.

Teaching

— They set challenging teaching and learning objectives which are relevant to all pupils in their classes. They base these on their knowledge of:

 — the pupils
 — evidence of their past and current
 — achievement
 — the expected standards for pupils of
 — the relevant age range
 — the range and content of work relevant
 — to pupils in that age range.

— They use these teaching and learning objectives to plan lessons, and sequences of lessons, showing how they will assess pupils' learning.

— They take account of and support pupils' varying needs so that girls and boys, from all ethnic groups, can make good progress.

— They select and prepare resources, and plan for their safe and effective organisation, taking account of pupils' interests and their language and cultural backgrounds, with the help of support staff where appropriate.

— They take part in, and contribute to, teaching teams, as appropriate to the school. Where applicable, they plan for the deployment of additional adults who support pupils' learning.

— As relevant to the age range they are trained to teach, they are able to plan opportunities for pupils to learn in out-of-school contexts, such as school visits, museums, theatres, field-work and employment-based settings, with the help of other staff where appropriate.

Monitoring and assessment

— They make appropriate use of a range of monitoring and assessment strategies to evaluate pupils' progress towards planned learning objectives, and use this information to improve their own planning and teaching.

— They monitor and assess as they teach, giving immediate and constructive feedback to support pupils as they learn. They involve pupils in reflecting on, evaluating and improving their own performance.

— They are able to assess pupils' progress accurately using, as relevant, the early learning goals, national curriculum level descriptions, criteria from national qualifications, the requirements of awarding bodies, national curriculum and foundation stage assessment frameworks or objectives from the national strategies. They may have guidance from an experienced teacher where appropriate.

— They identify and support more able pupils, those who are working below age-related expectations, those who are failing to achieve their potential in learning, and those who experience behavioural, emotional and social difficulties. They may have guidance from an experienced teacher where appropriate.

— With the help of an experienced teacher, they can identify the levels of attainment of pupils learning English as an additional language. They begin to analyse the language demands and learning activities in order to provide cognitive challenge as well as language support.

— They record pupils' progress and achievements systematically to provide evidence of the range of their work, progress and attainment over time.

— They are able to use records as a basis for reporting on pupils' attainment and progress orally and in writing, concisely, informatively and accurately for parents, carers, other professionals and pupils.

Teaching and class management

They have high expectations of pupils and build successful relationships, centred on teaching and learning. They establish a purposeful learning environment where diversity is valued and where pupils feel secure and confident.

They can teach the required or expected knowledge, understanding and skills relevant to the curriculum for pupils in the age range for which they are trained. In relation to specific phases:

a. those qualifying to teach Foundation Stage children teach all six areas of learning outlined in the QCA/ DfEE Curriculum Guidance for the Foundation Stage and, for Reception children, the objectives in the National Literacy and Numeracy Strategy frameworks competently and independently;

A range of work across the following subjects:

- history or geography
- physical education
- ICT
- art and design or design and technology, and performing arts independently, with advice from an experienced colleague where appropriate;

— They teach clearly structured lessons or sequences of work which interest and motivate pupils and which: make learning objectives clear to pupils employ interactive teaching methods and collaborative group work promote active and independent learning that enables pupils to think for themselves, and to plan and manage their own learning.

— They differentiate their teaching to meet the needs of pupils, including the more able and those with special educational needs. They may have guidance from an experienced teacher where appropriate.

— They are able to support those who are learning English as an additional language, with the help of an experienced teacher where appropriate.

— They take account of the varying interests, experiences and achievements of boys and girls, and pupils from different cultural and ethnic groups, to help pupils make good progress.

— They organise and manage teaching and learning time effectively.

— They organise and manage the physical teaching space, tools, materials, texts and other resources safely and effectively with the help of support staff where appropriate.

— They set high expectations for pupils' behaviour and establish a clear framework for classroom discipline to anticipate and manage pupils' behaviour constructively, and promote self-control and independence.

— They use ICT effectively in their teaching.

— They can take responsibility for teaching a class or classes over a sustained and substantial period of time. They are able to teach across the age and ability range for which they are trained.

— They can provide homework and other out-of-class work which consolidates and extends work carried out in the class and encourages pupils to learn independently.

— They work collaboratively with specialist teachers and other colleagues and, with the help of an experienced teacher as appropriate, manage the work of teaching assistants or other adults to enhance pupils' learning.

— They recognise and respond effectively to equal opportunities issues as they arise in the classroom, including by challenging stereotyped views, and by challenging bullying or harassment, following relevant policies and procedures.

As indicated by UNESCO statistics, with a world total of almost 59 million in 1997, teachers represent some 1.6 per cent of the world population in the age group 15-64 years and by some estimates the largest single group of professionals in the world. The growth in the number of teachers has been driven by a combination of growing school-age populations and rising enrolment rates.

The total number of teachers in formal education systems (in all countries and at all levels) increased by more than seven million in just seven years, rising from 52 million in 1990 to 59 million in 1997. More than two-thirds of these teachers are employed in developing countries, where their share with respect to the world total increased from 63.5 to 65.7 per cent between 1990 and 1997.

Between 1990 and 1995 the number of primary teachers has increased on average by almost 9 per cent in the developing countries, with a low of 2.2 in Eastern Asia and Oceania and a high of 25.5 in the Arab States, and by 17.5 per cent in the group of the least developed countries. The size of the population of official primary school age has grown correspondingly, increasing by 9 per cent in the developing countries, with a low of 3.5 per cent in Latin America and the Caribbean and a high of more than 16 per cent in the African region south of the Sahara.

The growth in the number of children of official primary school age, combined with efforts to expand access to basic education by reducing the size of the out-of school population, have created strong pressures on the demand for qualified teachers at the primary level in many developing countries. The ratio of the total population of children of primary school age (including both enrolled

Table 1
Percentage increase in the number of primary and secondary schoolteachers and children and youth of school age, 1990-95

	Primary school teachers (% increase)	*Primary school age children (% increase)*	*Secondary school teachers (% increase)*	*Secondary school-age youth (% increase)*
Developing countries	8.8	9.0	14.3	6.0
Sub-Saharan Africa	16.9	16.2	12.0	13.8
Arab States	25.5	15.1	23.8	9.0
Latin America & the Caribbean	12.2	3.5	11.6	5.9
Eastern Asia and Oceania	2.2	9.2	12.5	-4.5
Southern Asia	13.9	8.3	14.8	12.0
Least developed countries	17.5	12.5	16.4	13.9

and out-of school children) to teachers remains high in the group of the least developed countries, in sub-Saharan Africa and in Southern Asia, with an estimated mean of 57, 50 and 47 children of primary school age per teacher respectively (data 1995). The situation is exacerbated by significant numbers of secondary school age youth who are enrolled in primary education, as repeaters or late entrants. In some countries these represent over one-third of primary enrolment.

At the secondary level, the number of teachers has grown even more markedly over the same period, with a percentage increase ranging from 11.6 per cent in Latin America and the Caribbean to 23.8 per cent in the Arab States, while the youth of the (country specific) official secondary education age group increased on average, in the developing countries, by 6 per cent.

However, the size of the out-of-school population of secondary school age—more than 228 million, amounting to almost half of the total youth population of secondary school age (527 million) in 1995—gives an indication of the demand for qualified teachers that developing countries will need to meet in the future. Despite the efforts made during the 1990s to achieve the goals of the World Conference on Education for All that was held in Jomtien in 1990, many countries still experience severe shortages of teaching personnel and continue to face the challenge to train large numbers of new teachers at low costs and with few monetary incentives for retaining them. These continuing challenges form part of the concerns expressed, and the policy proposals for meeting them, at the World Education Forum held in Dakar in 2000.

Changes in pupil/teacher ratios

The ratio of pupils to teachers, which needs to be distinguished from class sizes, represents an important indicator of the resources countries devote to education. Since pupil/teacher ratios are broadly correlated with levels of GNP per capita decreasing the pupil/teacher ratios proves to be very difficult for some countries in the less developed regions even in situations where these ratios are clearly excessive. Where countries face increasing constraints on education budgets, the decision to increase or decrease pupil/teaching staff ratios needs to be weighted against the goals of raising access to education, providing competitive teachers' salaries, or investing in school infrastructures, equipment and supplies. At a global level, pupil/teacher ratios range, between countries, from 9:1 to 72:1 Pupil/teacher ratios in primary education vary greatly throughout the world from a low of nine students per teacher to a high of 72 students per teacher.

In 1998, three quarters of the 79 countries supplying these statistics for the 2000 EFA Assessment reported pupil/teacher ratios below 37:1, the number of such countries having slightly diminished since 1990. Over the same period, the number of countries reporting pupil/teacher ratios above 50:1 increased slightly, representing now around 11 per cent of the countries for which data are available. Teaching staff ratios by level of education in the OECD countries and the countries participating in the OECD/UNESCO World Education Indicators programme (WEI). The ratios are obtained by dividing the number of full-time equivalent students at a given level of education by the number of full-time equivalent teachers at that same level and in the same type of institution.

In general, higher levels of education witness lower student/teaching staff ratios The ratio of students to teaching staff at the primary and lower secondary levels varies considerably even across the group of OECD countries, ranging from 11 students per teacher in Denmark and Hungary to 32 in the Republic of Korea at the primary level, from ten in Austria to 35 in Mexico at the lower secondary level, and from ten in Norway to 27 in Mexico at the upper secondary level.

In general, the ratio of students to teaching staff ratio declines as the level of education rises. In the countries participating in the WEI project, student/ teaching staff ratios are on average higher than in the OECD countries. The average ratio of student to teaching staff exceeds 34 students per teacher in the Philippines and Zimbabwe at the primary education level and in Mexico and Brazil at the lower and upper secondary education levels, respectively. The relative position of countries for this indicator tends to remain fairly similar both for primary and secondary education in OECD countries, while larger differences in the student/teaching staff ratios between the primary and the secondary levels are found in the developing countries included in this comparison.

These differences may indicate differences in the relative importance that countries pay to student access to teaching staff at a particular level of education, but they may also reflect delays in the adaptation of the teaching force to changing demographic conditions, changes in demand for education at certain levels, or differences in teaching hours for teachers at the different levels of education.

In developing countries pupil/teacher ratios are twice as large as in developed ones. In the less developed regions, pupil/teacher ratios in primary schools are more than twice as large as those in the industrialized countries, while in the least developed countries they are nearly three times as large. In some cases, the regional averages hide large variations between countries and over time. In sub-Saharan Africa, pupil/teacher ratios ranged in 1997 from less than 30 students per teacher in countries such as Botswana, Cape Verde, Ghana and Mauritania, up to more than 50 students per teacher in countries such as Benin, Central African Republic (77:1 in 1990), Chad (67:1), Congo (70:1), Gabon, Malawi, Mali (70:1), Mozambique and Senegal. Average values of the order of 70:1 mean that in these countries there are cases of more than 100 pupils per teacher. In some of these countries the situation deteriorated after 1990, such as for example in Benin, where the estimated pupil/teacher ratio grew from 36 to 56 between 1990 and 1997, and in Mali where the pupil/teacher ratio went from 47 to 71 during the same period.

In other countries, conversely, the pupil/ teacher ratio decreased significantly after 1990, such as for example in

Burundi, where it went from 67 to 50 students per teacher between 1990 and 1997, and in Togo, where it went from 58 to 46. In Southern Asia, Afghanistan and India stand out having an estimated ratio of 58 and 47 students per teacher respectively, in 1997. High pupil/teacher ratios, in some countries, are associated with double or even triple shifts of pupils during the day in the same school premises and with the same teacher. While allowing reductions in both the costs of school facilities and equipment and the costs of housing and training teachers, this has increased the burden on teachers and raises questions of the quality of education dispensed in such situations. High pupil/teacher ratios are associated with high rates of dropout in developing countries In many developing countries, high pupil/teacher ratios are among the factors associated with high dropout rates. This demonstrates the inextricable relationship between quantity and quality, so that where the quality of the provision deteriorates, enrolment levels tend to decline.

Conversely, a decline in pupil/teacher ratios may indicate improvements in quality, provided that it is accompanied by increasing or stable enrolment ratios and low rates of repetition and dropout. An analysis of the demographic composition of the teaching force can provide important insights into the state of the teaching profession. The following analysis focuses on two demographic variables, the age profile of teachers and the proportion of women teachers at different levels of education. The employment status of teachers is also considered.

Age profile

The age profile of the teaching force reflects not only the supply of teachers and the rate of renewal of the teaching force, but also provides a proxy for teaching experience. For countries with a very young teaching force, questions related to experience, staff turnover and guidance arise, while for countries with large numbers of teachers in their forties or fifties there are implications for future teacher shortages, and other questions of how to adapt teacher qualifications to changes in demand arise, not least in the rapidly changing area of information and communications technology (ICT). Finally, countries with large numbers of older teachers reaching retirement age need to be concerned with forward planning of teaching staff requirements. The age profile of teachers shows different patterns in relation with the level of development of countries.

In many developed countries the age distribution of teachers is skewed towards the older age groups, particularly at the secondary level, a factor in recent concerns over emerging teacher shortages in these countries as large numbers reach retirement age. Among OECD and other European countries, only Bulgaria, Latvia, Lithuania and Estonia have 50 per cent or more of the teaching force aged below 40 at the primary level. Germany and Sweden have a relatively old teaching staff at the primary level, with over 70 per cent of teachers over the age of 40. The percentage of teachers under the age of 30 ranges from around a fourth in Luxembourg and the Slovak Republic to less than a tenth in Germany and Italy. At the upper secondary level, the pattern is similar in most countries, although teachers at this level tend to be older than primary teachers in Belgium, Finland, Italy, the Netherlands and Switzerland. Cross-country differences in the proportion of young teachers, as well as differences between levels of education within countries, can be explained, in part, by the typical completion age of pre-service teacher education and training.

In four out of the eight WEI countries for which comparable data are available, over 30 per cent of primary teachers are under 30 years of age. In Indonesia, over 50 per cent of primary teachers are aged below 30 years. The proportion of younger teachers is large also at both the lower and upper secondary levels, where between 28 and 53 per cent of teachers in all countries except Chile are aged between 30 and 39 years. In China, Indonesia, Jordan and Tunisia, over 70 per cent of both lower and upper secondary teachers are under 40. A separate compilation of 14 countries from Africa, Latin America and Asia drawn from International Bureau of Education (IBE) data in the mid-1990s confirm this pattern: primary and secondary teachers under 40 ranged from over 60 per cent in Argentina to almost 90 per cent in Jordan. A smaller proportion of teachers fall into the 40 to 49 year-old age group, while up to 5 per cent of teachers are in the over 60 category in Chile and Israel. The large proportion of young teachers in these countries indicates the shortage of experienced teachers encountered in countries that are rapidly expanding enrolment and implies a need for systems of guidance and supervision. It also implies currently lower wage-bills, where average salaries increase with the ageing of teaching forces and their moving up the salary scale. In this respect, it has been observed that countries with fewer teachers in the older age groups, such as Brazil and Jordan, provide higher monetary incentives to the most experienced teachers, while countries with older teaching forces, such as the Philippines, pay relatively lower premiums to experienced teachers.

The proportion of teachers under 30 years of age is very high in some of the least developed countries, where there tend to be very few experienced teachers The proportion of younger teachers is highest in many of the least developed countries. In eight out of 14 countries that participated in a study on the conditions of primary school in the least developed countries, more than 45 per cent of the teaching force was aged 30 years or younger. In Bhutan, Burkina Faso, Cape Verde, Ethiopia and the Maldives the percentage of teachers aged 30 or younger ranged between 55 and 65 per cent. Several factors may contribute to this, including demographic growth and the expansion of enrolment in recent years, unattractive working conditions of teachers leading to high rates of early departures from the teaching profession for better paid jobs and a generally lower average life expectancy, including—more recently—the high rate of mortality among teachers due to AIDS in sub-Saharan Africa.

Gender profile

The percentage of female teachers varies considerably across the world. However, it rose in all regions during the 1990s, continuing the trend observed during the 1980s. In general, the education sector is a more important source of employment for women than for men in developed countries, influenced by opportunities to combine employment and family responsibilities and better pay rates and career advancement potential relative to other occupations, whereas the opposite is often true in developing countries. The countries where teaching is still mainly a male profession are mostly in sub-Saharan Africa and in South Asia, although also in these regions the 1990s marked a move towards slightly higher percentages of female teachers. Women generally outnumber men as teachers at the lower levels of education, which have traditionally been associated with a lower level of pre-appointment qualifications and lower salaries, although the trend is towards a reduction of these differences, especially in developed countries.

In all regions, except the Arab States and Southern Asia, more than nine out of ten teachers at the pre-primary level are women. The proportion of female teachers is also very high at the primary level in the developed regions, the countries in transition and Latin America and Caribbean, whereas in the others, typically less developed regions, it is about 50 per cent or less. In general, it is in the regions where girls' access to school is lower (sub-Saharan Africa and Southern Asia in particular) that the percentage of female teachers is lowest, and in some sub-Saharan countries actually declining. At the secondary level, female teachers represent approximately half or more of the teaching force in the more developed regions and countries in transition and between 30 and 40 per cent in the less developed ones. In most of the developing regions, the trend was towards higher percentages of female teachers at all levels of education between 1990 and 1998, the largest increase being recorded in the Arab States where the proportion of pre-primary female teachers increased by 16 percentage points during this period. In some countries, higher access of women to the teaching profession, especially at the basic levels, has been encouraged as a measure to increase enrolment of girls in regions with persisting gender disparities.

In the OECD countries, pre-primary and primary teachers are predominantly women, with 65 per cent or more female primary teachers in all countries except Denmark and Luxembourg. In secondary education the percentages of male and female teachers show a greater level of similarity, and men outnumber women in vocational upper secondary education in most countries.

At the tertiary level, which is generally associated with much higher salary levels and professional status, male teachers make up the majority in all countries for which data are available. The breakdown of the percentage of women by age bands gives an indication of the trend in the "feminization" of the teaching forces.

In most OECD countries, the proportion of women is higher among younger teachers In almost all OECD countries for which comparable data are available, the percentage of women is higher among younger teachers than among older ones. The Republic of Korea is the OECD country where the feminization of the teaching force proceeded at the fastest pace: the proportion of women among teachers aged under 30 is 45 percentage points higher than among those aged 50-59 years at all levels of education. Other countries that have a higher proportion of women in younger groups of teachers include the Netherlands, Belgium and Germany at the primary level (with differences among age groups that range between 22 and 27 percentage points) and Austria, Germany, and the Netherlands at the secondary level (with differences ranging between 30 and 33 percentage points).

Among the countries participating in the WEI programme, the highest increases in the proportion of women teachers are observed in China and Malaysia at the primary level and in Jordan and China at the upper secondary level. These data, however, do not permit to establish whether the lower percentage of women at the older age groups is exclusively due to the feminization of the teaching force, or to the fact that women may be inclined to leave the profession more easily as a result of different life-cycle events, such as marriages, child rearing, etc.

The access of women to directing positions in schools is one of the indicators of gender disparities in the education sector and in the labour force in general. Despite the increasing feminization of the teaching profession, women are still underrepresented in management positions in schools in the majority of countries. A survey on gender differences in education in the EU countries revealed that women were far less likely than men to hold directing positions. Only pre-primary schools that are separate from primary schools are largely under the responsibility of women. Both in 1985-86 and 1992-93 the percentage of women heads was much lower than that of female teachers. Only in Scotland did it exceed 50 per cent at the primary level. At the secondary level the percentage of women heads was even lower, with less than one-third of such positions occupied by women, except in Ireland (42 per cent in 1993).

However, in all countries supplying data except Belgium and, at the secondary level, Scotland, the percentage of women heads increased between 1985 and 1993. Data reported for 1994-95 revealed continued incremental gains at both primary and secondary levels in a number of European countries. Noting similar patterns in these other OECD countries, many factors may be playing a part in these patterns, including turnover rates, age profiles of head teachers, changing status of such positions which reduce attractiveness for men, and increases or decreases in the number of schools.

The trend towards greater prevalence of women in management positions (including both heads and deputy heads) is confirmed by ILO data on a larger selection of countries from all income groups. In all countries that reported data, except Egypt, Jordan and Syria, the proportion of women managers in primary education increased between 1985 and 1994 and in some countries the increases were considerable.

In various high- and middle-income countries the percentage of women in directing positions was over 60 per cent in 1994. A similar trend is reported at the secondary level, where the increase in the proportion of women among school heads and deputy heads is positively correlated with the increase in the proportion of women teachers. However, women managers remain severely under-represented in some high income countries (such as Australia, Cyprus, Denmark and Republic of Korea) and in most low-income countries reporting data.

Full-time and part-time teachers

The proportion of teachers working on a part-time basis can be an indication of the relative flexibility of the education labour market, of which the public sector has the largest share. In all European and OECD countries for which comparable data are available, the majority of teachers are under full-time contracts. On average, less than one in five teachers works part time at the primary and secondary levels taken together. In some countries the trend is upward, but this is by no means universal. The proportion of teachers working part time varies considerably among European countries and by level of education, with typically a higher incidence of part-time work at higher levels of education. While in Italy all teachers are employed full time at all levels of education, in Sweden the percentage of part-time teachers at the upper secondary level makes up 74 per cent of the teaching force and in the Netherlands 59 per cent. In Germany and the Netherlands, however, 54 per cent of primary teachers work part time.

The majority of part-time teachers are women at the lower levels of education The majority of teachers who are employed part time are women at the primary and lower secondary levels while the distribution is more even at the upper secondary level. Although this reflects the gender composition of the total teaching force, the gender gap among the part-time teaching staff is even higher than among teaching staff employed on a full-time basis. Nevertheless, review of OECD data suggests that there is a clear-cut relation between the degree of feminization and the proportion of teaching jobs that are part time, in either primary or secondary education. Large variations in the proportion of part-time teachers are also found among WEI countries. Among these countries, part-time teachers are not reported in Jordan, the Russian Federation and Zimbabwe, while in Argentina they represent from 75 to more than 90 per cent of the teaching staff depending on the level of education. However, in some developing countries, high percentages of part-time teachers may be due to the fact that many teachers teach in more than one school, often a public one and a private one, because of the very low level of their public salaries. In the three countries with the overall highest percentage of part-time teachers, that is Argentina, Indonesia and the Philippines, the highest proportion of part-time teachers is at the pre-primary education level, while in Chile part-time teachers represent more than 20 per cent of the teaching staff at the upper secondary level.

Pre-service Qualifications and Professional Development

Pre-service subject matter knowledge and skills and professional training, "acquired and maintained through rigorous and continuing study", are both essential prerequisites for an effective teaching force. The CEART has continuously upheld the validity of these principles for an effective teaching profession and quality education.

The qualification required for entry into the teaching profession is often used as a proxy for the quality of the educational inputs. Qualification requirements are also a key policy lever for governments to influence the quality of instructional delivery. In general, it is important to distinguish between academic training (i.e. subject-matter instruction) and professional training (i.e. pedagogical instruction), which is often combined with periods of work experience. The ILO/UNESCO Recommendation considered the completion of secondary education and some professional training as the minimum qualification level for prospective teachers. Since then, there has been a worldwide trend towards the generalization of pre-service teacher training at the level of tertiary education, either in university or non-university equivalent level institutions. This trend has been reflected in international recommendations on appropriate levels of training and professional development which advocate as a minimum a first-level university degree or its equivalent. However, there are still differences among countries as to their position in respect to this trend, depending on their stage of development and of that of their education systems.

Fairly detailed and comparable data on the preservice training requirements for teachers are available for the OECD countries, other European countries outside the OECD, and the developing countries participating in the OECD/UNESCO World Education Indicators programme. These data include information on the number of full-time equivalent years of teacher training formally required to become a fully qualified teacher for each educational level taught, the type of educational qualification obtained and the organization of professional training.

In the OECD, the duration of pre-service training for primary teachers varies from three years in Austria, Belgium, and Spain to five-and-a-half years in Germany. For lower secondary teachers, the duration of pre-service training is higher than that for primary teachers in just above half of the countries, whereas it remains the same for all other countries. Pre-service training requirements for teachers at the upper secondary level are higher than those for teachers at the primary level in all countries except Australia, the United Kingdom and the United States, where training requirements are the same at all levels of education. Among the countries where the requirements for lower secondary teachers are already higher than for primary teachers, most do not require additional study time for the upper secondary level. Exceptions to this pattern are Austria and Germany, where requirements differ between all three levels. The average duration of training for upper secondary general teachers ranges from a minimum of three and a half years in Australia to six years or more in Germany, Spain and Italy. New primary teachers must earn a tertiary qualification in all developed countries and many countries in transition At the primary level of education and beyond, a tertiary qualification is required for entry to the teaching profession in all OECD countries as well as in the EU pre-accession countries for which comparable data are available.

In Austria, Belgium, Denmark, and Hungary an ISCED 5B qualification is required for entry to the profession at both the primary and the lower secondary level of education, while in Portugal, Bulgaria, Lithuania and Poland a Tertiary-type B qualification is only sufficient at the primary level. For entry to teaching at the upper secondary level of education, an ISCED 5A qualification is required in each of the countries presented here. With the exception of Denmark and some groups of teachers in Austria, an ISCED 5A qualification is also required for new teachers in upper secondary vocational programmes. Also all WEI countries train their teachers at tertiary level A tertiary qualification is required also in all WEI countries for entry into the teaching profession at all levels of education. The only partial exceptions are Brazil and Paraguay, where primary teachers have the choice of a secondary-level programme leading to an ISCED 3 qualification, or tertiary-level training. In Brazil, this secondary-level programme will however disappear by 2007.

In some countries, primary to upper secondary teachers have the same qualification requirements, such as in Uruguay, and in Chile, the Philippines and the Russian Federation. In other countries, secondary teachers have higher qualification requirements, such as in Brazil and Malaysia. In other countries yet, such as in Indonesia, Peru and Thailand, prospective teachers at all levels of education are allowed to complete their training by means of different paths leading to either ISCED 5B or ISCED 5A qualifications. Finally, while all WEI countries, like OECD ones, generally train their teachers at the tertiary level, the duration of the preservice training is usually shorter in WEI countries than in OECD ones, especially at the upper secondary level. In general, the length of the overall teacher training can also be affected by whether professional training occurs concurrently with subject-matter instruction, or consecutive, i.e. following the subject-matter course.

In most countries, the consecutive organization of training tends to take longer than the concurrent one. For teachers at the primary and lower secondary levels of education, the concurrent model of pre-service training is adopted in all OECD countries except in France, where pre-service training is organized according to the consecutive model, and in New Zealand, the United Kingdom and Ireland, where professional training can be either concurrent with or follow the completion of subject-matter studies. For teachers at the upper secondary (general) level, the organization of pre-service training varies more widely between countries. In Austria, Denmark, France, Ireland, Italy, the Netherlands, Norway and Spain, pre-service training is usually organized according to the consecutive model, while in Australia, the Czech Republic, Finland, Germany, Greece, Portugal and the United States it is usually concurrent. In Belgium, Hungary, New Zealand, Turkey and the United Kingdom, pre-service training can follow either models.

Current pre-service requirements cannot serve as a proxy for the qualifications held by the existing teaching force. Pre-service teaching requirements have, in fact, changed substantially in many countries over the years, as it can be seen from the description of initial teacher training in the EU countries during the 20th century.

One-third of the 83 countries that provided data on teacher qualification for the Year 2000 EFA Assessment reported that all of their primary teachers had at least the minimum academic qualifications required by national authorities for teaching in primary education and eleven of these countries reported that their teachers had all received the minimum teacher training required. However, since both indicators are based on minimum national qualification and training standards, care should be taken in comparing countries, as these standards may vary greatly between countries. The academic qualification rates of teachers reported were often higher than teacher training rates.

Some countries indicated that in order to meet the increasing demand for teachers in line with the rise in primary school enrolment rates, they had placed higher priority on recruiting staff with relevant academic qualifications, than on expanding the teacher training provision in their countries. In at least half of the countries of almost all world regions more than 90 per cent of teachers meet the nationally defined academic qualification In almost all regions of the world the median proportions of teachers with the required academic qualifications were higher than 90 per cent, except in South and West Asia where it was .82 per cent. The median proportions of teachers reported to have received the minimum training required were around the same level in Central Asia, Central and Eastern Europe, and East Asia and the Pacific.

In South and West Asia, sub-Saharan Africa and Latin America and the Pacific the rates were between 70 per cent and 80 per cent on average. However, in order to compare the level of qualification and training of the teaching force across countries, the level and length of the education and training course that corresponds to the required qualification in the countries concerned would have to be taken into account which is not generally possible. One cross-national study that collected information on the level of education of current teachers is the Third International Mathematics and Science Study (TIMSS).

The mathematics and science teachers of eighth-grade students provided information on their level of education.

While the qualifications of mathematics teachers are not necessarily representative of the level of qualification of all teachers, this indicator does show the range of qualifications held by both new and experienced teachers in an important subject area. In nine out of 16 countries, over 90 per cent of the students are taught by mathematics teachers holding a bachelor's or higher degree. Most teachers of eighthgrade mathematics students have at least some formal teacher training as part of their educational qualifications.

Indicators programme, where in general the majority of teachers have obtained tertiary qualifications and undertaken some teacher training. In some countries there are, however, large variations between levels of education. All primary teachers have a tertiary qualification in Jordan and the Philippines, while these are less than two out of ten in China and Tunisia In ten out of 13 of the WEI countries, 90 per cent or more of the upper secondary teachers have a higher education qualification, their percentage being lower only in Argentina, Egypt and Peru.

At the primary level, conversely, the number of countries with 90 percent or more of tertiary qualified teachers decreases to five. Brazil, China, Egypt and Tunisia are the countries with the largest variations in the level of qualification of the teaching force by level of education: the percentage of primary education teachers holding a tertiary qualification in these countries ranges between 13 and 23 per cent.

In many of the least developed countries the majority of primary teachers have at most a lower secondary qualification However, there are a number of countries in the developing world that are still suffering severe shortages of qualified teaching staff. A survey sponsored by UNESCO and UNICEF on the conditions of primary schools in the least developed countries collected data on this from 14 countries. In Cape Verde and the United Republic of Tanzania over 60 per cent of primary school teachers had obtained only a primary qualification in 1995, while in Benin, Burkina Faso, Equatorial Guinea, Togo and Uganda most teachers had obtained a lower secondary qualification. In Ethiopia and Zambia over half of the staff had an upper secondary qualification. In Cape Verde, Togo and Uganda, some 30 to 50 per cent of the teachers had received no professional training. These data, together with those on the educational background of teachers, give an idea of the massive effort made in these countries to rapidly expand enrolment, employing primary or lower secondary school leavers with no professional preparation as teachers. Although the sample sizes do not allow for generalizations, these results give an indication of the kind of problems faced by these countries and the distance that remains to be covered to ensure that all teachers in the developing world have an upper secondary qualification and one or two years of professional training.

The role of professional development

In-service training, continuing and further education, and the upgrading of teachers are different terms used to refer to teachers' continuing professional development. Although the main focus of teacher education in most countries continues to be on pre-service training, the need for in-service updating and renewing of knowledge, skills and capabilities is now widely acknowledged. In developed countries the age structure of the teacher population indicates that, for the majority of teachers, 15 to 20 years have passed since they received their initial training. In developing countries substantive proportions of teachers have received virtually no training. Beyond these considerations, the pace of change in the knowledge and skills needed by students and the rapid development of the technology of education suggests that continuing professional development must be a priority for educational policy. Unfortunately, there is little comparative information available. A recent review by the Centre for Education Research and Innovation (CERI) examined developments in eight countries, noting some shifts from individual career-oriented training towards whole school development activities. It was observed that much professional training was fragmented, not sufficiently focused on the real needs and interests of teachers, and perceived by teachers as a top-down offer rather than as a participatory continuing education enterprise.

Where in-service training is obligatory, Scotland provides teachers with 50 hours of training during the school year plus five days outside the school year. In Sweden and in Finland teachers have five and three days per year respectively of in-service training. In Greece, the initial training is extended by in-service training in which teachers have to take part three or four time during their career, every five or six years. In the other EU countries in-service training is generally on a voluntary basis, except in the case of individual promotion or reforms requiring particular training. While it is difficult to measure the availability of inservice teacher training programmes or their acceptance and use by teachers, the financial resources invested in these provide another way to assess their volume and importance. In none of the European countries supplying data does the spending share for in-service training exceed 2 per cent, while in some cases it was much lower than 1 per cent. Although these figures suggest that investment in serving teaching staff still is of low priority for formal in-service teacher training programmes, other evidence needs to be taken into account, including the ways teachers spend their working time, in order to assess whether low costs are not due to a successful integration of the professional learning of teachers into the day-to-day operation of schools.

In the developing world, where substantial proportions of teachers do not meet newly introduced qualification and training requirements, in-service training is mainly aimed at upgrading teachers' qualifications and has a significant impact on educational budgets. Not all of this upgrading, however, takes place in educational institutions, as distance education is one of the approaches often used for this purpose. The preparedness of governments to invest in the ongoing development of their teachers, through a coherent system of educational provision and incentives, as well as the willingness of individual teachers to invest in their own development, will be important for improving the quality of education.

Teachers Working Conditions

There is a clear link between the status of teachers and their working conditions, particularly their salaries and employment profiles. One of the guiding principles stated in the ILO/UNESCO Recommendation is that working conditions should be such that they will enable teachers to concentrate on their professional tasks, and promote effective learning by students. In particular, salaries should provide teachers with the means to ensure a reasonable standard of living and to invest in further professional development. They should also reflect the importance of the teaching function and take into account the qualification and experience required by teachers together with the responsibility they carry. Moreover they should compare positively with salaries paid in other occupations requiring similar qualifications.

Working time and teaching time

A teacher's contractual working time includes all working hours specified in the teacher's contract or conditions of service. It includes the statutory hours devoted to actual teaching as well as the statutory hours (when specified) devoted to teaching- related activities, such as lesson preparation, correction, in-service training, staff meetings, student support and extracurricular activities. Contractual working time represents an important element of teachers' working conditions and, together with class sizes, provides a measure of the workload of teachers. Besides, together with factors such as student/ teaching staff ratios, students' hours of instruction and teachers' salaries, the amount of time teachers spend teaching and working outside the classroom influences the financial resources which have to be devoted to education. Governments paying teachers relatively high salaries may choose to impose greater workloads on teachers. Conversely, governments may limit teachers' workloads in order to attract people to a profession that might not be well paid. Other options include holding down salary increases so as to maintain levels of employment in times of austerity.

Working patterns of teachers vary widely between countries, making it difficult to undertake international comparisons. In some countries, only teaching time is fixed and it is assumed that teachers will accomplish other duties without prescribing the time to be spent on these in their contracts. In other countries, teachers are also formally required to spend some time every day/week working on non-teaching activities. This nonteaching time can be devoted to activities such as the preparation of lessons, correction of assignments and tests, professional development, support of students, and meetings with parents. In still other countries, teachers are required to be at school for a mandatory number of hours each week but the organization of this time is specified at the school level. In general, the non-instructional component of teachers' work has been estimated to account for between 10 and 50 per cent of a week's work in European countries. While teachers' working time is not directly comparable across these organizational models, data on working time can give an indication of the level of effort formally required of teachers in different countries.

In Eritrea, Cambodia and Nicaragua primary teachers work 48 hours per week, which corresponds to the number of hours of three working weeks in Kyrgyzstan and Bolivia. In six out of 70 countries, teachers' statutory working time is lower than 20 hours per week, while in nine countries teachers are required to work more than 40 hours per week. These considerable variations in the workload of teachers are presumably due to the fact that, in the first group of countries, working time may not expressly include non-teaching activities, while in the second group of countries, the time to be spent on non-teaching activities may be prescribed in the contract or conditions of service of teachers. This, in turn, confirms the difficulty of comparing teachers' working time across countries. In some countries the number of specified working hours per week changed during the 1990s, decreasing by between three and 10 hours per week in six countries and increasing by between one and five hours per week in five countries. In most of the countries the contractual weekly workload of teachers did not change, confirming the results of the 1996 International Labour Organisation (ILO) survey on working hours trends.

Comparisons of working time to teaching time across countries are useful to explain, at least in part, variations in working time and the organization of the latter. Teaching time is relatively uniform across EU countries, while the largest variations in working time are determined by the time prescribed for non-teaching duties According to Euridyce data, most countries have some statutory time allocated to nonteaching activities in the school. In the case of England and Ireland (at the primary level), the working time allocated to teaching and other activities is specified by school heads, whereas in the other countries there is a statutory specification of how the working time of teachers is organized between teaching and other duties. While teaching time is relatively uniform across countries, variation between countries in the total annual time that teachers are formally expected to work is primarily determined by the amount of time prescribed for non-teaching activities. At the secondary level, the shortest working time is found in Luxembourg, France, Belgium, Ireland and Germany, where full-time teachers are only required to be at school for the specified number of teaching hours.

Conversely, the longest working hours are in Denmark, the Netherlands, Austria and Spain, where the load of formal non-teaching working time is the heaviest at all levels of education. An alternative source of information on teaching and working time comes from the Third International Mathematics and Science Study (TIMSS), where the mathematics teachers of eighth-grade students were asked about the weekly amount of time that they had formally prescribed to them for teaching and for nonteaching activities. The total scheduled time of eighthgrade mathematics teachers varies between 13 hours in Hungary and 28 hours in the Republic of Korea. In Belgium, Ireland and Norway, teachers of eighth-grade mathematics students reported that they spent less than two hours per week of formally scheduled time, on average, on non-teaching activities, while in the Czech Republic, Hungary, Japan, the Republic of Korea and the United States teachers spent ten hours or more. The latter countries, along with Canada and Sweden, tend to have the largest proportion of formally scheduled time devoted to curriculum planning. In most countries non-teaching time is devoted to the supervision of students.

Teaching hours refer to the statutory time teachers are required to teach. The number of teaching hours per week provides an indication of the teaching load of a teacher in a typical working week, although it does not allow comparison with the overall teaching load. A lighter weekly workload may be coupled, with a longer working year, while a high number of teaching hours per week may be compensated by longer holidays. The weekly teaching load varies widely from a low of 18 hours for both primary and lower secondary teachers in Saudi Arabia to a high of 36 hours for primary teachers in Bangladesh and 25 hours for secondary teachers in Ghana. These variations are confirmed by data on the statutory annual teaching time in the OECD countries and the developing countries participating in the OECD/UNESCO World Education Indicators programme. At all levels of education there are wide variations between countries in the number of teaching hours per year. Teachers in Australia, the Philippines, Sri Lanka and United States spend almost twice as much time teaching (950 hours or more) as do teachers in Hungary at all levels of education and those in the Republic of Korea, Spain, Tunisia and Turkey at the secondary level, where the number of teaching hours per year is comparatively low (around 580 hours or less). While

In almost all OECD countries (except Mexico and the United States), teaching hours are higher in primary education than in secondary education. In the OECD countries, the average number of teaching hours in primary education is 801, in contrast to 716 hours in lower secondary education, 662 in general upper secondary education and 692 in vocational upper secondary education. In the developing countries participating in the WEI programme, teaching hours are, on average, slightly higher and, unlike the situation in the OECD countries, they remain the same between primary and upper secondary education in two-thirds of the WEI countries and even increase in Argentina, Paraguay and, to a lesser extent, Malaysia. One explanation for this pattern is that, given the high costs of training teachers for higher levels of education, developing countries need to ensure that they maximize the returns to this investment. Trend data suggest that teaching time was relatively stable during the 1990s OECD data show that the annual teaching load of secondary teachers did not change substantially between 1990 and 1996, confirming ILO trend data on a larger selection of countries. Within the OECD, the largest changes were reported at the lower secondary level, in Belgium (French-speaking community) where annual teaching time increased by 17 per cent, and Portugal, where it decreased by 12 per cent.

Class size

Class size is a measure of the average number of students in a teacher's classroom during a school period and represents an important indicator of the working conditions of teachers, as well as the learning conditions of students. Smaller classes are valued because they may allow students to receive more individual attention from their teachers. Significant reductions in class size have sometimes been shown to be related to gains in achievement but there is no conclusive evidence that reducing class sizes is always the most effective policy option for improving students' achievement. Lately it has been pointed out that smaller classes do make a difference in pre-primary and initial primary education and have had positive results for low-income and minority children in some countries. In general, the effect of class size should not be considered in isolation but in relation to changes in teaching methods and classroom organization; recent research in the United States has noted better teacher/student interaction, reduced disciplinary problems, and more group and overall instruction time in smaller classes.

Shifting the focus from cognitive outcomes to social and affective ones, research indicates that the main effect of smaller classes often relates to gains in teacher attitudes and instructional behaviours, and there is evidence that both teachers' and learners' stress is less in small classes. At the same time, smaller classes are more expensive. There are potential tradeoffs between smaller classes on the one hand and the instruction time that can be devoted to each student, the teaching load for teachers, and costs on the other. Given differences in the organization of instruction, it is very difficult to obtain direct estimates of class sizes. Often pupil/teacher ratios, which can be more readily obtained from existing data and for a wider range of countries, are used as a proxy for class-size, although the relationship between the two measures is complicated by teacher workload, instruction time for students and other institutional and instructional factors. Pupil/teacher ratios are generally much lower than average class sizes, as in many countries a considerable proportion of the teaching staff is not actually allocated to teaching or is employed on a part-time basis. Pupil/teacher ratios may also be higher than class sizes, as for example in systems with multiple shifts of students taught by the same teacher. Therefore, while the pupil/teacher ratio is an important indicator of the resources that countries devote to education and, at times, a proxy for measuring educational quality, it is less suitable for measuring teachers' working conditions.

In the case of mathematics instruction, the IEA Third International Mathematics and Science Study (TIMSS) provides a direct estimate of class sizes for fourth-grade and eighth-grade students in almost 40 countries. In most participating countries, the average size of eighth-grade mathematics classes is smaller than 30 students. In 22 out of 38 countries that participated in TIMSS 1999, eighth-grade mathematics classes are less than 30 students. The smallest classes, with less than 20 students, are in Finland and Belgium (Flemish-speaking), while the largest ones are in the Philippines and South Africa, where students are, on average, in classes 2.5 times larger than in the former cases. Other countries with more than 40 students per class are the Islamic Republic of Iran, Turkey, the Republic of Korea and Thailand. An analysis of class sizes in middle- and low-income countries from data collected by the International Bureau of Education (IBE) shows that class sizes remain large in most developing countries.

In all countries, the smallest classes are in pre-primary education, which may reflect the largely private nature of early childhood education in most developing countries as well the limitations posed by the child-caring function at this level. In primary and secondary education average class sizes remain large, above 40 or 50 students per class, in virtually all low-income countries and some middle-income ones. In developing countries, class sizes in different grades are affected by the internal inefficiency of education systems, due to high rates of repetition and dropout and low survival rates. In Southern Asia, Latin America and the Caribbean and Africa South of the Sahara, less than three out of four pupils reach grade 5. In the least developed countries taken together the proportion is even lower, with only around half of the pupils remaining in school after grade 4. Indeed, many students drop out between the first and second grade. This situation results in overcrowded classes at the first grades of primary school that become progressively smaller at higher grades.

The UNESCO and UNICEF study on the conditions of primary schools in the least developed countries gives an idea of the magnitude of the decrease of class sizes in subsequent grades of primary school. Class sizes averaged at the primary education level hide these variations and the sometimes extremely difficult working conditions of teachers in the first grades. In Uganda, Togo, Madagascar, Nepal and Ethiopia, which are among the countries with the highest number of students per class in grade 1, class sizes in grade 5 or 6 are half that in grade 1. Indirect estimates of class sizes can also be used. One approach is to estimate class size as the average per country of the total number of students per school divided by total number of classes per school. Another approach is to estimate class size as the student/teaching staff ratio multiplied by the intended student instruction time and divided by the statutory average number of teaching hours. This measure is equivalent to weighting each class by the number of hours for which it meets during the year and it can be used as a proxy for class size if the assumption is made that all classroom teachers are fully occupied with teaching duties.

Estimated class sizes in lower secondary school range from 50 to 12 students per class. Based on these estimates, a class in Mexico, with 50 students, comprises the number of students of four classes in Belgium. All the countries participating in the OECD/UNESCO World Education Indicators programme for which data are available are at the high end of the scale, confirming the difficulty of lowering class sizes in developing countries, although in some countries, such as Peru and Uruguay, the estimated average number of students per class size is below 25. At the other end of the scale there are countries such as Australia, Belgium (Flemish-speaking), Finland, Norway and Switzerland, where there are not more than 15 students per class on average, based on this estimate.

Teachers' salaries

Teachers' salaries can be assumed to relate closely to the quality of the teaching force. The level of teachers' salaries can affect both the decisions of qualified individuals to enter the teaching profession and the retention of current teachers. The relative level of teachers' salaries can thus have an important impact on the composition and quality of the teaching force, affect the ability of education systems to recruit better than average individuals and retain the most skilled teachers. At the same time, the pressure to improve the quality of education is often under tight fiscal constraints and teachers' salaries and allowances are the single largest factor in the cost of providing education, accounting for two-thirds or more of public expenditure on education in most countries. OECD data permit comparisons with the annual statutory salaries at the beginning of the career, after 15 years of experience and at the top of the scale of teachers with the minimum level of qualifications required to be certified as a teacher of public primary and secondary education. Statutory salaries, which refer to scheduled salaries according to official pay scales, should be distinguished from the actual wage bills incurred by governments and the average salaries of teachers because they are not affected by the age composition of the teaching force and are more comparable across countries.

There are significant differences between countries in the salaries they pay their teachers. In the OECD, annual statutory salaries of public primary schoolteachers with 15 years' experience and the minimum training required range from below US$10,000 in the Czech Republic and Hungary to over US$40,000 in Switzerland, with an average of US$27,525. A primary teacher in Switzerland, the country with the highest statutory salary with 15 years' experience, is paid more than five times as much as a primary teacher in Hungary where the statutory starting salary is lowest, and more than four times as much as a primary teacher in the Czech Republic, even after adjusting for purchasing power parities. Other countries where the statutory salary of teachers with 15 years of experience is more than US$2,000 lower than the OECD country average are Greece, Finland, Iceland, Italy, Mexico, Sweden and Turkey as well as all WEI developing countries for which comparable data are available. This difference has of course a large impact on the variation in education costs per student.

Statutory salaries for teachers relative to per capita GDP provide some indication of the economic status of the teaching profession and the extent to which a country invests in teaching resources, relative to its financial capacity. Trend data show that, despite increases in teachers' salaries in real terms, the position of teachers in relation to average per capita GDP has weakened in the majority of OECD countries. Between 1994 and 1999, mid-career salaries of primary and lower secondary teachers decreased in relation to GDP per capita in all OECD countries reporting data, except Greece and New Zealand.

At the primary level, the OECD average for mid-career salaries relative to GDP per capita was 1.32 in 1999, compared to 1.42 in 1994, and at the lower secondary level this value decreased from 1.50 in 1994 to 1.36 in 1999. In Ireland, the mid-career salary of a lower secondary teacher relative to GDP per capita was 2.23 in 1994, but this value decreased to 1.39 in 1999. In general, minimum salaries are below GDP per capita in EU and OECD countries, while mid-career and maximum salaries are above GDP per capita. Despite the gradual narrowing of the gap between salaries at the beginning and at the end of the career observed in many of the EU countries between 1965 and 1993, an analysis of the current position of salaries relative to GDP per capita in European and OECD countries shows that length of service continues to represent a source of significant differences between teachers' salaries. While only a minority of countries at all levels of education pay initial teachers' salaries at or above GDP per capita, the mid-career and maximum salaries are above GDP per capita in the large majority of countries. When teachers' salaries are compared to national per capita income, many middle- and low-income countries reach positions that are comparable to, or higher than, those in OECD countries.

The ratio of teachers' salaries to GDP per capita reflects patterns of relative productivity that vary greatly between sectors in accordance with a country's level of development. This ratio is generally higher in developing countries than in more developed countries, because of the greater productivity in the service sector than in the rest of the economy. Unlike what happens in the majority of OECD countries, starting salaries for teachers with the minimum requisite qualification are above GDP per capita in seven out of WEI countries at the primary level, and at the secondary level in all countries except Indonesia, Uruguay and Peru.

Mid-career salaries of teachers with the minimum level of training exceed twice the national per capita income in the Philippines, Jordan, the Republic of Korea, Thailand, and Tunisia at all levels of education, in Malaysia for lower and upper secondary teachers, and in Switzerland and Brazil for upper secondary teachers only. In contrast, they are lower than GDP per capita in the Czech Republic, Hungary, Iceland and Norway. While the Czech Republic and Hungary have both relatively low GDP per capita and low teachers' salaries, other countries with low GDP per capita, including Jordan, the Republic of Korea, Thailand, the Philippines, and Spain, have comparatively high teachers' salaries. At the other end of the scale, Norway and the United States, two countries with relatively high GDP per capita, spend a below-average proportion of their wealth on teachers' salaries, while Switzerland spends an above-average proportion of its relatively high GDP per capita on teachers' salaries.

An even more relevant benchmark for the level of teachers' salaries than national per capita income is the earning of other workers, particularly those with equivalent qualifications. Statutory salaries of primary and upper secondary teachers have been compared with the 10th, 50th and 90th percentile of the distribution of gross annual earnings of full-time wage and salary workers in OECD countries. This comparison shows that although primary teachers in most of the reporting countries fare relatively well when compared with other full-time wage and salary workers, teachers in the Czech Republic, Finland, Hungary and Sweden receive comparatively low compensation. The general pattern is similar in secondary schools. In most OECD countries teachers' salaries are lower than those of equally qualified workers. In most of the countries for which data are available, primary teachers' statutory salaries after 15 years' experience are lower than the average earnings of other highly qualified workers, except in New Zealand and, for secondary schoolteachers, France, Germany, Sweden and Switzerland. Teachers' salaries in the Czech Republic and Hungary are at most 40 per cent of the average salaries of university graduates. In interpreting these comparisons, other aspects of working conditions of teachers have to be taken into account, such as teaching loads and total working time compared with those of other professions.

The unfavourable position of teachers in relation to other qualified professionals in both OECD and non-OECD countries has also been noted by the ILO, along with recent efforts made in some countries to establish higher salary scales in relation to other public sector jobs.

Teachers' working conditions are determined not by any of the indicators presented in the previous sections in isolation, but by their combination. When governments decide on their education budgets, they need to make trade-offs between factors such as the level of teachers' salaries, the size of classes, the number of teaching hours required of teachers and the intended instruction time planned for students.

In lower secondary level of education OECD countries has been used as a benchmark to allow comparing national policy choices. The difference between the teacher salary costs per student in each of the countries and the average over all countries has been decomposed into four main components that measure how much (or less) than the average is spent per students on significant determinants of educational costs:

a) the level of the statutory salary for teachers after 15 years of experience;

b) the intended annual hours of instruction for students;

c) the statutory number of teaching hours for which full-time teachers are expected to teach; and

d) class sizes

In Peru teachers are paid the second lowest salaries among the countries considered (US$4,235 per year), while in the Philippines, although teachers' salaries are still at the lower end of the scale, they are paid more than twice as much. However, in the Philippines teachers work longer than average hours (1,176 hours per year) and teach larger classes (50 students), while in Peru the teaching load is below the average (648 hours) and class sizes are at the average level, which reduces the salary disadvantage of teachers but adds to the salary outlays of governments per student.

New Zealand and the Republic of Korea are, with around US$1,700 of annual salary outlays per student, just above the average of countries. But both countries make very different decisions about other aspects of teacher working conditions: while in New Zealand annual teaching hours are, with 930 hours, comparatively high (which reduces the costs per student by US$275) they are, in the Republic of Korea, comparatively low (507 hours), thus increasing salary outlays per student by more than US$600. The converse is true when looking at class sizes.

In the Republic of Korea, class sizes are well above the country average, thus helping to reduce salary outlays per student by almost US$500, while in New Zealand class sizes are below the country average. Switzerland, Austria and Denmark show the highest teacher salary costs per student, with US$4,315, US$2,857, and US$2,814 respectively. In Switzerland, high salary levels are counterbalanced by a comparatively high teaching load (860 hours per year), while in Austria and Denmark, the reverse is true (658 and 644 hours per year). In all three countries, comparatively small classes reduce the workload of teachers but add between US$604 and US$1,086 to salary outlays per student.

In some countries, high teacher statutory salaries are compensated by a high teaching time or larger than average class sizes, while in other countries low salaries are combined with large class sizes and large teaching loads. In Germany, the Republic of Korea, Japan and Switzerland annual statutory salaries are, with between US$38,000 and US$52,000, the highest among the countries compared.

In Switzerland, this effect on salary costs per student is only in part compensated by a larger than average teaching load and in Japan by a lower than average instruction time for students. In the Republic of Korea, the effect of larger than average class sizes reduces the salary level effect by more than half. That is, while teachers in the Republic of Korea are well compensated for their work, they have to cope with very large class sizes. Conversely in Germany, Japan, and Switzerland teachers are not only well remunerated but they also teach classes with fewer students than average, and in the latter country this effect increases the salary outlays per student by more than US$1,000.

In Indonesia, Peru, Uruguay, Hungary and the Czech Republic teacher salary levels are the lowest, between less than US$2,000 and US$9,000. In Indonesia, class sizes are larger than average, which reduces even more the salary cost per student but adds to the workload of teachers. In some countries, a higher than average time of instruction for students is the only factor increasing the salary outlays per student above the average of countries.

In Uruguay, the Philippines and Indonesia instruction time for students is highest, with an average of between 1,231 and 1,467 hours of instruction per year in lower secondary education. The effect of this factor, which increases the salary outlays per student by between US$330 and US$650 above the average of countries, is largely compensated by lower than average salaries and larger than average class sizes in both Indonesia and the Philippines.

Moreover, in the latter country, teaching hours are higher than average, which further contributes to reduce salary costs per student but aggravates the working conditions of teachers. In some countries, a lower than average teaching load is compensated by larger class sizes, while in other countries smaller than average class sizes add to a low teaching load increasing salary costs per student.

In Spain, Sweden, the Republic of Korea, Hungary and Tunisia, annual teaching hours at the lower secondary level are relatively low (less than 600 hours); as a result more teachers are required to cover the total demand for teaching. This adds significantly to salary expenditures per student. In Spain, Sweden and Hungary smaller than average class sizes add to this effect whereas in the Republic of Korea and Tunisia larger class sizes compensate for the lower teaching workload. At the other end of the spectrum are Australia, the United States, New Zealand and the Philippines, where teachers are required to teach for more than 900 hours per year, which adds to the burden on teachers but frees up resources for other purposes. In Australia, the United States and New Zealand, the positive effect of the large teaching load on salary outlays per student is largely compensated by comparatively higher salary levels while in the Philippines teachers have both a high teaching load and comparatively low salary levels.

In the Philippines, larger than average class sizes compound the high teaching load. In some countries, large class sizes reduce the teacher salary costs per student In the Republic of Korea, Tunisia, Thailand, Mexico, Chile and the Philippines class sizes are comparatively high, with between 37 and 50 students per class on average. In all of these countries, this reduces salary outlays per student, in the cases of Mexico and the Philippines by almost US$700, and thus helps to provide resources for other purposes.

Teacher Indicators

Policy-makers are paying increasing attention to which educational, social and economic factors contribute to improved education and learning and enhanced returns to investment in education. The process of teaching is at the heart of education and the expertise, pedagogical know-how and organizational and technical competence of teachers are widely considered to be central to educational improvement. This shift in the focus of policy attention, coupled with a generally increasing demand for sound and comparable quantitative evidence, has also helped to strengthen the statistical knowledge base on teachers and teaching. In cooperation with relevant national agencies, international organizations, including the European Commission, the IBE, the ILO, the OECD, and UNESCO, are working on the establishment of reliable and internationally comparative statistics on the qualifications, salaries and labour market position of teachers and on their working conditions.

Aspects of the status of the teaching profession and its service conditions for which methods and instruments for the compilation of internationally comparable information have been developed include:

— teacher demographics;
— part-time/full-time employment status;
— student/teaching-staff ratios;
— length of pre-service training;
— statutory teaching time;
— statutory teachers' salaries, in absolute and, to a more limited extent, relative terms.

For example, through the World Education Indicators programme, developing countries are currently working with the OECD on establishing comparative standards and methods. The UNESCO Institute for Statistics has held regional workshops in a wide range of countries with the aim to cover and analyse these issues more in depth. The ILO is examining improvements in salary and hours of work among different sectors, including education. While progress is being made, there are important aspects of the situation of the teaching force where relevant and internationally comparable data are either non-existent, or where a lack of consistency in the underlying concepts, definitions and data collection instruments render the existing data inadequate for the purpose of international comparisons.

While some comparable measures of statutory teaching has proved far more difficult to measure and compare total teacher workload, including non-instructional and non-school based activities. While comparable measures of student/teaching staff ratios can usually be calculated, differences in classroom organization (particularly at the higher levels of education) make it very difficult to compute and compare class sizes (which are much more closely related with the employment conditions of teachers than student/teaching staff ratios). For some countries, separating teaching staff from other educational personnel proves to be very difficult, in particular for countries in which teachers have significant non-teaching responsibilities. Measures of the competitiveness of the employment conditions of teachers are often still limited to comparing salaries and working time with other groups of workers.

The quantification of instructional practices and classroom organization is proving to be very difficult. The big investment in cross-national assessment of student learning achievement in recent years has not been matched by a corresponding investment in the assessment of teacher learning achievement. How much teachers in the different countries actually know, either in the field(s) they are supposed to teach, or generally, is one of the biggest gaps in our knowledge about teachers internationally.

Information on the availability, use and effectiveness of information and communications technology in education, while improving rapidly, remains unsatisfactory. A framework for comparing trends towards the autonomy of educational institutions, including the participation of teachers in decision-making processes, does not yet exist. National institutional structures and the nature and organization of educational programmes vary greatly among countries and therefore make international comparisons difficult.

The revised International Standard Classification of Education (ISCED-97) provides some help but considerable work remains to be done in implementation of these standards. There are also areas where differences in the methods and data collections instruments that are applied by different international organizations make comparisons difficult. Filling some of the data gaps, e.g. those on teaching and learning processes, teacher learning achievement, or the integration of information technology into teaching and learning, requires extensive surveys and observation studies which are usually beyond the reach of standard international data collection programmes that can be administered on a regular basis.

However, as the OECD Education Indicators programme has shown, many of the data gaps mentioned above can be addressed with relatively simple and inexpensive annual data collections, which are based on a set of definitions, methods and data collection instruments that are annually reviewed and updated collaboratively by participating countries. The necessary data can often be derived from existing national sources that are then projected to international standards using statistical methods.

Many of the concepts and definitions presented in the following are derived from the OECD annual data collection on education statistics. The following provides basic considerations for the development of internationally comparable statistics on teachers and their working conditions. Collecting data on teachers and their working conditions is complicated, among other factors, by national differences in the work organization for education personnel.

In some countries "teachers" also assume significant non-teaching duties, at times including those of a school principal, whereas in other countries there is considerable functional differentiation, with various pedagogical, administrative and indirect support functions carried out by specialized personnel other than teachers. Other problems arise from the fact that countries differ in their practices in counting teachers without active teaching duties or persons who work occasionally or in a voluntary capacity in educational institutions.

A first prerequisite for obtaining internationally comparable statistics on teachers is therefore that countries adjust their data to reflect a standardized statistical concept of a teacher that can be distinguished consistently from other staff with special pedagogical, administrative, and professional functions, as well as from indirect support personnel. For statistical purposes, in OECD indicators work, a teacher is defined as a person whose professional activity involves the transmission of knowledge, attitudes and skills that are stipulated to students enrolled in an educational programme. This definition does not depend on the qualification held by the teacher nor on the delivery mechanism but, instead, is based on three concepts:

— Activity, thus excluding those without active teaching duties

— Profession, thus excluding people who work occasionally or in a voluntary capacity in educational institutions.

— Educational programme, thus excluding people who provide services other than formal instruction to students (e.g. supervisors, activity organizers, etc.), whether the programme is established at the national or school level.

In this definition, principals, presidents, vice-principals, and other administrators without teaching responsibilities in educational institutions, as well as teachers without active teaching responsibilities for students in educational institutions, should not be classified as "teachers", but as "other professional personnel". Since the combinations differ between countries, often considerably, it may be desirable to separate the teaching and non-teaching components statistically, i.e. in terms of hours spent on each of them. In order to provide for a basic set of indicators on teachers, at least the following information should be collected:

1) education personnel by type of institution (public, government-dependent private and independent private), personnel category (teaching staff, administrative and professional support staff and other support personnel), mode of employment (full-time, part-time, full-time equivalent), and gender; and

2) teaching personnel by level of education, type of programme taught, type of institution, mode of employment, gender and age groups.

The basis for defining teachers and other educational personnel could be the International Standard Classification of Occupations (ISCO-88) developed by the ILO. ISCO-88 provides definitions of managers, teaching professionals at all educational levels, associate teaching professionals and a range of support staff based on defined tasks and responsibilities. Dealing with differences in national institutional structures Another difficulty that needs to be overcome in international comparisons is to ensure that the institutions and levels of education that teachers are serving are comparable across countries.

Institutional structures and how they relate to different levels of education differ widely among countries. In addition, teaching staff often work in more than one level or type of educational programme. Thus, the separate collection of staff statistics for "general and academic" education and "vocational and technical" education poses several conceptual and technical problems in countries that do not have a reporting system which classifies teachers by the level of education and the type of educational programme in accordance with ISCED-97 a priori. In these cases, for the purpose of reporting headcount data, teachers should be pro-rated according to the time they are assigned to the corresponding levels and type of educational programmes.

The full-time equivalence of part-time teachers (or other education personnel) is then determined by calculating the ratio of hours worked by part-time teachers over the statutory hours worked by a full-time teacher during the school year. For the purpose of reporting headcount data, teachers should be pro-rated between those levels, educational programmes, types of institutions, and functions to which they are assigned. That is, teachers in different types of programmes should be divided proportionally to their number of statutory working hours. Where full-time equivalents are reported, data on teachers should be pro-rated according to their statutory working time at the different levels, educational programmes, types of institutions, and functions.

Fulltime teachers who receive additional contracts/ remuneration to perform additional teaching tasks, should be counted only once, as one full-time teacher, for the purpose of collecting headcount data, but with a fulltime equivalence factor greater than one. This methodology would ensure that the employment variable (full-time/ part-time) is reported more accurately, while the numbers reported by level, educational programme, type of institution, and function would be subject to some error (though not necessarily bias). The alternative (i.e., reporting full-time teachers as multiple part-time teachers in the different aspects) would destroy the employment variable and also bias the overall count of individuals employed in education.

Adequate instruments for the collection of data on pre-service training have been developed by the OECD and are reported routinely in Education at a glance. These instruments report the requirements for preservice training for new teachers based on ISCED-97. To reflect differences in the models of teacher training, a distinction between the concurrent training model and the consecutive model needs to be made. The data on pre-service training requirements can easily be converted into the total number of years of education and teacher training. The duration of preservice training for new teachers then refers to the typical number of full-time equivalent years of teacher training formally required to become a fully qualified teacher in a given country.

Countries differ widely in the way they measure teaching and working time. To obtain meaningful comparisons, the national concepts of teaching and working time need to be translated into an internationally comparable basis. Defining and measuring "working time" is quite difficult for many groups of workers, including teachers. For this group, the difficulties in measuring working time arise mainly from the fact that part of the working time can be spent outside of the school.

In some countries, full-time teachers are required to be at school for a specified number of working hours per week. In other countries or school systems, full-time teachers are only required to be at school for a specified number of hours for teaching. In yet other countries, there is no mandatory or formal amount of time that teachers must spend working, although there may be a customary amount of time that all civil servants work. The situation can be complicated further when teachers' work hours are set at the local or school level or when teachers can set their own work hours, based on the number of classes they are assigned to teach.

To deal with these differences adequately in international comparisons, appropriate taxonomies must be developed and estimation methods provided that allow countries to convert national data into the respective international categories. In order to obtain meaningful international comparisons of statutory teaching time, the national concepts of teaching periods need to be converted to the number of 60-minute unit equivalents. Periods of time formally allowed for breaks between lessons or groups of lessons should be excluded from teaching time, although they should be included in the measurement of working time.

In order to avoid that comparisons of average teachers' salaries are distorted or the comparisons rendered more complicated by the age distribution of teachers it seems generally preferable to report salaries on the basis of statutory salaries rather than actual average wages. Since pay scales differ between countries, it is important to base international comparisons on standardized anchor points in pay scales. For example, to capture the beginning of the pay scale, one can collect data on the average statutory gross salary per year of a full-time classroom teacher with the minimum level of training to be fully qualified at the beginning of his or her teaching career.

Similarly, to capture the end of a pay scale, one can collect data on the average statutory maximum gross salary per year of a full-time classroom teacher with the highest level of qualifications. Finally, it is often useful to compare the salaries of an experienced teacher during mid-career. The OECD defines this as the average statutory gross salary per year of a full-time classroom teacher with the minimum level of training to be fully qualified and who has 15 years of experience.

One of the difficulties encountered when examining teacher compensation is that teachers in some countries receive substantial additional bonuses in addition to the amount received based on their educational qualifications and experience. It is useful to measure these as the difference in salary between what a particular teacher receives as earnings for work performed at a school and the amount they would be expected to receive given only their level of experience. Such bonuses need to be classified and reported consistently. The OECD applies a classification for bonuses that distinguishes between bonuses related to educational, certification or training qualifications higher than the minimum qualification required, particular work assignments and responsibilities or subjects taught, outstanding performance in teaching and circumstances such as location, family responsibilities or age.

The ILO's data on average salary rates are meant to exclude bonuses and allowances other than cost-of-living allowances, while average earnings data are meant to exclude social security premiums and benefits and irregular bonuses (year-end, one-time), which accrue over a longer period of time than one pay period. Furthermore, teachers in some countries may receive additional non-monetary bonuses that are often difficult to value in monetary terms. Indicators on salaries can be expressed in absolute terms as well as in relative terms. For relative teacher compensation, GDP per capita or the average earnings of salary workers are often used as benchmarks. A more appropriate reference point, though more difficult to obtain, consists of the earnings of a person with a similar generally tertiary level qualification.

As teaching and learning evolve and the social and economic context of education undergo profound transformations, the demand for comparative information on the teaching profession will also change. A set of indicators on teachers and the teaching profession can therefore not be static but must adapt to these changes while providing a sufficient degree of stability to permit reliable analyses of trends. A prerequisite for the effective functioning of any indicator system is that it is being developed through a close dialogue between social partners, policy-makers and analysts, subject matter experts and statisticians.

Pofessional Development Programmes

Effective professional development programs that are known to make a difference to the quality of teaching support teachers to develop their classroom practice. Programs that provide further credentials are important for developing the professional status of teaching, establishing teaching standards, and assisting in career growth, etc.

However these training programs do not always provide adequate linkages and ongoing support with classroom practice, and therefore actual instructional practices are often not changed, and the quality of teaching and student learning is hindered. Therefore, the following section will focus on the characteristics of effective professional development programs that tend to improve classroom practice.

An initial determination of what are the needs, interests, and strengths of teachers and other staff is essential before professional development activities are designed. For example, do participants need an induction program to support their initial teaching experience, and what training, if any, do they already have on which to build? Will the program provide specific new knowledge and skills needed by the participants or is it for refining already acquired knowledge and skills?

Effective programs are well planned, and tend to be formal in nature. Some of these programs focus on improving the performance skills of individual staff, or on organizational or curricular issues that will affect the whole staff, and some programs for small groups of staff. An overall strategic framework for the long-term effort is necessary.

The overall planning needs to consider how various needs might be met: peer coaching; action research in the classroom or school; visits to other classrooms or schools; visits by outside specialists, officials, and consultants; meetings with parents and other community members; short meetings; whole day activities held at the school or another location; retreats for the entire staff; longer development workshops; whole semester release; use of teachers' centers; resources shared in school clusters; district level training; and long-term programs in centralized institutions.

The programs also need to be structured to reduce anxiety and fear of change, and the activities proven to be clear improvements from existing practice. Apart from close consultation about their needs, teachers, principals and other local participants along with administrative officials need to be involved in the next planning steps of the program. Some teacher education programs have been developed in local communities and later have been supported by central governments and international agencies.

In these programs, teachers, principals, and teacher educators worked as a team in the school to educate the community about its schools, the curriculum, and to learn a great deal about the characteristics of the local children and families. Locally recruited teachers develop a special role as mediators between mainstream culture of the school and the local culture of the pupils.

One example of this type of program is the Compensatory Education Project in Malaysia. This project attempted to improve the educational opportunities for the children of rubber states through heavy involvement of parents. It was distinguished by its flexibility and responsiveness to the needs of parents as they educated themselves to educate their children. Other approaches have been initiated at the central ministry level but successfully implemented at the local level. An example of this is the Nigerian Primary Education Improvement Project, which used mobile teacher educators to instruct teachers individually and in groups in six schools.

The project helped teachers achieve curriculum understanding and effective lesson application. Based on these experiences, educators have argued for the importance of rethinking traditional approaches for teacher training. Three other examples of teacher programs that use high levels of participation for planning and implementation are the Escuela Nueva in Colombia, the NEU in Guatemala, and the Compensatory Program to Address Educational Lag, or PARE, in Mexico. In all cases, the emphasis is on the formation of learning communities and changing the traditional role of teacher to be a facilitator of student learning.

The curriculum of the program needs to provide a balance of pedagogy and subject matter as opposed to exclusive emphasis on one or the other. It should also include practical methods to teach subject matter, child development, and learning theories in ways that are relevant to the student context, ways to evaluate teaching and learning, multigrade classroom management, and ways to develop parent-school-community relations through participatory learning strategies such as discussion, simulations, and teaching practices.

Many teachers do not teach as effectively as they could because they do not understand students, how they learn, and classroom dynamics. The pedagogical component of effective inservice programs often contains four key elements: i) methods for helping teachers acquire specific skills for teaching the existing curriculum; ii) methods for teaching meaningful rather than just rote learning; iii) methods for developing in pupils positive attitudes to lifelong learning; and iv) methods for helping teachers engage in curriculum development.

Joyce and Showers suggest that five essential components should be in training programs: i) presentation of theory or description of skill or strategy, ii) modeling or demonstration of skills or models of teaching, iii) practice in simulated and classroom settings, iv) structured and open-ended feedback about performance, and v) implementation.in the actual classroom. However, the most critical component is that the inservice programs include provision for ensuring implementation in the classroom of the acquired learning, and that ongoing support facilitates this.

While basic teaching and classroom management skills are important, especially for new teachers who may have little initial preparation for the job, it is also essential that teachers develop good evaluation and decision-making skills. Mastery of skills shaped by judgments about how student learning can best be achieved, and positive attitudes are important areas to develop. Peer coaching, self-evaluation, and reflective group discussion are some inservice techniques that might be adopted to enhance this critical thinking.

Teachers in rural areas face special problems that may need more emphasis in the inservice programs-dealing with isolation, working within the local community values and expectations, multigrade teaching techniques, administration of small schools and heavier workloads, rural familiarity and lack of privacy, difficult housing and sanitary conditions, safety and value concerns, and resource acquisition issues. In the study by Gibson on preparing teachers for rural education in Australia, it was recommended that not only was there a need for specialized programs of teacher education and induction for rural teachers, but that staffing practices and policy guidelines in departments of education needed to reflect national policies to appoint such teachers only after they are provided with adequate training and support.

Programs that focus on continuous development to guide, monitor, and support necessary skills, knowledge, and new ideas tend to be more successful in bringing about change at the classroom level than those that seek quick fixes to fill up deficiencies or those that simply provide a qualification. Tatto reports that inservice programs typically focus on helping teachers implement new curricula in conjunction with state values and educational reforms.

This ongoing support is essential for effective transfer of skills and is easiest developed through the school-based model. The main support comes both from within the school environment (e.g., principal, other.teachers) and personnel from the larger education system and community. At the level of the principal, the quality of teachers' work and student learning tends to be enhanced when the principal: i) sees that the resources are available to provide adequate support to teachers, sufficient learning materials, and well maintained learning facilities; ii) pursues high instructional standards by clearly and frequently stating in concrete terms the school's mission, curricular goals, and expected teaching behavior; clearly and frequently expresses high expectations of pupils and the school's focus on learning as its central purpose; iii) coordinates and manages the learning process; iv) communicates regularly and effectively with teachers, parents, and others in the community; and v) maintains high visibility and accessibility to pupils, teachers, parents, and others in the community.

At the teacher level, support to help the application of new skills into the classroom includes: i) coaching about classroom skills and management from mentors and peers; ii) a continuing study group with other teachers with similar inservice experiences; iii) coordination of the inservice with the regular supervision of teachers; and iv) provision made for traveling consultants to visit teachers. At the level of the larger education system, effective support happens when the system: i) delegates authority and responsibility for improvement to the schools themselves; ii) communicates expectations or exerts pressure for successful academic results; iii) provides important services to schools such as advice and training about instructional practices and management, resources needed to achieve instructional goals, and protects the school from political turbulence; and iv) monitors and evaluates schools' academic performance, recognizes successes, and provides support to overcome weaknesses.

Motivation is likely to be enhanced for the inservice program where increased salary or other benefits are ensured. At the level of parents and community, support for the ongoing work of teachers may be in several forms: i) seeing that pupils come to school healthy and prepared to learn; ii) providing financial or material support for the school's operation; iii) communicating frequently with school staff; iv) assisting with instruction both at the school and in the home; and v) assisting with school governance with meaningful authority.

There are various organizational models that are used to provide professional development for teachers, either as ongoing support, or for training at various stages of the teaching career. Several models are described here. The one noted for its effectiveness in changing classroom practices is the school-based model. The continuous or life-long professional development model is not well developed in many educational systems, but its principles are strongly supported in current debates on the importance of ongoing support for teachers.

The other models provide important support for various needs such as the establishment of an adequate stock of teachers quickly, and credentials from formal institutions. The models that do not have the school setting as their prime focus would have a greater effect on teacher performance where this linkage to classroom practice could be strengthened. Combinations of the various models should be considered, depending on the local context.

One of the challenges with this model is to match an appropriate incentive system and career path with actual improvement in teacher performance, a challenge that countries such as Singapore and Malaysia have been struggling with. It is the model of life-long learning-ongoing professional development. This model had the strongest support both from the survey of Andrews et al. and other experts, and works best when a combination of the following in-school activities are used: i) individual consultations between the teacher and the supervisor or other experts, especially with Organizational Models.emphasis on classroom supervision; ii) observation of excellent teachers, discussion, peer coaching, and mentoring; and iii) visits to other classrooms and schools.

Peer coaching, in which two teachers observe each other's classes with the objective of helping each other improve their instructional abilities, has become increasingly popular along with mentoring programs. The school-based model is very effective for long term guided learning. The support and participation of the head teacher or other designated "director-organizer" is essential.

The school-based programs should be controlled jointly by teachers, outside officials, and head teachers. School clusters (such as those employed in Thailand, the Philippines, and Sri Lanka) are very helpful to share scarce material and human resources. Core schools tend to host educational resource centers developed and operated jointly in the cluster. The learning action cells in the Philippines exist at the school, district, and regional levels and are used for school evaluation and staff development for both teachers and principals.

Similar organizational patterns operate in Nepal, in the Cianjur project in Indonesia, and in the school zones in Zambia. Small schools, in particular can benefit from clusters of schools teaming together.

The growth of distance education in both industrialized and developing countries as a possible cost-effective, more flexible learning approach compared with conventional means is significant. However, in the study of Andrews et al., distance education was not strongly supported as a model for effective delivery, but this may have been a reflection on experiences of poorly developed and supported programs. Robinson also reports that while not all courses have been of good quality or have worked well, "distance education can be effective on a large scale and in rural areas where the least qualified teachers are to be found and they can be instrumental in developing teachers' knowledge and skills and in supporting a decentralized program of inservice training, strengthening resource centers, and school clusters." Factors that have made a difference to the success of distance education programs include:

— adequate support infrastructure, e.g., communications, transport, library resources;

— adequate up-front funding knowing that in distance education there are often high initial and low recurrent costs;

— strong policy backing and credibility of programs;

— high quality materials and acceptance of high standards;

— up-to-date curricula based on recent research on learning;

— well designed self-study materials;

— opportunities to have continuous practice of the learning in the classroom;

— continuous mentoring, guidance, and support with instructors and other teachers/peers;

Effective and efficient control, management, and monitoring from the central education system is necessary. Mathison suggests that feedback informing facilitators on the modes of presentation, involve-ment, relevance, adequacy of facilities, and instructors etc., is valuable. However, she states that an effective evaluation must also investigate whether attitudes and practices of participants have actually changed for the better, and whether these changes are manifested in classroom and school practices and processes. Mathison states that in general terms, a good evaluation of an inservice teacher education program should:

— adopt an explicit standard to good inservice teacher education against which any particular inservice program can be judged Evaluation of Inservice Programs.;

— value the effects of inservice programs on teachers' needs for professional experiences;

— expect and appreciate inevitable differences among teachers and schools in efforts to change educational practices, and take a more longitudinal perspective on educational change that might occur as a result of inservice education;

— expand the venue for the evaluation beyond the inservice experience and into the school, classroom, or wherever change might be manifest; and

— require the expenditure of more resources to conduct serious evaluations.

Evaluations of teacher performance are usually conducted for two purposes: to make judgments about a teacher's performance, and to provide useful information to improve the teacher's instructional practices. A key factor here is the appropriateness of the criteria for the purpose of the evaluation. Peer and self-evaluations are often used to improve teaching proficiency. While supervisor evaluations from principals and other supervisory staff are also helpful in providing development information, these evaluations are also often used as the basis for terminating or retaining teacher employment; for higher salary awards, tenure, promotions, or other career related benefits.

Professional expertise is something that develops with guidance and more teaching and life experiences. New teachers should not be expected to have the same degree of confidence and proficiency as teachers who have been teaching for several years. However, by the time they have an evaluation for licensure, or the equivalent, many of the more developed educational systems have expectations that the new teacher be able to:

— Plan lessons that enable students to relate new learning to prior understanding and experiences;

— Develop rapport and personal interactions with students;

— Establish and maintain rules and routines that are fair and appropriate to students;

— Arrange the physical and social conditions in the classroom in ways that are conducive to learning and that fit the academic task;

— Assess student learning using a variety of measurement tools and adapt instruction according to the results; and

— Reflect on their actions and students' responses in order to improve their teaching.

Peer evaluations are advantageous because they encourage collegiality among staff and reduce job isolation. Two common types of peer evaluations are peer coaching and mentoring. Peer coaching involves groups of individuals voluntarily agreeing to observe each other's teaching, offer advice for improvement, and solve problems together. A relationship of mutual trust and respect must be developed first. Three steps often need to be in place to make the coaching time effective:

i) the observation experience needs to be planned beforehand to agree on what the lesson will be about, what the observations will focus on, and how the information will be gathered, etc.;

ii) during the observation sufficient, clearly taken notes are recorded in positive terms with the view of supporting the efforts of the teacher; and

iii) observations are shared, often with the observed teacher making a self-evaluation first and then brainstorming possible improvements etc.

Mentoring involves one person-the mentor-usually a more experienced staff member who provides assistance and guidance to another person to grow professionally. As with peer coaching, there must be a relationship of trust and respect as well as adequate time for the mentor to get to know the mentee very well.

Self-evaluations require teachers to collect information about their own teaching. This is a non-threatening, nonintrusive means of collecting data. Such reflection is needed to develop professionally as well as to make technical adjustments to lessons and management, etc. However,.because the teaching task can be busy, it is sometimes necessary to have another observer in the classroom to identify particular strengths and weaknesses in instructional practice, particularly for inexperienced teachers.

Supervisor evaluations are more formal sessions and involve another staff member who has authority over the teacher. In general, teachers tend to be more wary of such evaluations because the judgments often affect career opportunities and go beyond providing information for self-improvement. It is advisable to let the teacher being evaluated know the criteria and procedures to be taken during the evaluation.

Student evaluations can provide useful information about instructional effectiveness and the learning environment, although not all researchers agree that this practice is sound. However, to minimize limitations of the sorts of questions asked of school students, and for opinions for which they lack expertise, other sources of information should be used such as project work, essays, and other products in student portfolios that provide examples of what students have learned.

Teacher portfolios, like student portfolios, contain a variety of information about performance. Typically, they include curriculum and other materials prepared by the teacher, evaluation information gathered from others, and examples of student work.

One of the attributing factors for the success of the teacher education program is that it began as an idea from the Ministry of Education rather than by the project, thereby encouraging ownership and motivation. The program particularly targets small schools in scattered and distant locations where teachers are often very isolated.

In this program, teachers are provided with the organizational support they need to take responsibility for their professional development and to improve their teaching practice and student learning. Initially, teachers are helped to write a proposal for a grant competition to secure funding for a teacher-learning project.

School-based training (SBT) has been operating since 1994 in several areas of Egypt as pilot programs for English teachers at the preparatory level. The main goal of SBT is to provide inservice training to increase.the effectiveness of teachers through training and mentoring at the school site.

Preparatory school teachers receive materials on basic classroom teaching techniques. These materials are based on the instructional text and can be used immediately by the teacher to make classroom teaching more interesting and effective. SBT activities increase communication and sharing of ideas among the English teaching staff at participating schools.Transferring the SBT activities and ideas to other English classes in a school gives the senior teacher increased responsibility for professional development, and increases the status of the senior teacher. Teachers in participating schools develop a better rapport through working together to integrate SBT activities into their classes.

All teachers in the school receive new material and observe demonstrations. SBT provides a positive focus for inspectors' school visits, classroom observations, and meetings with teachers. Among the most motivated teachers, SBT encourages creative thinking and problem solving. SBT involves inspectors as demonstrators, trainers, observers, and evaluators; and it strengthens the relationship between the supervising inspector and the senior teacher in a participating school by focusing on professional development.

SBT can serve as a link between a centralized "spectrum" type of inservice training course and the local training courses. It is responsive to specific needs and includes schools identified by the inspector general and the inspectors. Developing a centralized file or library of teacher-produced materials that can be borrowed from and added to is also suggested.

In response to poor results in the second International Association for the Evaluation of Educational Achievement Science study in South Australia, the state government allocated funds for the development and implementation of a teacher professional development program that would improve the quality and quantity of science and technology taught in primary schools in the state of South Australia. Two long-term models of professional development are used in the public school system in South Australia.

The first is an in-school professional development program that involves the appointment of "teacher coordinators." All schools are allocated teacher coordinator positions based on the number of students they have. These positions provide teacher release for specific foci that are identified by an individual school. For example, one school may target a subject area such as mathematics, while another may choose issues such as gender equity or behavior management. The coordinator positions are advertised statewide and teachers are invited to apply for the one or two-year positions. In general, the coordinators are released from the.classroom one day per week to develop the school's program, organize the school's resources, and work in classrooms with teachers.

The second model is known as the "Focus School Project," and also operates on a statewide basis. Projects are funded for two to three years. However, because of the intensity of the program and the expenditure involved in teacher release, a limited number of schools can be involved. Schools within the local districts are clustered together to enable joint professional development activities, the sharing of resources, and the dissemination of information. There is generally one focus school selected per district cluster.

Bibliography

Anderson, W. M., "Rethinking teacher education: The multicultural imperative", *Music Educators Journal*, 78(9), 52-55,1992

Appelbaum, P. M., & Enomoto, E. K., "Computer-mediated communication for a multicultural experience", *Educational Technology*, 35(6), 49-58, 1995.

Banks, J. A., "Teaching multicultural literacy to teachers", *Teaching Education*, 4(1), 135-144, 1991

Barker, K. H., "Teacher education for international goals", Phi Delta Kappan, 47, 220-27, 1965.

Bennett, L., "Social studies in the preparation of elementary school teachers", *International Journal of Social Education*, 7(3), 76-80, 1993.

Bruce, M. G., Podemski, R. S., & Anderson, C. M., "Developing a global perspective: Strategies for teacher education programs", *Journal of Teacher Education*, 42(1), 21-27, 1991.

Fox, W., & Gay, G. "Integrating multicultural and curriculum principles in teacher education", *Peabody Journal of Education*, 70(3), 64-82, 1995.

Gonzales, F., "Creating education that works: Building bilingual teacher competencies", IDRA Newsletter, 20(10), 4-6,8, 1993.

Hadley, M. B., & Wood, R. W., "International perspectives in teacher education", Action in Teacher Education, 8(3), 57-63, 1986.

Margerison, P. S., "Changing hearts, changing minds: Encouraging student teachers to use multicultural literature", *English Education*, 27(4), 258-267, 1995.

Rivers, W. M., "Curriculum, student objectives, and the training of foreign language teachers", Babel, 23(2), 4-10, 1988.

Tisher, R. P., & Wideen, M. F., "Research in teacher educational international perspectives", Britol, PA: Falmer Press, 1990.

Index